MONEY

Recent Titles in
Contributions to the Study of World Literature

Reworlding: The Literature of the Indian Diaspora
Emmanuel S. Nelson, editor

Caliban in Exile: The Outsider in Caribbean Fiction
Margaret Paul Joseph

Sitting at the Feet of the Past: Retelling the North American Folktale
for Children
Gary D. Schmidt and Donald R. Hettinga, editors

The Anna Book: Searching for Anna in Literary History
Mickey Pearlman, editor

Writing and Reality: A Study of Modern British Diary Fiction
Andrew Hassam

Shakespeare's Proverbial Themes: A Rhetorical Context for the Sententia
as *Res*
Marjorie Donker

Promptings of Desire: Creativity and the Religious Impulse in the Works of
D. H. Lawrence
Paul Poplawski

The Second Best Bed: Shakespeare's Will in a New Light
Joyce E. Rogers

Literary Selves: Autobiography and Contemporary American Nonfiction
James N. Stull

Storied Cities: Literary Imagining of Florence, Venice and Rome
Michael L. Ross

Women Writers in Russian Literature
Toby W. Clyman and Diana Greene, editors

Writing the Good Fight: Political Commitment in the International Literature
of the Spanish Civil War
Peter Monteath

MONEY

Lure, Lore, and Literature

Edited by
JOHN LOUIS DiGAETANI

PREPARED UNDER THE AUSPICES OF HOFSTRA UNIVERSITY

Contributions to the Study of World Literature,
Number 55

GREENWOOD PRESS
Westport, Connecticut • London

Library of Congress Cataloging-in-Publication Data

Money : lure, lore, and literature / edited by John Louis DiGaetani ;
    prepared under the auspices of Hofstra University.
        p. cm. — (Contributions to the study of world literature,
    ISSN 0738-9345 ; no. 55)
    Based on papers presented at a conference held at Hofstra
University.
    Includes bibliographical references and index.
    ISBN 0-313-29219-1 (alk. paper)
    1. Money in literature.   I. DiGaetani, John Louis.
II. Hofstra University.   III. Series.
PN56.M547M66   1994
809'.93355—dc20   93-39359

British Library Cataloguing in Publication Data is available.

Library of Congress Catalog Card Number: 93-39359
ISBN: 0-313-29219-1
ISSN: 0738-9345

First published in 1994

Greenwood Press, 88 Post Road West, Westport, CT 06881
An imprint of Greenwood Publishing Group, Inc.

Printed in the United States of America

∞™

The paper used in this book complies with the
Permanent Paper Standard issued by the National
Information Standards Organization (Z39.48-1984).

10 9 8 7 6 5 4 3 2 1

Copyright Acknowledgments

The authors and publisher gratefully acknowledge the following for allowing the use of their material in this volume:

Extracts from William Carlos Williams, *Paterson*, copyright 1951 by William Carlos Williams, reprinted by permission of New Directions Publishing Company.

Extracts from Molière's *The Misanthrope*, copyright © 1955, 1954 and renewed 1983, 1982 by Richard Wilbur, reprinted by permission of Harcourt Brace & Company.

"The Wings of the Dove" by Joann P. Krieg, reprinted with permission of Twayne Publishers, an imprint of Macmillan Publishing Company, from *Epidemics in the Modern World* by Joann P. Krieg, Copyright © 1992 by Twayne Publishers.

For Dr. Bruce Johnson

Contents

Part V. Money and English Literature

Acknowledgments

This book grew out of a three-day conference at Hofstra University on the topic "Money: Lure, Lore, and Liquidity." The conference was codirected by Dr. Herman Berliner, Provost, and Dr. Marcel Tenenbaum, Chairman, Economics Department. Most of the chapters began as papers given at that conference. I then selected and edited the papers for this book.

I would like to thank the Hofstra Cultural Center for sponsoring this conference, in addition to Hofstra University for providing funding for the conference. I would particularly like to thank Natalie Datloff of the Cultural Center for her valuable help. I would also like to record my gratitude to Dr. Bruce Johnson for his personal encouragement with the editing of this book.

Introduction

JOHN LOUIS DiGAETANI

The love of money is the root of all evil.
> I Timothy 6:10, The Bible

The lack of money is the root of all evil.
> George Bernard Shaw, *Man and Superman*

This collection of essays seems at first like a strange kettle of fish, but in its diversity is its strength. The book connects what at first seem like irreconcilable opposites: money and art—the realm of the real and concrete versus the realm of dream and fantasy. To accomplish this unusual—some would even say cynical—connection, a careful and well-planned approach is necessary, which is what I have tried to do with this anthology. Though 80 percent of the chapters involve art, a very important 20 percent involve a very slippery and complex subject, money—a term very hard even to define. And the term is so hard to define because its definition depends entirely on the context of its analysis.

As a result, this book is divided into five parts in an effort to systematize an approach to an oxymoron—money and art. In Part I, money is analyzed in terms of language and culture. How we understand money very much depends on our culture and our language. Part II connects money with history, showing how money was influenced by history and how money changed history. After these two broadly theoretical parts, designed to give the reader an understanding of the complexities involved in the subject, this book then applies many of these theories to various fields of literature. Part III discusses money as it appears in the literatures of Russia and America; Part IV analyzes the theme of money in French literature; and Part V, the largest section of this anthology, discusses money and its appearance in English literature.

By the end of this book, the reader will have a fuller understanding of the subject of money and literature. But why this combination? Some might see these two factors as deadly enemies, opposites rather than subjects that can be connected. There are some naive souls who believe that great art, in particular literature, should have nothing whatsoever to do with such sordid subjects as money and materialistic concerns. Some read literature to avoid these very realities. But few writers would have agreed that money is a subject that should be avoided in great literature. Great writers write about what interests first of all themselves, and then by extension humanity in general. And writers and artists have generally been very concerned about money and its influence on human life. Writers are not alone in this interest. George Bernard Shaw felt that money and society's distribution of money were the only subjects which art should concern itself with, but not all writers were this extreme. Most, however, showed a healthy interest in this topic because it interests most people, including the artists themselves.

Money, in fact, remains a subject which fascinates us all. We use it all the time, think about it often, but do we really understand it in all its ramifications? This book tries to analyze a topic close to all our hearts—money. And most of the greatest writers and thinkers from Plato to Freud and beyond have also been concerned about money, wealth, and social status in the human condition. Marx and Wagner decried materialism, Smith and Hegel tried to explain and justify it, and Ayn Rand tried to glorify it, but economic realities and all their implications permeate so many aspects of our lives.

"The worldly philosophers," the phrase Robert L. Heilbroner coined to describe the great economists, is a clever way to indicate the inevitable bond between money and philosophy. And Heilbroner, whether talking about the optimistic worldview of Adam Smith, the gloomy worldview of Malthus and Ricardo, the savage world of Thorstein Veblen, or the economically sick world of Keynesian economics, argued repeatedly in *The Worldly Philosophers* that economics belongs in the greater world of ideas because economic theories inevitably contain social, political, and philosophical implications. And it is hardly a coincidence that most golden ages in the arts correspond to golden ages in the stock market. During a period of economic boom, more people can afford to commission and buy works of art. The arts generally need a Maecenas—whether that be a wealthy patron, state funding agencies, or the federal government's National Endowment for the Arts. Horace and Virgil were lucky enough to have the wealthy and generous Maecenas; many current artists still need such people, unless they come from wealthy families themselves. So worldly philosophers, better known as economists, can tell us something about philosophy as well as money. But where can one begin an examination of this complex subject?

Using a variety of approaches and writing styles, the authors in this book analyze what some would call the cynical topic of money. *Money: Lure, Lore, and Literature* begins with a discussion of money's connections with language and culture. Robert Leonard writes of money and its pervasive influence on our language. Property rights systems and money are the subjects of Michael Haupert's chapter, where he examines in what sense money can be equated with real property. Catherine Lawson discusses the topic of money's connections with love, though some might argue that there should not be such a connection. Richard Doty's chapter on money discusses the age-old problems of forgeries and what governments do to protect their currencies. Forgeries of coins and paper money appear almost as soon as the original does. Ellen Stephens next analyzes to what extent money is a motivator for some, though not all, people. This section of the book ends with a particularly grim chapter, by David Courtwright, on the inevitable connection between money and drugs. Throughout, these authors indicate that the very definition of money changes with various societies and civilizations. *Money* is a term impossible to pinpoint for permanent definition because its cultural context controls its meaning.

Part II of this book discusses money in terms of its ancient history. Clifton Potter discusses how Queen Elizabeth I of England used money as a form of propaganda for herself and the Tudor monarchy. Thomas Luckett shows how money shortages in the eighteenth century ultimately became one of the major causes of the French Revolution. Andrew Economopoulos then analyzes banking in nineteenth-century America. For history, culture, and cultural symbolism, then, money has became a major chord. Governments' attempts to control money throughout history have generated a variety of social, political, historical, and artistic problems.

The remaining sections of the book provide the major focus of the book and discuss the connections between money and literature. Some simple souls may feel that the art form of literature should not concern itself with money, but few writers and artists would have agreed. In fact, the composer Richard Strauss was sometimes criticized for socializing with wealthy bankers and businesspeople instead of artists and writers. He defended himself by asserting that writers and artists wanted to talk only about money. Strauss's comic and cynical perception seems justified by many of the chapters in this book.

Part III discusses money as a theme in some American and Russian literature. Andrei Anikin analyzes Pushkin's use of the theme of money in his famous story "The Queen of Spades," a theme sustained in music by Tchaikovsky in his operatic version of the tale. Joann Krieg next discusses Henry James' *Wings of the Dove* in terms of money and health, examining the nineteenth-century view of health as economic capital. This chapter explains why virtually all of James' fiction describes and analyzes wealthy rather than poor people. William Carlos Williams' *Paterson* is next discussed in terms of its uses of the money theme in John Ulrich's essay. This chapter analyzes Williams' observations about credit and society, and how these interact through money.

French literature also produces many examples of writers' concerns about wealth. Alex Szogyi's "The Ultimate Seduction: Money and French Theater" provides an overview of the theme of money in French theater from the seventeenth to the twentieth century. Helen Harrison discusses Molière's *Tartuffe* in terms of money and the quest for some sort of unequivocal sign. Molière suggests, according to Harrison, the complex interrelations between signs and meanings about economic value. Flaubert's own obsessions with money certainly appear in *Madame Bovary*, and this obsession is the subject of Patricia Reynaud's chapter. Finally, John Frey discusses this same theme in the fiction of Balzac, Zola, and Gide. These major authors of the nineteenth and twentieth centuries in France concerned themselves with social status in society, and how that status depends on money.

The book ends with a long section on money's numerous appearances in English literature. Sandra Fischer analyzes Shakespeare's uses of wealth and money, discussing *Timon of Athens* in terms of economic realities in Renaissance England. Jeffrey Powers-Beck then shows how this same theme dominates Herbert's religious poem "Avarice." The South Sea trade in eighteenth-century Britain and how this trade influenced Defoe's *Robinson Crusoe* are analyzed by Lee Morrissey. I then write about Swift's *Wood's Halfpence Poems* and how money and metrical experimentation work together for the creation of a poetry of political propaganda. Jonathan Swift used his poetry as a means of keeping worthless English currency out of Ireland, and his poetical propaganda succeeded in keeping Woods' coins out of Ireland. Vanessa Dickerson next looks at how some nineteenth-century women writers used the theme of money. She indicates that the Victorian stereotype of women who were unaware of financial realities does not correlate with the fiction of the period. Charles Dickens, who arguably used the theme of money in all his novels, examines this subject centrally in *Martin Chuzzlewit*. Raymond Baubles' chapter analyzes Dickens' use of money in this novel. Finally, Robert Smart shows us how blood and money are unified through the threat of monopoly in Bram Stoker's *Dracula*. A novel which at first seems like a gothic thriller actually turns out to be a study of money and society.

Money: Lure, Lore, and Literature begins and ends by examining the connections between money and the arts. Art objects of course often become status symbols; in fact, some wealthy medieval merchants thought they could buy their way into heaven by paying for religious art in churches. In our own time, Sigmund Freud connected money with the anal stage in a child's development. And as we see at the end of the twentieth century the collapse of many forms of communism, we also witness how countries that formerly sought to create theoretically anti-materialistic societies adjust to the realities of a market economy. Money, it can be argued, connects with most aspects of the human experience, particularly literature. I believe this anthology of essays sheds some light on this very nexus.

Whether we earn it or spend it, inherit it or work for it, waste it or hoard it, reject it or dream about it, money and economic worries permeate our lives. Economic realities, says E. M. Forster in *Howard's End*, are the very "warp and woof" of life. And through this complex web of threads run social and political conflicts, religion, personal values, self-awareness, art, literature, and perhaps even our very souls. Throughout *Money: Lure, Lore, and Literature* a variety of experts use a variety of writing styles and approaches to examine the many complexities of what is resting every day right in our purses and pockets. Can art and literature afford to ignore such an omnipresence?

_____ Part I

Money, Language, and Culture

Money and Language

ROBERT A. LEONARD

Money and language are both highly abstract social conventions. Although we deal with them daily on what appears to be a concrete level, they both really exist only as social contracts: money and language are, if you will, all in our minds. Money, further, constitutes such an important domain that when it intersects with areas of language that have important social functions—slang and jargon, for instance—we observe speakers investing much effort and creativity. Money and language also intersect in that the names of currencies are expressed in language. Techniques and principles of historical linguistics help fill in the histories of the spread of currencies and innovative money-related concepts. So we will discuss the social contract aspect of language and money; examine the dynamics of some money-related slang and jargon; and first, explore the history of some currencies and currency names.

In 1974 I was traveling along the East African coast researching regional dialects of the Swahili language. In an antique and jewel shop in the town of Malindi, in Kenya, I noticed some old coins for sale: silver dollars. Not U.S. dollars but 1780 Maria Theresa dollars, minted in Austria. The coins had not been imported for sale, the owner told me, but had been bought from local families. How did these coins find their way to that corner of Africa, and, especially intriguing to an American, why were they *dollars*?

Malindi is an ancient port. Called Ma-lin by medieval Chinese sailors, it was founded by Swahili-speaking peoples who for many centuries had traded with Arabs, Indians, and other folk who found themselves blown to the east coast of Africa by the seasonal monsoon winds. Vasco da Gama came there in 1498, and it was colonized by the Portuguese, the Omani Arabs, and the English. Malindi received ships up from South Africa, down from the Red Sea, and regular shipping from Bombay via Mombasa. Germans and Italians came, and even the Americans came in their clipper ships. But these dollars, as we will see later, had not come on clipper ships.

The currency names *dollars*, *pennies*, *pounds*, and *shillings* serve as good illustrations of a tenet of historical linguistics regarding the movement of words from one language to another. The words most likely to be borrowed, or "imported," into a language are those that refer to some new concept or artifact, as opposed to what is termed *core* vocabulary. Core vocabulary are words such as the names for body parts, for immediate family members, and for numbers under five. These words are quite resistant to borrowing even if the speakers of one language have great power over the speakers of the other. So it is unlikely that a language will adopt another's words for "hand," "foot," "sister," "brother," or "one, two, three," but not surprising to find that in English, *government*, *judge*, and *plaintiff* were borrowed from the French-speaking Normans who conquered England in 1066. Some recent loans of novel concepts into English from French are *cotillion*, *femme fatale*, *bon mot*, *detente*, *objet d'art*, and *déjà vu*. From German, English has borrowed names for new objects and cultural concepts such as *leitmotif*, *frankfurter*, *sauerkraut*, *pretzel*, *wanderlust*, *kindergarten*, and—*dollar*.

In 1516 in Bohemia, currently a part of the Czech Republic but then a possession of the German-speaking Hapsburg Empire, the Count of Schlick opened a rich new silver mine. This mine had been discovered in St. Joachimsthal, or the dale, the valley, of St. Joachim.[1] In 1519 the silver coin of St. Joachimsthal was first struck, and it became known as *joachimsthaler*. That means, literally, "of Joachim's valley." *Joachimsthaler* was shortened into *thaler*, the part of the word that means "of the valley." This "of the valley" coin was widely accepted, for it was minted to a predictably high quality. The spelling and pronunciation of *thaler* varied according to country and location, and we find, among many other variants, *taler*, *daler*, and, in English, even before 1600, *dollar* (*OED* 785).

The northern European countries also circulated *daler* coins known as *riksdaler* in Sweden and *rigsdaler* in Denmark; it was not until 1873 that the German *mark* replaced the *thaler* as the German monetary unit. There were other currencies known as *dollars*. The Spanish *peso*, otherwise known as a "piece of eight," was very well known in Spain and her New World colonies. The etymology of *peso* is fairly straightforward. The word is Spanish for 'weight' and meant "a coin of a certain weight of precious metal." Already by the end of the 1500s the peso was referred to in English as a *dollar* (Barnhart 291) because it had the same general value as other widely circulated coins called *dollars*. The *peso* was well-known in North America during the time of the Revolutionary War almost two hundred years later. Throughout the colonial period the English had done all they could to keep the North American supply of coins low, and the colonials used whatever coinage came into their hands. This was often the *peso*, or the *Spanish dollar*.

The colonials reckoned in *pounds*. George Mason wrote from the Constitutional Convention declaring that he hoped he and the other delegates would be successful in their noble task; it was difficult work. "I would not, upon pecuniary motives, serve in this convention for a thousand pounds per day" (Vaughan 341). In 1782, in an apparent effort to distance the new United States of America from its former colonial master and ongoing opponent Britain, Thomas Jefferson suggested to the Continental Congress that the *dollar* be established as the currency of the United States. As indeed it was, in 1785 (Barnhart 291). However, these new continental dollars were not adequately backed and they depreciated sharply. It became difficult to find sellers who would accept them. (The British widely circulated counterfeit paper continental currency, and this, of course, did not add to the dollar's acceptability.) *Not worth a continental* was a contemporary phrase dismissing something as worthless.

George Mason wrote of pounds; Shakespeare writes of dollars in *Macbeth*, act 1, scene 2:

> Nor would we deign him burial of his men
> Till he disbursed at Saint Colme's inch
> Ten thousand dollars to our general use.

King Duncan is being briefed on an attempted Norwegian invasion of Scotland. The king of Norway, he is told, has been forced to pay the sum of ten thousand dollars before being allowed to bury his men. The time context of Macbeth is the years 1040–1057, when the historical figure Macbeth indeed ruled Scotland. A reasonable question might be, "Why *dollars* in *Norway* in about the year *1040*?"[2]

Remember that dollars started in Bohemia, in 1519. One of the places to which they spread was the Scandinavian countries. By the time Shakespeare wrote *Macbeth* around 1605 Norway was ruled by Denmark, and thus its monetary unit was the *rigsdaler* or dollar of northern Europe. A Norwegian king of that time might well be required to pay up in dollars. But in the year 1040, 500 years before the first *thaler* was minted? The answer, one supposes, is that Shakespeare cared more for his play's comprehensibility to contemporary audiences than he did for historical accuracy. One can similarly envision a 1990s playwright having a 1700s German speak of payment in *marks*, even though, as we noted, the mark only replaced the *thaler* in 1873.

The dollar that I saw in Malindi was a silver *thaler* or *dollar* of the Hapsburg empress Maria Theresa. Such coins were first struck in 1751.

Maria Theresa died in 1780 and since then hundreds of millions of the coins have been minted, all dated 1780. Mussolini used Maria Theresa dollars to finance his invasion of Abyssinia (today's Ethiopia) in 1935. Over twenty million of these same dollars were minted in Bombay during World War II. As of the 1960s they were minted still in Austria and circulated at a slight premium over the value of the silver itself, in the area of the Red Sea (Morgan 29). Given the direct trade links of Malindi with the Red Sea area, and especially its trade with Bombay, it would have been surprising had there *not* been Maria Theresa dollars in Malindi.

When the British came to colonize East Africa, they brought with them their English money, known as *sterling*. "How much is that in sterling?" one might hear, asked about a price quoted in dollars. The units of sterling are of course the *pound* (or *pound sterling*), the *shilling*, and the *penny*, counted in *pence*. *Pound* and *pound sterling* started out, as one might imagine from the other meaning of the world *pound*, as weights. *Pound* comes from the Latin *libra pondo*, which means "a pound by weight." The interesting thing here is that *pondo*, the word that we get *pound* from, doesn't mean "pound" in Latin—it means "weight." *Libra* is the word that means "pound." Notice that our abbreviation for *pound* is not *pd.* or some such, but *lb.*, as in *libra*. A pound started out as twelve ounces, corresponding more or less to a troy pound, still used by goldsmiths and jewelers. But as early as the thirteenth or fourteenth century things got confusing because a pound of sixteen, not twelve, ounces was used for items bulkier than gold and jewels.[3] In fact, the pound varied according to place and according to what was being weighed and could be anywhere from twelve to twenty-seven ounces. So pounds of different weight were used for cheese, wool, salt, hay, and so forth. Edward III stepped in and made the sixteen-ounce pound the standard "merchandise of weight," or *avoirdupois*. This pound contained 7000 grains, as opposed to the troy pound of 5760. (The Scottish pound contained 7608.9496.) But all this was too late to affect the pound sterling, which had been fixed at a pound: a twelve-ounce pound weight of silver (*OED* 1201–2).

The term *sterling* originally referred to the English silver penny of Norman times. The editors of the *Oxford English Dictionary* say that the word represents a hypothesized late Old English word *steorling* "coin with a star" (from *steorra* "star"), since some of the new Norman pennies had on them a small star. A competing explanation is that *sterling* is a form of *staer*, the name of the *starling* bird—there were four birds on some pennies. But then, given how other related vowels evolved, the word would have derived normally as *starling* and not *sterling*. Another explanation (that dates from 1300) was that the word was actually *Easterling* from the coin makers of Easterling. This seemed plausible on two counts. First, that a coin would be called after the locale where it was struck—remember *dollar*—and second, that such a term would be short-ened by usage—*dollar* is a good example again. However, the first syllable in *Easterling* is stressed (*Ea*sterling), and from all the observations linguists have made of how languages do and do not change, it seems improbable that *Easterling* would indeed shorten to *sterling* (*OED* 3044). In any event, a *pound* was defined as a pound of sterling pennies, those pennies being famous for their high quality and adherence to a fineness standard of 925 parts pure silver per thousand. This standard became known as sterling silver. The now-familiar *pound sterling* was originally a *pound of sterlings*.

There were pennies well before sterling. The origin of the term *penny* is of great antiquity, likely dating back to a common Germanic age (*OED* 2121), before the time that German and English and Norse started to split off from the common Germanic language in the fourth century to develop into separate languages. There are related forms—one in Old Norse, *pengar*, meant "money" (*OED* 2121) and one in Old High German, *pfant*, meant "pawn or surety" (*OED* 2103). So there were well-established Saxon pennies by the time of the Normans. The Normans took the word over when they conquered England and transposed their money system into Saxon terms. The Normans used the Roman system of the *libra* or "pound" (whose entrance into English we discussed), consisting of twenty *soldi* and a *solidus* of twelve *denarii*. The Saxon word *scilling* became used for the *solidus* and the *penny* for the *denarius*. Notice that the abbreviation for penny in amounts such as *3s4d* for "three shillings four pence" shows a *d* for *denarius*. *Shilling*, formerly *scilling*, originally meant a "piece cut off" and was used for broken pieces of coins and silver. It had already evolved into a term for a precise amount of money by the time the Normans appropriated it (Morgan 18).

So far we have looked at terms denoting various amounts of gold and silver. But there are modern units of currency that trace their origins to other items of value: for example the Greek *drachma*, and the Ghanaian *cedi*. The *cedi* comes from the Akan group of languages and means "cowrie." Cowrie shells are the best known and most widely used of what are called "ornamental currencies." For several thousands of years cowries have been used as payment in India, China, and the Middle East. Their use has continued in historical times in Asia, Africa, and the Pacific, a range one author describes as "from Nigeria to Siam, and from the Sudan to the New Hebrides" (Morgan 12). Perhaps their range was even further. Although cowries come only from the Indian and Pacific oceans, they have been found in pre-Viking burial tombs in Sweden and Norway dating from the fifth and sixth centuries A.D. (Heyerdahl 305).

Cowries were convertible into gold and other currencies. The great Arab traveler Ibn Battuta wrote in 1343 that in the Maldive Islands, south of India, four hundred thousand cowries were equivalent to a *dinar* of gold. In the early 1500s a Portuguese sailor wrote that in Bengal small cowries were "used as petty cash, being considered better than copper" (Heyerdahl 157–58). A monetary expert wrote in the 1960s, "Even now [the cowrie's] use is not quite extinct, and when the Japanese invaded New Guinea in 1942 they distributed cowries so freely as to cause a sharp fall in their value and in the words of an aggrieved district officer, 'endanger the economic and financial stability of the district' " (Morgan 12). In 1975 a Swahili friend, Sawiti bin Mohamed, took me to the northern Kenyan village of Ishakani just south of Somalia and showed me the cowrie trade there. There was basket upon basket of shells waiting for export. Most were perforated and woven into strings or belts (like ones found in tombs). Sawiti reported that when he was a schoolchild in the 1940s every day the schoolmaster would break school and take all the children to the shore. There he would send them into the shallow water to collect cowries to be divided among the village's families. (Sawiti also remembered that if he didn't collect enough he'd be whipped and sent out again: cowries were serious business.) The cowrie was central to the town's economy and the shells were exported far and wide. I saw no modern evidence of cowrie use as money, rather only as barter or sale for cash.

The scientific name of the money-cowrie is *Cypraea moneta*. *Cypraea* is from the Latin *Cypria*, a name of Venus (*OED* 1305). *Moneta*, from which comes our word *money*, was the name of a goddess, probably a Carthaginian goddess, considered identical to the Roman goddess Juno. During the third century A.D. Rome was allied with Carthage during the Pyrrhic War. Tradition says that the Romans sought Juno's advice about the best way to wage war. They were told that if they proceeded correctly their money—always important in war—would not fail. In gratitude they established their mint in her temple, the temple of Juno Moneta. *Moneta* came to mean "a mint," and "money" in general (*OED* 1836). Well-minted Roman coins date from this period.

While coins are essentially metal discs, metal "tool money" came first. It worked its way from northern Europe to the Mediterranean, and in Homeric Greece basins, rings, tripods, axes, and spits were used as currency. These were originally bronze, and later iron. The ancient *drachma* was a coin equivalent to six *obol* coins or weights. *Obol*, or *obolos* in Greek, is related to the word *obelos*, Greek for "iron spit." The value of a *drachma* was originally a handful—six—of iron spits (Morgan 12–13). *Drachma* itself originally meant "as much as one can hold in the hand," and thus its value became fixed vis-à-vis the current standard of worth: iron spit tool currency.[4]

Far from the intrinsic worth of a currency like an iron spit is the mere promise of the *banknote*. A *banknote* was originally a note issued by a bank that pledged to repay a depositor. The banknote in its modern sense originated with London goldsmiths who in the seventeenth century began to perform several banking functions. By 1670, along with the name of the depositor the words *or bearer* were added, and notes began to circulate instead of coins (Morgan 23–25). Of course banknotes, paper money, are no longer redeemable at a bank in gold or other precious metal, at least in the United States. Probably the last such note most of us have seen was the *silver certificate*, redeemable in silver by the U.S. government until 1967, and withdrawn from circulation a number of years ago. Our present United States money is *fiat* money: it has value because the issuer says it does. All money has value only if we all agree that it has value. That, of course, is part of the definition of money. The more a medium of exchange has intrinsic value the further away from money it becomes; exchange of items valuable in themselves is *barter*. So money needs no intrinsic value. That fact, and the reality that a certain piece of green paper with drawings on it currently has worth, while a nearly identical paper in, say, orange does not, together illustrate an important quality that money shares with language: arbitrariness.

In English we call a cat a *cat*; in French the animal is called *chat*, in Spanish it is *gato*, in Swahili *paka*. There is no natural connection between the sounds in *cat* or *gato* or *paka* and the animal those sounds represent. The relationship between the words and the meaning is *arbitrary*. There is no natural or God-given reason that a cat should not be called a *tac* or a *jabbo* or any other sequence of sounds we can think up. All that matters is that the speakers of the language *agree* that a word mean what it does: meaning in language is a social contract. Why should this be so? Let us examine some nonarbitrary "natural" words and meanings. *Plop* has a natural connection with its meaning, as does *splash*, and *hum*. Similarly, the word for "cat" in the Thai language is *maew*, clearly imitative of the animal's cry. In Swahili the word for "cattle" is *ng'ombe*, imitative of lowing cattle. But think how quickly we would run out of things that we could say if we could only say what we could imitate the sound of. How to express "red" and "green," let alone "truth" and "justice"? How could we represent the sound made by the present, past, and future?

The vast majority of words and grammatical items in a language—in all languages—mean what they do because they are *arbitrarily* attached to their meaning by the agreement of the speakers of the language. It is this arbitrariness that allows human language to have evolved into a system capable of efficient, flexible, and virtually infinite representation and expression of meaning. In much the same way it matters not if a dollar is printed on green paper or orange paper, or if money is given expression in silver, aluminum, paper, or plastic, or as a notation in a book or an excitation of electrons in a computer chip. It is the very immateriality of the substance in which money is expressed that gives money such vast advantage over the clumsy and inefficient barter systems from which money evolved. The linguist De Saussure held that language is a form, not a substance. The same is true of money.

Language and money are connected in other ways as well. Money engenders great creativity in language. Slang terms abound that deal with money (although there are far more that deal with sex). Here are a few older slang terms for money: *dough, jack, spondulics, rhino, simoleans, mazuma, gingerbread, kale, moss, long green, salt, dust, insect powder, tin, chink, blunt, brass, dibs, chips, beans, rocks, clinkers, plunks, horse nails, iron men, mopuses, bucks, bones, wad, oof, ooftish, yellow boys, thick 'uns, shekels, barrel* (chiefly political), *velvet* (money gained without effort), *palm oil* (bribe or tip), *the needful, the ready, the actual, corn in Egypt, plum* (£100,000), *grand* ($1000), *monkey* (£500), *century* (£100 or $100), *pony* (£25), *tenner* (£10 or $10), *ten spot, fiver, five spot, cart wheel* (silver dollar), *bob* (shilling), *tanner* (sixpence), *two bits* (quarter). These are from a 1936 source (Mawson 313).

It is easy to think of a few from those days that they missed: *moolah* and *greenbacks* for money in general and a *fin* (from Yiddish *finif*, related to German *fünf 'five'*) for "five bucks," a *sawbuck* for ten dollars and a *double sawbuck* for twice that. In addition to *two bits*, meaning a "quarter," there is *four bits* for a "half dollar," and *six bits* for "75 cents." Remember that the *dollar* currency that was the immediate forerunner of our U.S. *dollar* was the *peso*, the Spanish dollar. Further remember that the British severely restricted the coin supply in the colonies. All coins were scarce, but small change was very hard to come by. The peso was worth eight *reales* and called a *piece of eight*. It was often actually cut into bits to divide it into reales (Junge 77). Two bits, or two reales, was a quarter of the Spanish dollar and this is the origin of the term regarding U.S. dollars. Reales, or should I say parts of reales, also live on in the Southern term *picayune*, which means "something tiny or insubstantial." Its original Louisiana meaning was "a Spanish half-real coin," which was worth, of course, only 6¼ cents (*OED* 2164).

The evolution of money terms marches on. Recent field collections of slang and jargon terms in the New York dialect area reveal some new "coinages." In current street slang in New York City *cent* is used to mean a "dollar," as in "I only got fifty cents on me tonight" and "I only won twenty cents in that game." Gamblers refer to a "thousand dollars" as a *dime*, "five hundred" as a *nickel*, "one hundred dollars," as a *dollar*. When placing a bet with a bookie, one says, "I want *five times* on the Jets" to place a $25 bet, *ten times* for a $50 bet, and so on, each *times* an increment of five dollars. While one of the functions of slang and jargon is to conceal meaning and activities from outsiders, the above terms probably serve more to establish the insider status of the speaker than to conceal the meaning of what is being said.

Language with intent to conceal certainly abounds, however, and no less in the realm of money than elsewhere. Such intent is found in secret used-car sellers' jargon, which allows sales staff to discuss prices in front of a customer without the customer being aware of the amount or, often, even that a price has been comunicated. For example, upon seeing interest in a particular car, one of the staff may leave the showroom, look up what the car cost the dealer, and compute a price based on their desired markup. He or she can return and in front of the customer tell the other employee, "Oh, Jack, that was line 48 you were asking about." *Line 48* means the price is $2400. *Line 36* would mean $1800, *line 50*, $2500, and so on, each two-line increment equaling a hundred dollars.

Other inventive street slang usage finds the word *money* itself used as a stranger's name, as in, "Yo, money, want to help me change this tire?" The term *money-grip* means "friend." Technology always leaves its mark. Coins themselves were quite an innovation, and it was a major advance in the history of money when in the seventh century a pattern was engraved on the punch as well as the die used to mint coins. This allowed coins to be stamped with a design on both their sides, and different denominations were distinguished by different designs on their reverse (Morgan 13–14). We saw how the star design on a silver coin likely gave rise to a new term, *sterling*, that came to mean "money" in general. The word *silver* used to be used for "money" in general (especially in Scotland) (*OED* 2826). Then the stars, the sterling, on the silver came to mean "money."

An analogous situation now presents itself involving more modern materials. For some time, the word *plastic* has been used in slang with the meaning "money." Now on some of this plastic (a certain brand of debit card) there are three letters, *m-a-c*. Just as the stars on the silver gave rise to a new term for money, this *m-a-c* on the plastic has done the same. My most recent slang collection netted the term *mac* with the general meaning "money." From silver to star, from plastic to m-a-c. Just as plastic has supplanted silver, so *mac* may supplant the sterling star, and instead of referring to money as *sterling*, perhaps (who knows) we will all someday refer to it as *mac*. Were such a term to become successful, it would be just another reflection in language of the continuing evolution toward more and more abstract expression of the concept of money.

NOTES

I wish to thank fellow African linguist Wendy Saliba for her help in gathering data, and for her insightful comments on drafts of this chapter. All responsibility for errors and omissions, of course, remains mine.

1. *Joachim*, off the subject of money, means "established by God" in Biblical Hebrew and was the name of a king of Judah who was defeated and sent into

exile by Nebuchadnezzar. The reason this king's name was so popular in Christian Europe, and why it was thus available as the name of the valley that gave rise to the dollar, is that it was believed to be the name of the Virgin Mary's father. With the rise of the cult of Mary in medieval times the faithful wanted to venerate Mary's father along with her mother, Anne, as a saint. Yet nowhere in the Bible is he named. Joachim is the name that medieval Christian tradition commonly ascribed to the father, thus causing it great popularity (Hanks and Hodges 177–78).

2. One less-than-serious historian has suggested that 1040 was even then a mystically significant number for dollars.

3. If troy weight is at all familiar to most Americans today, it is only from the backs of grammar school composition books that listed the number of grains in a pennyweight and scruples in a dram. An original and continuing motivation for the adoption of the metric system is that British Imperial and U.S. Customary units of measure are overly complicated—among other intricacies, there are three different systems of weight: troy, avoirdupois, and apothecaries'. Notice that for practical purposes, we try to avoid all but avoirdupois. From a communication standpoint, the customary system is very inefficient. There are liquid *pints* and dry *pints*, each indicating a different volume. There are fluid *ounces*, indicating volume, as well as troy and apothecaries' *ounces*, which are the same weight, and avoirdupois *ounces*, which are a different weight.

4. The word *drachma* also survives in English as *drachm* or *dram*, originally the weight of the Greek coin: in apothecaries' weight ⅛ of an ounce and in avoirdupois weight 1/16 of an ounce (as if further evidence were needed of the complexity of the system vis-à-vis the metric). Although there are apothecaries' and avoirdupois *drachm*, there is no troy *drachm*. A *fluid drachm* equals 60 minims or drops (*OED* 1971:795).

REFERENCES

Barnhart, Robert K. *The Barnhart Dictionary of Etymology*. New York: H. W. Wilson, 1988.

Brugmann, Karl. *Comparative Grammar of the Indo-Germanic Languages*. Vol. II. London: Kegan Paul, Trench, Trubner, 1981.

Coffin, Joseph. *Complete Book of Coin Collecting*. New York: Coward, McAnn and Geoghean, 1976.

Hanks, Patrick, and Flavia Hodges. *A Dictionary of First Names*. Oxford: University Press, 1990.

Heyerdahl, Thor. *The Maldive Mystery*. London: Unwin Hyman, 1986.

Junge, Ewald. *World Coin Encyclopedia*. New York: William Morrow, 1984.

Lehmann, Winifred P. *Historical Linguistics: An Introduction*. New York: Holt, Rinehart, and Winston, 1962.

Lyons, John. *Introduction to Theoretical Linguistics*. Cambridge: University Press, 1968.

Mawson, C. O. Sylvester. *Roget's Thesaurus of the English Language in Dictionary Form*. Garden City, N.Y.: Garden City Books, 1936.

Morgan, E. Victor. *A History of Money*. Middlesex, England: Penguin, 1965.

Morris, William, and Mary Morris. *Morris Dictionary of Word and Phrase Origins*. New York: Harper and Row, 1977.

The New Columbia Encyclopedia. New York: Columbia University Press, 1975.

Oxford English Dictionary (Compact Edition). Oxford: University Press, 1971 (abbreviated as *OED* in the text).

Vaughan, Alden T. *Chronicles of the American Revolution*. New York: Grosset and Dunlap, 1965.

2

Determining Efficient Property Rights Systems for Money

Michael J. Haupert

There is the story of the old man who, when asked why he had never married, replied that he had never found a woman worth a whole cow.

The literature concerning the evolution of money centers on various explanations, but all touch upon the central theme that the development of money was a social institution, occurring without the aid of any central organizing body. These social institutions, however, did not prevail. In every case, the state eventually took over the control of the money supply. Eventually it proceeded to monopolize the money supply, restricting certain property rights associated with the production, introduction, and circulation of money. The aim of this chapter is to examine existing and potential money systems in order to identify the characteristics associated with the most efficient method of assigning the property rights to its production and control.

DEFINITION OF MONEY

For the purpose of this chapter, I will define money by touching upon its three major functions and the different forms they can take. The interest in doing so is in assessing these functions' roles in determining the most efficient form of assigning the property rights to money. That is, to whom should the legal right to produce money belong? Should it be exclusive (e.g., a government monopoly) or competitive? If the former, who should enforce this exclusivity, and how? Or, in the case of the latter, should there be a system of quality control or some other form of regulation?

The three major functions of money are a medium of exchange, a unit of account, and a store of value. Money serves as a medium of exchange by serving as one of the two goods exchanged in every transaction. In a pure barter system, goods are exchanged between parties in such a way that each gets what he ultimately desires. For example, a shoemaker will trade his shoes to a farmer for milk. The problem with this system is that it promotes a double coincidence of wants problem. That is, the shoemaker desiring a quart of milk must not only find a farmer willing to trade a quart of milk, but that farmer must at the same time be in need of a pair of shoes. The presence of money as a medium of exchange facilitates trade by eliminating the need to find a trading partner who both demands what you are selling and sells what you demand. Instead, all goods are sold for the medium of exchange, and in turn all goods are purchased with it.

As a store of value, money allows individuals to protect their purchasing power over time. Money will hold its value—at least in the short run—so that it can be exchanged for the same amount of goods today as tomorrow. For this reason, gold is a much better money than ice cream—especially in warmer climates. This feature of money is important because it allows consumers to separate spatially and temporally their demand and supply. No longer must they simultaneously demand and supply, but instead can sell goods, such as their labor services, at one time in one market, and demand at another time in another market. If the store of value is the same as the medium of exchange, then this is directly possible and lowers transaction costs—the sum total of all costs associated with a transaction or exchange. These costs include searching for the desired good; identification of the quality of the good; measurement of the attributes of the good, such as its weight, length, or purity; the writing of contracts to cover the exchange of complex goods, such as land or labor services: and the costs of enforcing exchange contracts. Transaction costs are decreased because traders don't have to convert their store of value into the medium of exchange before buying or selling.

Finally, money serves as a unit of account. The values of all other goods are measured in terms of the money. In our economy we measure the values of apples, automobiles, and oil not in terms of how many oranges it takes to purchase a barrel of oil or an automobile, but in terms of how many dollars we must trade for each. The cost of trading is decreased if the value of everything is measured in terms of one good. This facilities exchange because relative prices are much more easily calculated. Furthermore, if that one good is the medium of exchange, then there is no need to measure the medium of exchange in terms of the unit of account.

The next question I will address is what money is made of. There are two polar cases to consider, with a spectrum of variations in between.

On the one hand is commodity money, such as gold or silver, which has an intrinsic value. At the other extreme is pure fiat money—inconvertible money that is declared legal tender by the government. The U.S. dollar is an example of a pure fiat money. In between exists fully backed convertible paper money, which is convertible on demand into some commodity or other good with intrinsic value. The virtues of these various kinds of money will be discussed later.

EVOLUTION OF MONEY

The dominant theme in the literature on the evolution of money is that money evolved without the intervention of the state. It evolved as a response to various social needs—but it was initially a social institution, the idea of a state-sponsored money being a foreign and future one. George Knapp argued that money is merely what the government declares it to be. He begins his book by saying that "money is a creature of law. A theory of money must therefore deal with legal history" (Knapp 1). However, even he amended his statement by later admitting that money is "a commodity which had obtained a special use in society, first by custom, then by law" (Knapp 3). On the basis of this evidence, the question of interest then becomes one of determining under what circumstances a socially accepted money will evolve. The answers are many and varied.

A common thread in most money evolution theories concerns information constraints and specialization. This approach is especially supported by Alchian, King, and Plosser. Alchian emphasizes the existence of the cost of identifying goods—which includes the cost of knowing of the good's availability (where and when it can be purchased), attributes (size, color, quality, etc.), and terms of trade (conditions of sale). He argues that individuals can profit from specializing in identifying and providing information about a specific good. Jewelers, for example, specialize in identifying the quality and authenticity of diamonds and other precious gems. The cost of identifying goods makes barter a costly method of exchange on either of two margins. First, it is costly to identify the attributes of the goods that one is not a specialist in identifying. Second, if one chooses to deal only in goods in which he or she specializes (e.g., if a wheat farmer trades only wheat with specialists in the various goods he or she desires), then the double coincidence of wants problem arises.

In this context, the good that is sufficiently and cheaply identifiable by many, as if they were all specialists in that good, would become money. In order to facilitate trading, the good with the lowest cost of identification will emerge as the money in the economy. That good will become the medium of exchange (Alchian 112).

Alchian contends that the existence of specialists—persons with informational advantages concerning the attributes, availability, and terms of trade of a good—is what fuels the existence of money. If the costs of identifying some good are generally low in a society, that good will become the medium through which information costs can be decreased and hence exchange made more economical. The increased costs of trading due to the increased number of transactions which must be made when dealing with an intermediary good instead of direct barter are over-whelmed by the decrease in the costs associated with bartering. Most notably, it is the high costs of searching and identification necessary in barter due to the double coincidence of wants problem which make barter so expensive. It is the existence of the possibility for exchange which spawns specialization. Without specialists in each good, even the presence of an easily identifiable good would not be enough to encourage trade and thus spawn that identifiable good as money.

This idea is not too far removed from Karl Menger's theory concerning the evolution of money. Menger stressed the degree of "salability" of a good as the determining factor in what became money. According to this theory, money developed over time as merchants frequenting markets and fairs observed that there were certain goods which were in more demand than others, making it easier to trade those goods. This helps explain the existence of cows, tobacco, shells, and slaves as monies in various economies at various times. Eventually merchants realized that direct barter could be superseded by an indirect trading system in which the intermediate good was one with a high degree of salability—one whose value reflected the general economic situation and which could be obtained over time and across distance. That is, the good which becomes money is the one that people are most certain will be accepted by the next person in exchange for goods at a predictable rate of exchange (Menger 245).

Jones, like Menger, believes that the commodity that will develop as money will be the one that is most salable. However, he goes further than Menger in explaining exactly what that "most salable" good is. It is the good that the greatest number of people desire, and therefore will be most in demand at markets. This will not be hard for people to observe—even those without a demand for that good (Jones 757–75).

All potential traders enter the market with some idea of the probability of exchanging their goods directly. Those who succeed will upgrade their probability estimates. Those who don't can observe those goods that do trade more easily, and reevaluate their probability estimates accordingly. What develops is a secondary wave of demand for those goods most in demand by others. People who didn't previously demand the good will demand it now, not for consumption, but for indirect trade.

King and Plosser combined this idea with the notion of the Alchian specialization theory to put forward their hypothesis concerning the evolution of money. The greater the identifiability of a good, the greater its salability because more people are specialists in that good, and hence willing to accept it in exchange for goods because of the relatively low costs of doing so (King and Plosser 93–115). Therefore the good which evolves as money will tend to be the one that is most easily and cheaply identifiable in the society in question. The cost of identification includes the cost of discerning the "real" money from a counterfeit.

None of these arguments precludes the possibility that more than one good could evolve as money. Indeed there exists no theory which asserts that only one money should exist. Hicks addresses this by discussing the evolution of a dominant money. Historically, this is observed as the recurrence of the king's money as the one that tended to dominate the others. There are reasons for this to occur naturally, due to market forces, without the necessity of a law prohibiting other currencies or requiring the use of the king's money. The reason for the dominance of the king's money is its wider geographic range of acceptability—a result of its being relatively more identifiable than any other monies as a consequence of the king's guarantee, which further decreased the transaction costs of exchange by making the money perfectly identifiable. The king's guarantee took the form of a stamp on a metal coin certifying its weight and fineness as measured by the king.[1]

What determines which of several competing monies will become dominant? The one which displays the features of dominance: trust, wide recognizability, and wide circulation—not just local acceptability, such as an IOU or personal note that many be accepted in an area where the issuer is personally known. Trust refers to the confidence people have in the money's salability—that is, must possess the characteristic that the person accepting it believes that it can in turn be traded.

The name brand value of a firm will depend on its reputation, and the critical issue for any bank is the degree of confidence that it can establish. Money is not accepted unless people believe that they can exchange it for goods and services. Money does not have to be legal tender to be accepted. It does, however, have to be "what one might call common tender, i.e., commonly accepted in payment of debt without coercion through legal means" (Timberlake 438). The belief that others will accept the money in exchange for real goods and services is the underlying principle which keeps all money systems operating. If a money lacks the confidence of the people that it will be accepted as a means of exchange by others, it will cease to circulate as a money.

TRANSACTION COSTS

What are the effects of the evolution of a money on the transaction costs of exchange? The presence of a money, as noted above, serves to facilitate trade on certain margins—specifically by decreasing information and search costs. In addition, there are certain margins of trade on which the use of money results in costs that are not present in barter. This includes money's effect on relative prices and price stability, as well as the costs involved in detecting and punishing counterfeiting and enforcing the control of money or the way it is handled, for example, government regulations on banks to ensure that they don't mismanage the money supply.

There is no denying that money is an efficient institution. After all, the evolution of money was voluntary—there was no law enforcing its use. Therefore, if it had been less costly to use some other method of exchange, that method would have prevailed, not money. Jones argues this way, presenting a model of exchange in which a money evolves voluntarily from a system of pure barter because the benefits of money exceed the costs. He shows that given the possibility for a system of pure barter, mixed exchange, or pure money, the pure money system will prevail (Jones 757–75).

However, the argument that a monetary economy is superior to a barter economy does not preclude arguing about which particular type of money system is best. While indisputable evidence indicates that some type of money is superior to no money, the same cannot be said about the efficiency of the current state monopolization of the money supply as opposed to some other allocation of the property right to the supply of money. An attempt to determine with whom the property right to money supply should lie—whether it should be the state or private firms—must be dealt with by comparing costs and benefits. For example, what are the benefits of government monopolization of the money supply, and do they outweigh the costs? Conversely, what would be the benefits of a privately controlled money supply, and what would be the costs in such a situation?

First, it must be determined what the costs and benefits are, and then how to measure them. The former determination I will discuss in this chapter, the latter must await significant future research. The benefit to the state of controlling the money supply is the ability to inflate it in order to increase expenditures. If the state can inflate the money supply, that is, increase it at will without regard to the current needs of the economy, it need not raise as much money through taxes—and lower taxes translate into more votes. In addition, an inflated money supply allowing for increased expenditures is a very low-cost (in terms of real resource costs) method for the government to increase expenditures. All that need be done is to bear the cost of printing a few extra pieces of paper—a cost which is negligible. Of course these benefits must be considered net of any costs incurred to produce them—such as the erosion of faith in the money that accompanies inflation, as well as the inflation of future prices the government must also face.

The problem with unstable prices is that they decrease the quality of money services by decreasing the certainty of the value of money in the future as well as the value in the current period. If the state determines it beneficial to inflate the money supply by, say, 10 percent per year, then this imposes a 10 percent per year cost on the holders of money in terms of higher prices.

The benefits to society resulting from government control of the money supply include the state's advantage in providing necessary services that accompany the presence of money in an economy. One example is the problem of counterfeiting. There are high start-up costs associated with the prevention of counterfeiting which the government is willing to undertake when it supplies the money. These costs include the cost of supplying a money that is easily recognizable, yet sophisticated enough so that it cannot be easily counterfeited, as well as the costs of enforcing and monitoring counterfeiting.

In addition, the government is in a unique position to enforce and create laws in regard to money. These laws both promote money's acceptability, hence heightening its use, and guarantee against abuse of the money system by those outside the system (counterfeiters) as well as those within (banks). This latter point is accomplished by bank regulation, which is undertaken in order to ensure that banks do not mismanage the money supply for their own benefit at the expense of those who hold and use the money (Friedman and Schwartz 40). The former point is covered in the government's role as buyer of last resort. In the worst-case scenario, when nobody else will accept the government-issued money, you can always use it to pay your taxes to the government.

The major disadvantage of the state's possessing a money supply monopoly lies in the fact that the government has the incentive to do all of those things against which it protects us. It has an interest in counterfeiting (in such a case it is referred to as seignorage), especially when the situation arises that a commodity money's intrinsic value falls below its trade value. The temptation then exists for debasement in an attempt to capture the available profits. For example, if the value of one pound of silver is one dollar, the government can profit by issuing silver coins bearing the inscription "one dollar," but weighing only eight ounces. The government then has the remaining eight ounces of silver to use as it pleases. As mentioned earlier, the government also has an incentive to mismanage the money supply to manipulate it for its own purposes. This fear is certainly borne out in historical analysis by considering the several instances of state inflation used to help pay for wars or retire debts.

It is due to arguments such as these that proponents for a system removing the monopoly from the government get their greatest ammunition. Some argue for a return to a commodity standard, which is inherently free from government intervention, while others, such as Friedman, while not advocating a return to the gold standard, do push for a money growth rule whereby the state cannot manipulate the money supply at its own discretion, but instead must allow it to a grow at a steady, predictable rate.

A perfectly competitive money supply is also susceptible to problems concerning incentive. If a competitive supply of money exists, it seems that each individual supplier would have the incentive to inflate his own supply of money in order to capture the potential profits from doing so. Klein argues differently, however, claiming that as long as each individual money is distinguishable from all others, this will not occur because a profit-maximizing money producer will take into consideration the brand name value attached to his money (Klein 423–53). Inflating the money will cause a decrease in the quality of the money's services and therefore cause an exodus from that money into other available monies. This argument seems to hold in historical perspective. During the free banking era in the United States competition certainly prevailed, with over 1500 banks each producing its own currency, the value of which was in part a function of the reputation the issuing bank had established (Haupert 73–80).

Klein derives a model for a competitive money supply system showing that the profit-maximizing scheme for each money-producing firm would mean not inflating the money supply. This would also maximize the value of money services to the consumer. This value is composed of prize level stability as well as confidence, both of which depend on the money supply record of the firm. A firm which tries to profit by inflating the money supply will be run out of business as people switch out of its unstable money in favor of another money, losing confidence in its certainty for future prices. Therefore, it will be in a firm's best interest to maintain stable prices. This in turn decreases the cost to users of the uncertainty of a money's value, as well as the costs of having to switch to an alternate money to avoid inflation (Klein 423–53).

The cost to competing money supply firms of supplying information concerning the stability of their money may be great if there are high start-up costs associated with the dissemination of information. If this is so then a monopoly may be the most cost-efficient method of supplying money (Friedman and Schwartz 45). The problem with this system is that while it may further decrease the information costs by eliminating the need to compare the stability of various monies, at the same time it provides a higher cost of uncertainty as regards the potential for inflating the money supply. A monopoly has an incentive to inflate the money supply for its own purposes, since it is not in danger of losing any of its business to competitors.

Balancing these potential costs is the problem that if a firm decides to do this, it faces a loss of owner capital as people flee the money supply system, causing decreased money demand, or sue for breach of contract. Either way the owners face a loss of their investment in their firm—a problem which doesn't seem to face a government monopoly, which may arguably have a greater incentive to renege, since the person doing so has no investment in the state. At the same time, those controlling a state money supply have little incentive to take any risk involved in improving the efficiency of the system, since they themselves would accrue none of the gains, that is, greater potential profits, of doing so, but would bear the costs of failure by way of losing their jobs (Friedman and Schwartz 45).

RESOURCE COSTS

Another way to approach the question of who should control the supply of money is to focus on what constitutes the most efficient type of money. This issue has often been discussed, but never satisfactorily resolved (Friedman and Schwartz, Garrison). The debate boils down to one basic question: is it more efficient to use a commodity money or a pure fiat money? When discussing commodity money, the standard most often used is gold. Since it is unclear that the costs of any other commodity money, such as silver, copper, lead, or tin, would be appreciably different, the arguments of the gold standard proponents will be cited as the arguments for commodity money in general.

The general cost considered for the use of commodity money comes in the form of the resource costs employed in maintaining it. These costs include the mining, minting, coining, and guarding of the gold. Additional nonresource costs of using a gold standard include the costs it imposes on the price level in terms of rigidity. This argument proceeds along the lines that with a fixed supply of gold the quantity of money cannot be increased fast enough to accommodate economic growth. The result is that the price level must constantly decrease as the money-to-goods ratio decreases. Since prices change slowly, the result is disequilibrium and misallocation. While such a money system prevents a monetary authority from inflating the money supply for its own purposes, it also prevents it from adjusting the money supply to match economic growth and thereby reduce the possibility of allocation problems.

Proponents of commodity money argue that comparing the resource cost of a gold standard with a paper fiat money misses the point, because the real costs of a paper money are not the real resources employed in supplying it. Furthermore, the gold standard is a net-benefit system, so measuring the resource costs compared to a fiat system does not reveal the true cost-benefit comparison of the two systems (Garrison).

The only way to make a true comparison of the costs of the two types of money systems is to compare opportunity costs, thus taking into consideration all of the costs and benefits associated with each system, not just the pure resource costs. The total costs of a pure fiat currency include only the negligible resource cost of printing the money. However, several other costs are related to using such a system, including the costs imposed by different political factions trying to gain control of the printing press, and the costs imposed by various special interest groups to persuade those in control. These costs include both the costs involved in the use of resources to try to influence those in control of the money supply, and the costs imposed on the economy as a result of such struggles. These costs include the instability of the price system due in part to uncertain expectations which impose costs concerned with trying to figure out what the monetary authority will do, as well as the related costs associated with adjusting to expected authority actions and the subsequent costs due to failure to properly adjust and/or predict monetary authority movements. In addition, there are costs associated with inflation, in the form of unstable prices as well as the resulting costs of inflation-induced misallocation of resources. Further, the uncertainty of future prices caused by this imposes a cost of searching out alternate stores of value.

On the other hand, the implicit assumption is that commodity money wastes valuable resources which could be used for other purposes if a less costly money were used. However, it is not at all clear, and in fact there is historical evidence to the contrary, that the existence of a pure fiat money would mean the end of commodity money. Just because gold is no longer money, there has been no end to gold mining, minting, and guarding. History has shown that gold is a good substitute for fiat money, and the elimination of gold from use as a medium of exchange does not mean its elimination from use as a store of value; hence we continue to deploy resources toward gold even though it isn't money. Furthermore, if a money system is administered irresponsibly, the result might even be to increase the demand for gold to such an extent that the total resources devoted to gold may be even higher than if paper money had not been used, and a more stable gold standard reigned instead.

Now that the costs of the two systems have been set out, a brief look at the benefits provided by both is in order. According to gold standard proponents, the major benefit of a gold standard is that it is a system that is stable, free from irresponsible tinkering by the government, and incapable of use as a source of power to threaten political and economic freedom—in other words, all of the things a pure fiat money is not. While Milton Friedman has asked how it would be possible to construct a money system that would act in this way (Friedman), proponents of the gold standard answer that no such system can be created—it can only evolve. Not coincidentally, those items originally evolving as money were commodities, such as gold, silver, tobacco, cattle, or shells. Reference here can be made to the positivist slogan that "what man has made he can also alter to suit his desires." So, argue the gold standard supporters, the resource costs associated with gold are far outweighed by the benefits of immunity from state intervention and resulting instability of money.

On the other hand, the proposed benefits of a pure fiat money include the opportunity cost of an alternate, commodity system—the tremendous resource costs involved with such a system that were mentioned above. Further benefits include those associated with monetary policy—the ability to adjust the money supply as necessary to changes in the economy. If the money supply can be harnessed and put in the hands of a monopolist, then monetary stability, defined as manipulation of the money supply in order to minimize unemployment and inflation, can be achieved. Other arguments center on the use of monetary forces to maintain stable prices by adjusting the money supply to the changes in production.

CONCLUSION

The performance of the current money system has been questioned repeatedly, both in terms of the type of money used and the property rights system existing around it. The current system has come full circle from a stage of independent instruments serving to fulfill the desired functions of a money, to one in which all three were embodied in one, and back again. Early in the evolutionary development of money, the prevalent form was a commodity money, which served most efficiently as the unit of account, medium of exchange, and store of value concurrently (during the depression the dollar bill performed these roles optimally). Only during times of decreasing prices will the dollar serve as a good store of value. In times of increasing prices, dollars lose real purchasing power, and are inefficient means of storing value.

Today we once again live in a world in which the three functions of money are largely separated. While in the United States the dollar is the overwhelming unit of account, it is losing favor as a medium of exchange to checking accounts, traveler's checks, and money market checking accounts. Indeed, except among the lower strata of income earners and in the black market, dollars have become largely a thing of the past as a medium of exchange. To an even greater degree the dollar has been replaced as a store of value. A myriad of highly liquid financial instruments, including money markets, Treasury bills, stocks, and commodities, have arisen, trading actively on secondary markets.

Of interest also are the state's effects on the transaction and resource costs of the money system. Given that the state has switched to a pure fiat system, are all of the costs of that fiat system due to the state? What would be different if a competitive fiat money were issued? In the free banking era, stable prices were more the rule than the exception, but to what extent was this due to the fact that the monies were backed by gold, and to what extent was it because of the competition?

Friedman and Schwartz address these questions when discussing their support for a government-controlled money. Another factor is the pervasive character of money, which means that the issuance of money has important effects on parties other than those directly involved. What remains very much open to question is what institutional arrangements would minimize those third party effects. A strong case has been made that government involvement has made matters worse rather than better, both directly and indirectly, because the failure of monetary authorities to pursue a stable noninflationary policy renders performance by private intermediaries equally unstable (Friedman and Schwartz 37–62). As yet there has developed no consensus on desirable alternative arrangements, let alone any effective political movement to adopt alternative arrangements.

In considering any alternative arrangements the political as well as economic ramifications of such changes must be taken into account. Keeping both of these questions in mind leads to a public choice perspective on the situation, that is, a focus on what institutions and policies will facilitate the operation of the free market. Once again, Friedman and Schwartz ask the interesting question when considering changes in the money system. They emphasize that two questions need to be asked: the narrower one being whether or not a proposed set of arrangements is economically viable, the broader, whether this set of arrangements would allow for stable political as well as economic equilibrium. That is, is its existence consistent with the political constitution, or would it generate political forces leading to major changes in the arrangement (Friedman and Schwartz 45)?

Research in these areas has unearthed several interesting questions but few, if any, answers. The broad question, stated once again, is what system of property rights in money would lead to the most efficient monetary institution. Within the scope of this research, however, there are a host of other questions that need to be answered first. Such fundamental issues as just how an efficient monetary institution is to be defined, on what margins this system can be enforced and substituted away from, and how resource costs would be affected by using different types of money in different property rights systems must first be answered before such a prodigious project can be satisfactorily completed. Given the gaping holes in each of these areas of research, the determination of an efficient property rights system from money will entail significant future research.

NOTE

1. Although a good may be relatively more acceptable than others, it may still possess attributes that are not readily observable, such as the weight and fineness of precious metals. The king's stamp acts to decrease these costs by guaranteeing the quality of the commodity. To the extent that traders trust this guarantee, the commodity becomes more identifiable.

REFERENCES

Alchian, Armen. *Economic Forces at Work*. Indianapolis: Liberty Press, 1977.
Friedman, Milton. *A Program for Monetary Stability*. New York: Fordham University Press, 1959.
Friedman, Milton, and Schwartz, Anna J. "Has Government Any Role in Money?" *Journal of Monetary Economics* 17 (January 1986).
Garrison, Roger. "The Cost of a Gold Standard." In *The Gold Standard: An Austrian Perspective*. Rockwell, Llewellyn, and Yeager, Leland B., eds. Lexington, Mass.: D. C. Heath, 1985.
Haupert, Michael J. "Investment in Name Brand Capital: Evidence from the Free Banking Era." *The American Economist* 35 (Fall 1991).
Hicks, John. *A Theory of Economic History*. Oxford: Clarendon Press, 1969.
Jones, Robert. "The Origin and Development of Media of Exchange." *Journal of Political Economy* 84 (December 1976).
King, R. G., and Plosser, C. I. "Money as the Mechanism of Exchange." *Journal of Monetary Economics* 17 (January 1986).
Klein, Benjamin. "The Competitive Supply of Money." *Journal of Money, Credit and Banking* 6 (November 1974).
Knapp, George Friedrich. *The State Theory of Money*. London: Macmillan, 1924.
Menger, Karl. "On the Origin of Money." *The Economic Journal* 2 (June 1892).
Timberlake, Richard. "Private Production of Scrip-Money in the Isolated Community." *Journal of Money, Credit and Banking* 19 (November 1987).

3

Money, Love, and Roses: Liquidity Preference Reconsidered

Catherine L. Lawson

INTRODUCTION

A popular song likens love to a rose, which flourishes only so long as it remains undisturbed in its natural state; anyone who ventures to pick it and thereby take possession of it is left only with thorns.

The thesis explored in this chapter is that what is true of love, as described in the song, is also true of wealth. At first blush, such a connection may seem far from obvious. Perhaps the initial images that we conjure up of either love or wealth do share some basic qualities—we may think of something a bit mysterious, alluring perhaps, and definitely elusive. Beyond this, however, there seems little room for comparison between the eminently practical "laws of motion" governing the creation and amassing of wealth, and the tender sentiments pertaining to love. Nevertheless, the resemblance of *both* wealth and love to the properties of the rose, has been incorporated into the perspective of some of the great economists. So much so, in fact, that these insights have attained the status of "truisms" and, as such, have been largely forgotten as ways of gaining fresh insight into the newly unfolding economic landscape. It is our purpose here to rescue them from this status and to reconsider what this perspective has to teach us about our current economic environment.

Our first task in what follows will be to establish that the patterns governing the behavior of the rose, growing only when left on the plant that bears it, apply as surely to the creation of wealth as to the affairs of the heart. To see this, we draw from the works of John Maynard Keynes and his lesser-known Polish contemporary Michael Kalecki. We then consider what it is that interferes with the steady creation of wealth, focusing on the contemporary significance of Keynes' preoccupation with liquidity preference and the casinolike tendencies of the financial markets. This leads into a discussion of the financial innovations characteristic of the modern environment. Finally, we conclude with a brief comment regarding the question of just who it is, in the end, that is left with thorns.

WEALTH AS A LIVING ROSE

In introductory economics courses we are all taught (and have readily observed) the simple fact that spending drives the economy. In a system where firms produce for a profit, the only way to ensure that they will continue producing and, thus, continue offering employment to the vast majority of the population, is to ensure that what they produce gets purchased. As the simple circular flow model of the economy demonstrates, when all of the income generated in the production process is spent on the output generated in that process then we have no problem. The value of output and the value of income generated in the production process coincide. Where problems crop up is in the withdrawal of some of this income from the spending stream in the form of savings (be they savings of businesses or households). As Keynes' "paradox of thrift" makes clear, efforts on the part of the community to save more may actually lead to less saving than before if, when this income is withdrawn from the spending flow, it does not find its way back into that flow in the form of investment spending on new capital goods.

This is all standard theory in basic economics. However, we are talking here about the circulation of wealth, and wealth cannot expand unless allowed to circulate, just as the rose cannot flourish after it is picked. This is suggested more clearly by conceiving of the savings in this picture as the income accruing to a particular class. It is commonplace that those parties with the largest incomes are those most likely to save. Indeed, those with very large incomes meet their consumption demands with a relatively small portion of their income, and the major issue becomes one of how to dispose of the rest.

It is this kind of starting point that characterizes the work of Michael Kalecki, the Polish economist credited with arriving, contemporaneously, at the same insights as Keynes.[1] His initial point of departure is the classical economists' division of society into two classes, workers and capitalists. Inserting this perspective into the simple circular flow model, we have the flow of income coming out of the production process conceived as being split into two parts: the wage income received by workers and the profit income received by capitalists. Wage income is all channeled directly back into the spending flow in the form of consumption expenditures. Profit income may or may not make it back into the spending flow. The portion of profits needed to finance the consumption of capitalists (which Kalecki believes to be relatively income-inelastic) is directly channeled into the spending flow, just as is the spending of workers. But what of the remainder?

This amount constitutes the current increment to the holdings of wealth by the individual capitalist (although the funds may be held by the representative of that individual, namely, the modern business firm). If the holder of this wealth behaves in the manner of the classical capitalist and reinvests the profits in the creation of new capital goods, then this means that income finds its way back into the spending stream. In this case, we get the requisite investment spending, the circular flow proceeds uninterrupted, and the real wealth of the community—its productive capacity—is augmented as well. If not, however, problems arise. Some firms hoping to sell their output—a feat necessary for the maintenance of the flow of profits to the capitalist class—find themselves disappointed. As a result, production is cut back, output falls, and *both* wages and profits are lost. Thus, Kalecki's famous dictum: "The workers spend what they get; the capitalists get what they spend" (*Selected Essays* ix).

Actually, this characterization of the problem is not so different from the scenario envisioned by Keynes, though the similarities are in some ways more obvious in his *Treatise on Money* than in the more well-known *General Theory of Employment, Interest, and Money*. Kenneth Boulding suggests that Keynes' *Treatise* discussion provides a "widow's cruse" theory of profits (Boulding 5). The reference is to a story in the Old Testament where oil is burned in a lamp (cruse) belonging to a widow. The more oil that is burned, the more plentiful becomes the oil available to be burned. Similarly, according to Keynes, the more of total income that is spent in the economy, the more successfully the system will create new income and wealth, thus providing for further spending.

To summarize this point, it is clear that wealth left undisturbed like a rose in its natural setting on the vine, circulating in the economy to finance spending on new capital goods, tends to grow. This is true from the perspective of the individual wealth holder, who adds to his or her personal fortune through increments of current profit. It is also true for the larger mass of people who, unknowingly, are dependent upon investment spending to augment consumption spending in order for their current employment to be maintained.

INCENTIVES TO PICK THE ROSE FROM THE VINE

Problems arise, in the arena of both love and wealth, when the human propensity to *cling* to the objects of one's desires gets out of hand. This propensity is especially aroused in the face of a heightened prospect of the loss of such objects. In the economic system, a heightened generalized fear about the prospects for earning profits prompts owners of wealth to reach for the maximum degree of control over what they have already amassed—in a word, to reach for *liquidity*. The Keynesian preoccupation with liquidity preference, therefore, can be seen in broad terms as a basic concern for the economic equivalent of "picking the rose from the vine."

The explanation for why fears about profitability might be expected to materialize on a regular basis is highlighted in Kalecki's work. It is not irrationality, nor "animal spirits" (Keynes' colorful phrase for swings in business confidence) that lie at the base of the fears that end up expressing themselves in a heightened preference for liquidity. Rather, it is the basic logic of the investment process itself. While we have emphasized so far the role of investment as a component of total spending, investment has as its ultimate objective the construction and installation of new capital goods—goods which augment the productive capacity of the economy. Once this addition to productive capacity is placed in operation, the total supply of goods being produced in the economy will be augmented, and the profit rate to be earned upon the sale of that output must be correspondingly attenuated. Thus, the general stimulus to profits that is provided by the boost in aggregate demand from investment spending is, at some point, offset by the increased supply of output that such spending ultimately makes possible as well. When this happens, further investment spending—a pursuit always motivated fundamentally by the general rate of profit—is no longer an attractive prospect. The inducement to invest falters, wealth owners pull back from investing, and alternative "resting places" for their accumulated holdings of wealth increasingly are sought out.[2]

Something similar is at work in Keynes' discussion of the long-run prospects for capitalism, as set out in chapter 16 of the *General Theory*. As capital becomes more and more plentiful over time, its return has to fall, for it is only on the basis of its scarcity that it earns a return at all. Were investment in new productive capacity the only possible abode for wealth in our economy, a falling rate of profit on such investment would simply have to be accepted by wealth owners. It would not, therefore, interfere with the capital accumulation process or with the maintenance of sufficient aggregate demand. The problem is that real capital investment is *not* the only abode for wealth: "there is always an alternative to the ownership of real capital assets, namely, the ownership of money and debts" (Keynes *General Theory* 212). Thus, the increasing reluctance to purchase real capital assets may engender at some point a wholesale shifting into other more liquid kinds of assets, and it is in this type of phenomenon that the significance of liquidity preference really resides.

This brings us to the contemporary relevance of these Keynesian/Kaleckian notions. What Kalecki's analysis makes clear is that the maintenance of an adequate inducement to invest is far from assured. Rather, it is likely that at least periodically difficulties will be experienced. This conclusion emanates from an examination of the internal structure of investment spending—the fact that it augments both demand and supply. There is little reason to believe that much has changed in this regard since Kalecki first described the problem. Keynes contributes even further to this picture by examining the means of holding and enhancing wealth that are available as *alternatives* to real investment. With regard to this factor, *much* has changed in recent decades—mostly, in an undesirable direction. The overwhelming changes that have occurred in the financial sector in recent years, the vast extension of this kind of activity, and its dramatically increased sophistication are critical factors in connection with the question of just how successfully wealth owners may be able to "pick" the rose from the vine, and how successfully others are able to cope with the consequences.

THE ROLE OF THE FINANCIAL SECTOR

Events in the financial sector may be interpreted fundamentally as symptoms rather than as causes of disturbances in the productive sphere of the economy. The logic of these financial sector events is derived from the changing role that the financial system is called upon to play in accommodating real sector activity. When activity in the production economy slackens, the financial sector begins to move away from the role of providing *complementary* goods and services which *facilitate* real economic activity, and toward one of providing *substitute* goods and services which offer *alternative* means of achieving the same goals. Thus, as investment instability erodes the rate of growth in aggregate demand, profits, and living standards (as it seems to have since the early 1970s), decision makers in the economy are able to seek recourse, at least partially, in the financial system.

Two general outcomes are particularly obvious. First, as the failure in investment spending reduces aggregate income, all of the various parties demanding goods—firms, consumers, government—are forced to resort to the increased use of *debt* finance in order to maintain and/or expand their levels of expenditure. Second, as wealth holders experience falling yields on investment in new capital goods, they seek out methods of *financial manipulation* (of both assets and liabilities) by which to protect and enhance their wealth. In each of these cases, reliance is placed upon financial institutions to facilitate these responses, and a primary means by which this is accomplished is through financial innovation. Thus, the innovative behavior of financial institutions is at least partly driven by the demands placed upon them in an environment of declining economic activity. An examination of the new practices of financial institutions, as well as the products and markets that they have introduced, reveals this basic linkage.

Three characteristics of what Wall Street insider Henry Kaufman calls "the new financial world" characterize contemporary financial firm operations (Kaufman 45). First, variable rates of return paid to lenders by financial institutions and paid to financial institutions by borrowers are increasingly the rule rather than the exception. Second, financial assets of a steadily increasing variety are securitized—meaning loans are made, pooled, and sold to other financial institutions who issue securities backed by the loans. Third, "proxy" instruments such as futures and options have become widely available for the purpose of conducting arbitrage and attempting to hedge risk. These characteristics enable and encourage financial firms to accommodate escalating credit demands of consumers, firms, and government. They also convey the impression that the increasing risks which accompany financial expansion can be, and are, effectively neutralized. Following Kaufman's critique of these practices, however, we can see that this may or may not be the case (Kaufman 43–59).

Financial firms, like others, have attempted to minimize their risk. This has been accomplished by transferring the risk to others through variable rate lending devices. From the perspective of the financial institution, the variable rate aspect of both their liabilities and their assets suggests that the spread between borrowing and lending rates is a given. Therefore, the only available means of enhancing profits is to increase the *volume* of credit outstanding. Thus, the debt expansion required by firms and households in their responses to investment instability finds itself translated into the incentive structure of the intermediaries who carry it out. "Spread banking" becomes the name of the game, not just for commercial banks, but for all financial institutions. Unprecedented debt expansion, accompanied by unprecedented default potentialities—in view of the variable rate characteristic—follow from such a practice.

The growing trend toward securitization, exploited by many financial institutions, is also problematic. It tends to reduce credit quality, hence, increase default risk, while at the same time attempting to hedge against such risk. Kaufman has dubbed this the problem of "credit without a guardian." Since the party granting the loan will be tied to the borrower for only a brief period, the incentive to scrutinize carefully the creditworthiness of the borrower is significantly impaired. Securitization appears to reduce risk by promoting diversification and marketability. But the weaker scrutiny of borrowers may lead to an increase in defaults sufficient to affect the market. All holders will not be able to sell out before the general credit quality deterioration becomes public knowledge.

Finally, the use of proxy instruments such as futures and options has become a preferred method by which intermediaries and large institutional investors attempt to reduce the variability of returns. While the markets for some of these instruments have their roots in hedging behavior connected with the production economy, the far greater share of activity arises from the hedging and arbitrage operations of financial institutions. As the size and complexity of financial markets grows, so too does the volume of proxies that are traded for these purposes. Many observers have warned of the tendency of this type of trading to attract and encourage speculative interests. Such interests, in turn, tend to increase market volatility. These warnings have found powerful validation on the stock exchanges in recent years.

These changes in financial institution operations all facilitate an emerging thrust toward increasing debt levels and increasing speculative activity—the very repositories of wealth that Keynes worried about as "alternatives to the ownership of real capital assets." What is important to recognize is that such patterns mesh well with, and are at least partially motivated by, the needs and desires of nonfinancial decision makers (households and firms) who are attempting to cope with declining economic performance. Some households undertake debt expansion in the attempt to preserve living standards in the face of declining income. Others resort to increased asset management and speculative activity for the purpose of maintaining an acceptable rate of return on accumulated wealth. Nonfinancial firms seek recourse to the financial sector to halt the slide in profits and overcome rising obstacles to the maintenance of sales. In this regard, rising debt and increased speculative activity both have a role to play. Thus, participants on both sides of the transactions which create debt and promote speculation have incentives to accelerate this activity. And financial institutions stand ready to accommodate them. The specific financial innovations which correspond to these activities are manifold. Only a sampling will be reviewed here for purposes of illustrating the predominance of these trends in the contemporary economy.

FINANCIAL INNOVATION

Throughout the 1970s and 1980s, a wide variety of innovative instruments emerged to accommodate the increasing demand for consumer credit. This was observable in mortgage finance, in the finance of consumer durables such as automobiles, and in the widespread availability of consumer credit instruments designed to suit just about any purpose. In the mortgage arena, lagging consumer demand resulting from economic slowdowns and interest rate increases led builders and mortgage lenders to come together to offer a wide variety of financing alternatives. The simplest of these, the adjustable rate mortgage, now provides the bulk of new mortgage financing. The obvious benefit of this device to the lender is a reduction in interest rate risk. However, it is clear that these loans do not actually alter that risk but simply transfer it from lender to borrower. This is true for most of the new types of mortgages that have been introduced over the last decade. The willingness of borrowers to accept such risk in order to afford home ownership indicates an attempt to meet consumption targets through changed financing devices in lieu of adequate personal financial capacity.

A similar dynamic has governed trends pertaining to other types of consumer debt. Auto loans offered with longer terms (up to ten years at some companies) have become commonplace, as has consumer auto leasing. With a lease format, the auto "buyer" is able to use debt for essentially 100 percent financing of the new car. Since the consumer does not own the car at the end of the lease, literally continuous debt finance becomes necessary in order to meet transportation demands. Bank cards, finance company credit lines, mortgage lender home equity loans, and retailer credit all tell a similar story. Each form of consumer credit was initially made available and then expanded in order to increase or, in many cases, maintain, the profits of the issuer. These programs offered consumers access to debt on a revolving basis to finance the purchase of just about any type of good. This debt has grown dramatically at the same time that real wages and creditworthiness have declined. Borrowers have sought to maintain their lifestyles despite the latter adverse developments. A billowing and worrisome volume of consumer debt has been the result.

Households have also sought to maintain the returns they earn on accumulated wealth. In attempting to accomplish this, they have resorted to both cash management schemes and sophisticated investment strategies. Cash management devices, such as NOW accounts, were unheard-of only a short time ago but are now commonplace. The general objective of these devices is the same as that of corporate cash management efforts, that is, to earn a return on the money balances that are acquired as a normal part of routine transactions. In order to earn an adequate rate of return on other financial wealth owned (such as their savings balances) households, like firms, have chosen to devote more and more resources to financial management. They have done so, however, by increasingly "institutionalizing" their savings—that is, by hiring large institutional investors such as pension funds, insurance companies, and stock and bond mutual funds to invest their money for them. This means that households of relatively modest means now share with their more affluent counterparts some of the clout deriving from a larger presence in the financial markets. This, in turn, has allowed them to invest in a steadily widening array of complex and esoteric financial instruments not readily available to them before.

The increased institutionalization of savings, while extending the financial investment opportunities available to households, has also promoted increased speculative activity in the financial futures markets. The institutional investor is charged with obtaining a high and stable return for the individual household with whose funds it has been entrusted. Failure to carry out such a task provokes a swift response from the increasingly financially sophisticated household (or its representative), who simply places the funds with another agent. A constant shifting and reshuffling of funds between alternative financial assets is undertaken in the pursuit of the highest possible return. This, in turn, contributes to market volatility and, thus, invites increased use of interest rate futures and options to stabilize returns on debt instruments, as well as stock index futures and options to stabilize stock portfolio values. As the search for higher yields increasingly becomes a global pursuit, foreign exchange futures and options also become important to stabilize foreign denominated financial asset values and yields. Again, all such activity is conducted in markets that are highly conducive to excessive speculation.

The financial transformation which has overtaken businesses is even more dramatic and more thoroughgoing than that of households. As more and more financial management has come to be conducted within nonfinancial firms, their status as primarily production units has given way to an identity defined equally, or more so, by their activities as financial units. This evolution from a focus on production to a focus on finance is evidenced in the contemporary phenomenon of nonfinancial conglomerates that wield as much influence in some financial markets as do leading financial institutions. General Electric, Ford, General Motors, and Sears are all examples of such firms. While the financial activities of most nonfinancial firms are far less extensive, such activity does provide a significant area of endeavor for a great many firms. The emphasis is generally not on selling financial services to the public, as with Sears, but on utilizing financial techniques for salvaging profits. This has led to both increased corporate debt burdens and a wide variety of "restructuring" measures involving financial manipulation of both assets and liabilities.

For a variety of reasons, firms over the 1970s and 1980s acquired progressively larger amounts of debt. Partly this was because internal sources of finance for investment spending (retained earnings and depreciation allowances) were not always adequate to finance such spending. This was especially true when such resources were being drained off into corporate "restructuring" activity (discussed below). Partly also, the debt expansion process is self-feeding to some degree. Interest payments on debt require increased future cash flows which may or may not be forthcoming, thus yielding a further impetus to debt creation. And, successful fulfillment of debt obligations inspires a relaxation of credit standards as time goes on. Thus, the commitment to larger amounts of debt emerged and the task became one of finding innovative means of keeping the cost of such funds low.

In an early example of innovative behavior geared toward this objective, firms in the late 1950s and early 1960s discovered that they could reduce their cost of short-term funds by competing with banks for large time deposits. They set up facilities to offer commercial paper to lenders as an alternative to large bank deposits. As the 1960s progressed and U.S. nonfinancial firms became more involved in international business, they became increasingly aware of the services offered by foreign financial institutions. Eurodollar borrowings became another source of funds, as they were often offered at lower rates than equivalent domestic loans. Innovative debt instruments materialized during the 1970s and 1980s at an astounding rate. Devices such as variable rate notes and bonds and callable bonds were introduced which allowed firms to continue acquiring more funds by reducing rates below what they would have been had adequate risk premiums been added to the prevailing fixed rates. The combination of a strong impetus for debt expansion and rising real interest rates also brought forth various innovations designed to defer, and in some cases reduce, debt servicing costs. Convertible bonds, offering a below-market interest rate in exchange for the option to convert each bond to a fixed number of shares of common stock after a deferral period, provide an example. A plethora of other examples—bonds with warrants, zero coupon bonds, zero coupon convertible bonds, and so on—were all developed with similar goals in mind, and the theme in all of them is one of increasingly complex financial claims on the firm, in lieu of higher current debt service.

At the same time that this debt explosion was under way, and partly as a motivation for it, another development was taking place in the corporate sector, that is, the aforementioned "restructuring" activity of nonfinancial firms. In the financial press, this term usually crops up in reference to the infamous mergers and acquisitions boom of the 1980s. This *has* been a major part of the increasingly speculative and predominantly financial adaptation which firms have made to a declining economic environment. Several important financial innovations facilitated this development, including the notorious and much-maligned junk bond market and leveraged buyout lending of banks. Less spectacular but equally widely practiced examples of restructuring behavior are also in evidence. These range from a proliferation of relatively innocuous cash management strategies, through the leverage-enhancing properties of practices such as stock buybacks and sale-leasebacks, to sophisticated financial maneuvers involving swaps of stocks and bonds and manipulations of pension fund liabilities. Presumably, most of these activities are legal and have been profit-enhancing. None of them, however, has unambiguously improved the real productive capacity or performance of firms. And the very existence of such techniques, to say nothing of their widespread use, testifies to the great extent of the efforts devoted by nonfinancial firms to the goal of augmenting profits through primarily financial means.

SUMMARY AND CONCLUSIONS

The foregoing review of the contemporary financial landscape, at least in its dominant features, has been conducted to suggest just how far we as a society have come in promoting the "alternatives to the ownership of real capital assets" that Keynes so feared. That this progression has occurred is clearly illustrated in the financial activity, just reviewed, of the business sector—a sector populated, after all, by the managers if not the owners of much of the wealth in the society. A good deal of business activity in the 1980s, such as the mergers and acquisitions boom, can be interpreted as the economic equivalent of "picking the rose from the vine." The response of an individual household to the resultant stagnation in the economy has depended upon the stratum of the income distribution in which it resides. For wage earners, the possibility of adaptation has been afforded through the development of a plethora of consumer debt vehicles. The longer-run consequences of this adaptation are as yet unclear. On the other end of the spectrum, the ability of wealthy households to find alternative repositories for their wealth has been clearly enhanced by the wide variety of financial investment devices made available by the processes reviewed above.

The task of definitively sorting out the positive from the negative features of this landscape is a complex one, and somewhat daunting. This is partly because financial innovations seemingly *have* allowed people to adapt to the declining performance of the economy in ways hardly imaginable in earlier times, including that of Keynes. Indeed, it may be because of these financial sector developments that we have not experienced an even greater decline in the economic system, not to mention outright collapse, despite the "picking" process described in the earlier portions of this chapter. Yet it also seems clear that the financial sector has promoted and extended this "picking" process and, in doing so, has contributed to the decline of the production economy.

While firm conclusions regarding these issues are difficult to come by, it does seem appropriate to offer, in closing, at least a preliminary conjecture: just who is it, anyway, in the realm of wealth as opposed to love, that is left with thorns? Again this is a complex question, but one thing does seem clear. In contrast to the earlier parallels that were drawn between love and wealth, we have here a clear difference between the two cases. Attempts by the possessive lover to "pick" the rose from the vine may leave him or her only with thorns. If so, it is clearly the hand of the wrongdoer that is injured. Not so with the economy. Unfortunately, it is society at large, and especially its most vulnerable members, that seem to be left paying the price when private wealth owners flee to liquidity and financial maneuvering. These thorns may be seen in the intensification of a wide variety of social problems—homelessness, crime, drug abuse, and so on—or in the more familiar macroeconomic measures of increasing unemployment and lost output. In view of this result, then, it is clear that the perspective explored in this chapter leads ultimately to a call for renewed inquiry into a fundamental and controversial issue: namely, the propriety of exclusively private, uncoordinated decision making regarding the deployment of wealth in our society.

NOTES

1. The substance of Kalecki's model of the business cycle is presented in concise form in his "Outline of a Theory of the Business Cycle" in *Selected Essays on the Dynamics of the Capitalist Economy*. His assessment of the possibility for sustained long-term economic growth is summarized in the *Theory of Economic Dynamics*. Interesting commentaries on Kalecki's work are contained in the books by Donald Harris and David Levine (see references).

2. This "resting place" imagery is developed by Frank Hahn in his work on macroeconomics and general equilibrium theory (see references).

REFERENCES

Boulding, Kenneth. "Puzzles over Distribution." *Challenge* 28 (November/December) 4–10.

Hahn, Frank. "Keynesian Economics and General Equilibrium Theory." In *The Microfoundations of Marcoeconomics*, ed. G. C. Harcourt. London: Macmillan, 1977.

Harris, Donald J. *Capital Accumulation and Income Distribution*. Stanford, Calif.: Stanford University Press, 1978.

Kalecki, Michael. *The Theory of Economic Dynamics*. New York: Modern Reader Paperbacks, 1968.

———. *Selected Essays on the Dynamics of the Capitalist Economy*. Cambridge: Cambridge University Press, 1971.

Kaufman, Henry. *Interest Rates, the Markets, and the New Financial World*. New York: Times Books, 1986.

Keynes, John Maynard. *The General Theory of Employment, Interest, and Money*. New York: Harcourt Brace Jovanovich, 1964.

———. *A Treatise on Money*. London: The Macmillan Press, 1971.

Levine, David. *Contributions to the Critique of Economic Theory*. London: Routledge and Kegan Paul, 1977.

4

Money: How Do I Know It's O.K.?

Richard G. Doty

The coin was originally invented to render the buying and selling of things easier and quicker. Instead of having to weigh or otherwise test each piece of gold or silver proffered in trade, each time it was traded, it was agreed that an authority respected by all should (1) ensure that there would be some sort of standardization among the pieces of metal being employed for commerce, and then (2) indicate that each piece had been inspected and was now being guaranteed, by means of a seal, punch, or other form of indelible statement. Bankers had so marked bullion before (and would continue the practice, in the Far East, until well into the present century); when *governments* began doing so, the first true coins emerged.

The best current evidence is that this was taking place, in western Turkey, by about 620 B.C. Within a short time, the coinage concept had spread to adjacent Greece, and from there to the rest of the Western world. Coinage appears to have arisen in a second center, China, at about the same time.

Shortly after the invention of coinage, the first counterfeits of those early coins began appearing alongside them. And forgery of one sort or another has been with us, at least as a threat, ever since. The counterfeit attacks our assumptions about the value of objects which are very close and very dear to us, objects whose very worth incorporates and stands for much more than a simple utility in the marketplace. This is because money itself has always stood for much more than a simple recording or storing of value. It addresses a number of psychological demands as well—the need for power, the need for solidity, stability, for something upon which we can depend. The coin, and its modern descendents, are thus emotionally charged objects, and when any one of them is proven false, every other one will be suspect.

Let me briefly illustrate this point. In the late 1950s, Congress decided that the motto *In God We Trust* should appear on our currency, just as it did on our coins. The change was effected over the next decade or so. Occasionally, notes printed prior to the introduction of the motto still surface in commerce. Whenever they do (and they are identical with newer issues in essentially every other respect), they are likely to be rejected by the public. Almost invariably, a minor panic will ensue as to the validity and safety of the older notes, with a temporarily heightened suspicion of *all* notes, old and new alike.

This is the sort of thing which governments fear most. In earlier days, there was not a great deal they could do to safeguard the safety and quality of their money because the primitive technology which mints employed to produce official coinage was easily available to anybody on the outside who might harbor felonious intentions. Simply put, this technology involved three pieces of hard metal, and one piece of soft. Two of the three pieces of hard metal were elongated cylinders, with a design engraved on one end. Bronze was the favored metal for dies, although iron was also used when available. The third hard piece of metal was the head of a hammer. The fourth soft piece of metal was a circular blob or blank of gold, silver, or copper, and it would be turned into a coin.

To do so, one of the dies was fixed in an anvil. The coin-to-be was placed atop the engraved surface of this die. The other die was then positioned atop the small piece of metal (numismatists refer to the latter as a planchet or flan), and the hammer was used to drive the designs of top and bottom dies simultaneously into its two sides, thereby creating the coin. Under ordinary circumstances, it would require several hammer-blows to complete the process, which is why many ancient coins show evidence of doubling in their designs. This method, primitive as it was, produced some of the great masterpieces in numismatics. But it was also a golden opportunity for forgers.

The early coin was vulnerable from several interrelated circumstances. First, it was fairly difficult to achieve a precise consistency of weight between one officially produced coin and another. Second, dies were carved by hand, and standardization of design was also impossible, given the technology of the times. A moment's reflection will lead to the conclusion that the complete consistency of faithful standardization is one of the most effective weapons against counterfeiting: if each coin is supposed to be identical with every other, and each coin produced by a government actually *is* identical, then the variant, the fake, will be relatively easy for the public to discern. But to achieve such consistency one needs an entire revolution in the way in which all commodities, including coins, are produced. And that lay many centuries in the future.

So the counterfeiters had a field day. Cast replicas of genuine issues were manufactured. Ingenious methods of taking a base-metal core, plating it with silver or gold, then striking it between two dies had been devised by around 400 B.C., and this method was fairly widely employed to create fakes in Greek and Roman days. During the last half century or so of the Roman republic, official minters sporadically created a distinctive form of coinage with a serrated edge, and it has been suggested that the odd edge was adopted as an anticounterfeiting device, a way of showing the public that the metal inside the coin was as good as the metal on its outer surfaces. It is likely that serrated coinage sprang from other causes, although it would have been a welcome addition to the meager arsenal of security devices available to governments in ancient times. Otherwise, states were restricted to increased efforts to achieve weight standardization, increasingly draconian laws against forgery, and, just possibly, an occasional attempt to mass-produce some of the elements on coinage dies. These recourses were insufficient: counterfeiters continued their work, and those without their tools or skills could take another tack: they could simply remove bits of precious metal from real coins, by clipping their edges, sweating off bits of metal from their surfaces, or even boring into their interiors, debasing the currency from the inside out. The methodology of monetary fakery in ancient and medieval times was a testimony to human ingenuity. It was also an ongoing annoyance for governments. But through all of this, there was one slight redeeming feature: the reason that counterfeiting remained an annoyance and not a crisis was that relatively few people used coinage. The great majority of the inhabitants of a given state lived on the land and were seldom engaged in commerce, seldom at risk from false money.

This situation began to change in early modern times. Commerce increased, as did the numbers of city-dwelling coin users. More coins were now required, and they would have to be of better quality, harder to forge. Governments came up with a number of coining improvements in the sixteenth and seventeenth centuries—machines to roll out metal into strips of a consistent thickness, machines to punch that metal into identical flans for coining, and, most importantly, two contrivances for the coining itself.

The first of these, called a Castaing machine after the man who supposedly invented it, imparted an ornamented edge to a round piece of metal, before it was struck into a coin. This fancy edge would render the cast counterfeit more difficult. It would also make it much harder to shave or clip coin edges, because there was now a new element which was supposed to be there, and that was the major reason for its use. The second new contrivance was a screw press, or *balancier*, which squeezed designs into the two faces of a coin flan, giving a sharp, consistent clarity to all portions of the design. This had been very difficult with the old, hammered method, and virtually any ancient coin will display weakness on portions of one or both of its sides. These various improvements expanded production possibilities to a limited degree, but they were primarily intended to safeguard the quality of circulating coinage. They were in place at most large mints by 1700, and governments now faced their numismatic adversaries with increased confidence.

For a time, this feeling was well placed: it is undeniable that the incidence of forging and clipping declined for several decades after the introduction of the new methodology. But the menace of fraud and counterfeiting began increasing at the end of the eighteenth century, as the first tremors of the Industrial Revolution began to make themselves felt. Rumblings of what was to come were being heard in Britain by the 1780s, in the United States by 1800, and in a west-to-east ripple across Europe as the nineteenth century progressed. Wherever the forgers intruded, they altered the nature of the economy, creating new demands on the production of money, ultimately changing the way it looked and the manner in which it was made.

As noted earlier, preindustrial times had found the majority of people tied to the land, existing in an essentially non- or premonetary world. Shackled as they were to old methods of payment in labor and in barter, they would need relatively few coins in their ordinary economic dealings. What few coins were required would have a tendency to be made from gold or silver for purchases of luxury goods in the cities.

But the Industrial Revolution changed everything. Its new factories cut through the old network of payment in kind and obligatory services. These new, larger workshops gathered laborers from wide areas, forcing them to live in unfamiliar places, among strangers, where the older methods of exchange could not possibly function. The only way to tempt prospective hands into this new, very different, and hostile environment was to offer to pay them *in cash*. And since wages were low, and the commodities needed by the average worker were also modestly priced (bread, cheap fabric for clothing, and the like), the new industrial order would require a huge number of fairly low-value coins.

This was a challenge which the typical eighteenth-century national mint could not meet. The need for mass-produced coinage caught these facilities off guard. The most modern improvements in productive capacity had, as we have observed, been introduced at least a century previously, when the coining capacity they allowed, fifteen to twenty pieces per minute, was considered adequate for all purposes. The new industrial classes would need many times the numbers of coins the most modern eighteenth-century mint was capable of producing. And the situation would grow worse as the industries grew and the proletariat expanded.

In the case of the pioneering industrial power, the counterfeiter thoughtfully stepped in to ease the burden. The most desirable British copper coin, the halfpenny, saw an increasing extralegal production (an irate correspondent of the *Gentleman's Magazine* complained that "not the fiftieth part" of halfpennies in current use were genuine—this as early as 1791). The back-alley coiners of Birmingham (the center of British metalworking, including, unfortunately, counterfeiting) also circulated white-metal discs as silver shillings and sixpences. The new industrial workers were receiving wages for daily purchases, but much of it was composed of worthless trash, and all of it was a target for the forger. And it is almost axiomatic that the lowest coinage denominations will be those to which the state exends the least protection against forgery; certainly, this was the case in eighteenth-century Britain. In sum, a crisis was developing in the country's monetary system, one which the British government was powerless to arrest.

But an individual prepared to meet the crisis head-on. This was Matthew Boulton, an industrialist from Birmingham, center of the forgery trade. Boulton is an immensely appealing character, and one of his major attractions for the modern historian is a real social conscience. He knew what the flourishing industry in counterfeits was doing to factory workers in his hometown, and he began to speculate on ways to solve the problem. In the process of finding a solution, he would redesign the coin.

He had a partner named James Watt. Boulton decided that one of his colleague's improved steam engines, harnessed to a coining press, might provide safer money for the poor, and more of it than anything possible with the customary technology. His tinkerings were yielding results by the late summer of 1789, and he obtained a patent for most of his improvements a year later.

His inventions solved the twin desiderata of greater production and safer coins. Production immediately rose from fifteen or twenty pieces per minute on an old, hand-powered press to forty-five per minute on one of Boulton's new ones—and ascended still higher as the industrialist refined his methodology. But the steam-powered press was most successful when it addressed the second problem: using the power of the new engine, Matthew Boulton would be able to create coins which, quite simply, could not be made outside his establishment, or an establishment which had purchased his equipment. The new money would be perfectly round, perfectly struck, with the vertical, smooth edges we associate with the modern coin. It must have that kind of edge, because it would have to be struck in a collar, in order to restrain the outward flow of metal under the greater force of Boulton's presses. But if coins could be sharply struck with the increased motive force, so could *dies*: in seeking to massproduce coinage, Matthew Boulton also discovered a means for the mass production, and hence absolute consistency, of the instruments necessary for striking the coins. Mass production of both coins and coin dies suggested a final feature which we have come to take for granted: very shallow relief, speeding up the coining process, gentler on the new dies, easier to replicate *on* those new dies. All of these attributes were at total variance with everything which had gone before, and they made all previous money, including counterfeit money, obsolete. By dint of great efforts (plus a few connections at court), Boulton obtained a contract to strike the Royal Mint's coinage for it in 1797. And the first thing he turned to was safe copper money for the new industrial poor. In time, he and his successors would sell minting equipment in addition to coinage, sending their presses and skilled engineers to erect and maintain them to Russia, Brazil, Denmark, Mexico, very nearly to the United States—and to Britain herself, where Boulton's presses struck England's coins from the time of George III to that of Queen Victoria. And to this day, every coin, and every coining press, owes an immense debt to Matthew Boulton.

In our century, the counterfeit coin has effectively disappeared, which is partly a tribute to the dream of Boulton and those who followed him. But the elimination of bad coinage has also been rendered possible by inflation and changing usage patterns. Coinage today is entirely base-metal in nature, and most of it has such a reduced purchasing power that it is not worth counterfeiting. For anything more expensive than a small candy bar or a daily newspaper, the world's industrial citizens employ paper money.

But that medium is dangerous too, and it is far easier to lose faith in the suspect note than in the questionable coin: on a very basic level, everybody knows that paper has no intrinsic value whatsoever, because, in the nature of things, paper simply *has* no intrinsic value. So if we are to take paper money seriously, it must be very reassuring indeed.

And this was where American ingenuity with the banknote supplemented British ingenuity with the coin. The United States created the first mass-producible, difficult-to-counterfeit paper note for a number of reasons, all of them based on stringent need. By the 1790s, the new nation was taking tentative steps toward modernizations, with the arrival of the earliest factories and the first of the new salaried workers. But the United States lacked specie to pay the new wage earners: we had as yet discovered no major local sources of metal, and the only other possibility, foreign coins, flowed out of the country as soon as they entered it, as payment for imported goods. Despite the lack of metal, those pioneer factory workers would have to be recompensed for their labor, and major new sources of capital would also have to be found were the American industrialization not to be curtailed as soon as it had begun. An unorthodox monetary source would have to be pressed into service. And so it was: paper money.

Now, the American people of 1800 were no fools: they knew perfectly well that paper money was a fragile medium, one very easy to counterfeit. They knew it because they had been forcing fake notes on each other for a hundred years, ever since the introduction of the medium in 1690, and because they had been the victims of a British plot to devaluate their currency during the Revolutionary War. So if paper were to be the mainstay of our particular corner of the Industrial Revolution, it would have to be produced in quantity, in so intricate, consistent, and perfect a manner that, just as with Matthew Boulton's coins, nobody outside the "official" printery could convincingly re-create it.

This would necessitate an entire battery of revolutionary printing methodology, in part made possible by that same Industrial Revolution responsible for the monetary crisis. Among many other developments, the spread of industry meant the availability of high-quality steel and powerful stamping and rolling presses. A gifted Yankee inventor named Jacob Perkins combined these two technological improvements on behalf of currency reform. He devised a way of engraving on a soft steel master plate, hardening it, transferring his design onto a soft steel roller, hardening that, and then using the roller to mass-produce faithful daughters of the intricate original engraving on any number of working, note-printing steel plates. By 1805, Perkins had devised and was printing the direct ancestor of every modern banknote. It could be created in any quantity desired and it was nearly impossible to replicate unofficially. But it made a tempting target, and so Jacob Perkins and his successors, men such as Asa Spencer, Asher B. Durand, and W. L. Ormsby, were forced to develop a continuing and growing arsenal of improvements, always attempting to gain on the counterfeiters. In the process, they brought the United States to that same position of preeminence in security printing as the British had earlier secured for coining.

These statuses have long since been lost: other mints were creating better coinage by the 1830s, and official and private printeries have gone far beyond our modest anticounterfeiting capabilities in the present century, with watermarks, security threads, holograms, micro- and multicolor printing, and optically variable inks. Indeed, we are currently introducing notes with a few of the tamer of the improved security devices in this country because it has now become dangerously easy to produce plausible replicas of United States currency by means of a very good color photocopier. In this tardy response, the Bureau of Engraving and Printing is simply following in the footsteps of earlier purveyors of official money: no innovation will ever be adopted until a state fears that its wares will not be accepted by the public it serves. That old question, Money: how do I know it's O.K.?, lies very close to the surface. And it must never be allowed to break through.

NOTE

This chapter represents some fifteen years of archival research in Great Britain and the United States, wide reading, and direct work as a numismatic curator with coinage and currency. So it is impossible to adequately cite all sources. But the following may help those interested in further study.

The Boulton-Watt papers are held in the Archives Department, Birmingham Reference Library, Birmingham, England. They are the necessary center of any research on Matthew Boulton and his career, and they form the major source for my upcoming book on the coining adventures of Boulton and his successors. Several British periodicals of the late eighteenth century, most notably the *Gentleman's Magazine* and the *European Magazine*, both from London, give precious insights into the counterfeiting problem and the coining shortage which spurred Boulton to action. (The comment on the percentage of genuine British halfpence in circulation is taken from a letter written by "S. S." on 16 September 1791 to the editor of the *Gentleman's Magazine*; the full text will be found on page 890 in volume 61, part 2 [October 1791] of that publication.) H. W. Dickinson's *Matthew Boulton* (1936) is still the standard biography. I have found it generally trustworthy as to personal information, woefully inaccurate as to coinage. Samuel Smiles' *Lives of Boulton and Watt* (1865) is still useful—but again, caution is recommended concerning Boulton's activities as a coiner. For information on Perkins, consult Greville and Dorothy Bathe's *Jacob Perkins: His Inventions, His Times & His Contemporaries* (1943), as well as *Perkins' Bank Bill Test*, published by that inventor in 1809 and, happily, reprinted by George Fuld in 1962. Gunnar Andersen's *Banknotes* (1975) is very useful for more modern printing processes, while Philip Grierson's *Numismatics* (1975) contains useful synopses of early coining methods—although the field deserves an expanded coverage which it still lacks. My own articles in volumes 56 and 57 of the *British Numismatic Journal* (1986, 1987) examine the relations of the firm Boulton founded with Mexican and United States mints in the early nineteenth century; they are primarily based on the Birmingham archival resources mentioned earlier.

5

Individual Differences in Money as a Motivator

ELLEN STEPHENS

Many theories have tried to explain the role money plays in motivating behavior, especially in job-related situations. Unfortunately, no theory to date has been useful in predicting how everyone will react in a given situation. When applied to the workplace, most theories have proved to be limited and inconclusive (Vroom & Deci, 1970). Often what was thought to be a motivating force creates the completely opposite effect and in reality actually works to reduce any motivation to do well that a person may have had (Salancik, 1975).

In applying need theories to work situations, money seemed to be more connected to the individual's economic conditions outside the job than to whether the individual found the job itself satisfying or dissatisfying (Ross & Zander, 1957; Vroom & Deci, 1970). On the basis of these findings, Lawler (1971) rejected applying need theories to money. He felt that in order for something to be called a need, it should be sought as an end in itself rather than as a means of obtaining other goals.

He saw the motivation to perform as being determined by two variables. The first was the effort to achieve a specific reward. A given amount of effort would be put into performance if that performance would result in obtaining a given reward and if that reward was seen as a positively valued outcome. The second was the concept of reward or valence. The reward value of the outcome stems from its perceived ability to satisfy an individual's needs. Therefore money acquires valence because it is perceived to be instrumental for obtaining other desired goals.

The reward value and effort probability combine to determine an individual's motivation. Because rewards can be either extrinsic or intrinsic in nature, an individual's motivation can be influenced by more than one outcome. To complicate this further, job content also affects the relationship between performance and the reception of intrinsically rewarding outcomes that influence motivation (Lawler, 1971).

Gellerman (1963), using anecdotal evidence, presented the idea that money has no intrinsic meaning for people but becomes an important motivating power when it starts to become the symbol of an individual's abstract goals. It is the individual's outlook on life that determines how he or she will respond to the opportunity to earn money. As a symbol, money can be interpreted as a projection device.

People who are high achievers tend to strive for personal improvement by setting challenges for themselves, but they also like almost immediate feedback on their performance (McClelland, 1961). Organizational research suggests that people use pay as feedback to gauge their accomplishments, especially when the amount of pay is seen as relating directly to the performance criteria (Lawler, 1971; Opsahl & Dunnette, 1966).

It seems as if monetary incentives place a value on a job, which in turn places a value on the person capable of doing that job. Individuals with strong achievement drives usually demand more of themselves, making the accomplishment of the task the end reward. Money becomes the symbol of achievement and adequacy, providing feedback of performance at a fairly reliable interval. The primary significance of money becomes its ability to measure the individual's success (Lawler, 1971).

As a projection device, money seems directly related to self-concept. If an individual sees himself as having the ability to move up within his profession, then money will be valued in a way that corresponds to this view. If he sees himself as a failure, money may have very little meaning to him (Gellerman, 1963; Lawler, 1971). This may relate even more directly to whether an individual has an internal or external locus of control. Individuals with an internal locus of control view themselves as having earned monetary rewards through their own efforts, which increases their intrinsic motivation, while those with an external locus of control view monetary rewards as being controlled by others, which tends to decrease their intrinsic motivation (Rotter, 1966).

The literature investigating locus of control and monetary rewards is scarce. A study by Earn (1982) provided contradicting results. Students scored on Rotter's Internal-External Locus of Control Scale performed a puzzle-solving task under paid or unpaid conditions. When the aspects of the rewards were kept vague, individuals high in internal locus of control demonstrated an increase in intrinsic motivation which corresponded to increasing pay, while those high in external locus of control demonstrated the expected decrease in intrinsic motivation with increasing pay. But in the second condition, where pay was contingent upon performance, increasing the pay decreased the intrinsic motivation in both groups.

A later study by Reeves, Olson, & Cole (1987) investigated the importance of individual differences in predicting intrinsic motivation, examining individual differences in need for achievement, anxiety, locus of control, and gender. Locus of control and the resultant achievement motivation interaction predicted the level of intrinsic motivation, supporting the idea that individual differences are important in predicting intrinsic motivation.

The one area that seems important to motivation but is mostly merely hinted at in the literature is the sex of the individual. Studies have been conducted exclusively with males (Salancik, 1975; Pinder, 1976) or have disregarded the data from female subjects because the measurement on the scales used had problems (Atkinson, 1978). A study by McLaren (1982) used vocabularies of motive and causal attributes to look at internal and external control in a sample of working women. The results suggest that the ambitions of women are connected with such things as their feelings of powerlessness, oppression, and self-blame and the active seeking of alternative social institutions. Of course, this study does not relate how the foundation of a woman's ambitions may be different from the foundation of a man's.

Gilligan (1988) did conduct a study that compared gender differences and similarities, although it pertained to moral orientation rather than motivation. Using a group of young adults, she compared their thinking concerning real-life dilemmas in terms of focus-on-justice or care perspectives. She found that although men and women used both orientations, women were more likely to be care-focused and men were more likely to be justice-focused in dealing with dilemmas.

RATIONALE AND HYPOTHESES

There are distinct differences in the way different individuals are motivated by money. The value given to money seems to be related to self-concept and the feedback money provides about the individual's performance. Of particular importance is the individual's need for achievement. Those who have a high need to achieve set challenging goals for themselves and tend to use monetary rewards as a measure of their success or failure. Since rewards are seen as feedback about their abilities, they usually increase intrinsic motivation. This same increase in intrinsic motivation is seen in individuals with internal locus of control. These individuals also regard the reward as being directly related to their performance or ability. Therefore the first hypothesis was that individuals having an internal locus of control would be more likely to respond to monetary rewards when these rewards are directly linked to performance and/or ability by the job criteria.

Likewise, individuals having an external locus of control see things as controlled by forces other than their performance. They do not see their abilities as leading to monetary rewards and often see these rewards as a method to impose control on their behavior. An increase in monetary rewards usually leads to a decrease in intrinsic motivation in these individuals. Therefore, the second hypothesis was that individuals having an external locus of control would be less likely to respond to monetary rewards linked to their performance and ability.

Although still vague, there seem to be distinct differences in the factors that are motivators for men and those that are motivators for women. Because the exploration of this area is still at an early stage it was impossible to predict what direction differences might take. Therefore, the third hypothesis was that monetary rewards would lead to different reactions or a different level of reactions in men than they would in women.

METHODS

Subjects

All participants were recruited from a college or a social organization located in northern New Jersey, except for 16 males who were recruited from a group of police applicants. Out of the 93 subjects, 37 withdrew from the study.

Of the remaining 56 subjects, 23 were male and 33 were female, with a mean age of 37.5 (ages ranged from 19 to 72). Forty-four worked full-time. Eight (1 male, 7 females) individuals were not employed and 4 females worked only part-time. Income levels ran from under $15,000 to over $75,000, with the mean income being $35,000.

Most individuals had completed high school, with 16 having some college (6 males, 10 females), 9 having already attained undergraduate degrees (4 males, 5 females) and 4 having attained graduate degrees (2 males, 2 females).

Design

This was a 2 × 3 mixed factorial design with three covariates. The factors are subject's sex and the three levels of monetary incentives that differ as explained below (within subject variables). The covariates were locus of control, age, and income.

Materials

Rotter's Internal-External Locus of Control Scale (1966) was given. A short semantic differential scale was used to rate the individual's concept of money and five related words which included *credit* and *salary*. Each word was rated on a five-point scale as being more closely related to one of a pair of opposite adjectives. There were six pairs of bipolar adjectives which included such concepts as valuable-worthless and ability-inability. These pairs were randomly arranged so that in some cases the more positive adjective appeared first and in some cases the more negative adjective appeared first.

There were seven statements which also related to the individual's concept of money. Each statement connected money or salary with a single concept such as equality, ability, or status. These statements were rated on a five-point scale that ranged from strongly agree to strongly disagree.

Scenarios represented the different conditions relating to the monetary incentives that were used to measure the subjects' reaction to monetary rewards. Each scenario described a hypothetical job offer in very general terms of jobs skills, potential for growth, and working conditions. One represented work conditions of a desirable nature, one work conditions that were extremely poor, and one work conditions that were neutral in nature. All presented pay that was contingent on ability and performance. In each situation the subject responded with the monetary incentive it would take for him to accept the position.

There was also a questionnaire pertaining to demographic information including age, sex, income, education, and employment history. All materials except the questionnaire were ordered by random assignment.

Procedure

The experimental materials were distributed to the subjects at the time of testing and collected immediately after the group had finished. There were several testing sessions at the college and at the social organization as well as one testing session at the police academy. Each session consisted of between 5 and 16 individuals. Upon distribution of the testing materials the subjects were read the instructions, which were also presented in written form.

RESULTS

The scores relevant to the hypothesis were those from Rotter's Internal-External Locus of Control Scale and the subjects' reactions to the monetary levels in the scenarios. Rotter's scale has a possible range of 0–23, with 0 representing the highest level of internal locus of control and 23 the highest level of external locus of control. Each monetary level had a possible range of 1–4 with 1 indicating no reaction to the monetary incentives and 4 indicating the greatest reaction. The means for these variables are presented in Table 1.

The first hypothesis, stating that individuals having an internal locus of

Table 1
Means, Ranges, and Standard Deviations for Variables Measured in Study*

	Locus of Control	Money I	Money II	Money III	Age	Income
MALES						
Mean	10.22	2.696	2.913	2.435	34	$40,000
Mode	12	1 & 4	3	2	-	-
Actual Range	3-20	1-4	1-4	1-4	21-64	$20-$70
Possible Range	0-23	1-4	1-4	1-4	19-72	$15-$75
Standard Deviation	4.42	1.222	.668	.843	.714	1.329
FEMALES						
Mean	9.52	1.727	2.667	2.515	36	$41,000
Mode	5 & 6	1	3	2	-	-
Actual Range	0-18	1-4	1-4	1-4	19-72	$15-$75
Possible Range	0-23	1-4	1-4	1-4	19-72	$15-$75
Standard Deviation	4.22	1.008	.736	.755	.992	1.281

*Based on sample of 56 subjects: 23 males and 33 females

control would be more likely to respond to monetary rewards when these rewards are linked to performance and/or ability by the job criteria, was not supported. Likewise the second hypothesis, stating that individuals having an external locus of control would be less likely to respond to monetary rewards linked to their performance and/or ability, was not supported. In other words, there was no relationship between locus of control and response to the monetary rewards.

The third hypothesis, stating that monetary rewards would cause different reactions or different levels of a reaction in males than they would in females, was upheld. A 2×3 mixed factorial analysis of variance was performed on the means for sex and the three scenarios (see Table 2). There was a significant main effect for gender ($F(1,55) = 7.76, p = .007$) with males overall scoring higher on the levels of monetary incentives than females.

The interaction of gender and money is portrayed in Figure 1. This interaction was significant ($F(2,107) = 4.61, p < .05$). Females ($M = 1.727$) were not as accepting of poor and neutral conditions as were the

Table 2
Summary of Analysis of Variance

Source	SS	df	MS	F	p
Between Groups					
Sex	5.84	1	5.84	7.76	.007
Error between	39.85	53	.75	----	----
Within Groups					
Money	6.78	2	3.39	4.20	.018
M x S	7.44	2	3.72	4.61	.012
Error within	86.35	107	.81	----	----
Total	146.26	165			

males (M = 2.696). But both sexes were just as likely to accept the position under excellent conditions.

The semantic differentials and statements investigating the subjects' concept of money had some significant correlations. Views of money correlated with views of authority (r = .6303, p = .001) and views of property (r = .6311, p = .001). Views of money also correlated with views on salary, although the correlation was slightly lower (r = .5439, p = .001). Salary also correlated lower with views of authority (r = .5386, p = .01) and property (r = .3921, p = .01). Authority also showed a correlation with property (r = .3929, p = .01).

Credit had a low correlation with money (r = .4238, p = .001) and salary (r = .4534, p = .001). This sixth statement, asserting that credit is the same as money, correlated with the subjects' views of credit, (r = .4756, p = .001) but showed no correlation with money. There also was a significant correlation between the sixth statement and the subjects' scores on Rotter's I/E scale (r = .3397, p = .01).

There were two significant correlations with the subjects' education level. The sixth statement showed a negative correlation (r = $-$.3830, p = .01), indicating that subjects with more education were less likely to regard money and credit as being the same; while the fourth statement, which relates community status to income, showed a positive correlation (r = .3393, p = .01), indicating that subjects with more education were more likely to consider community status to be related to income.

Figure 1
Mean Level of Monetary Incentive Chosen in Poor Work Conditions,
Neutral Work Conditions, and Excellent Work Conditions

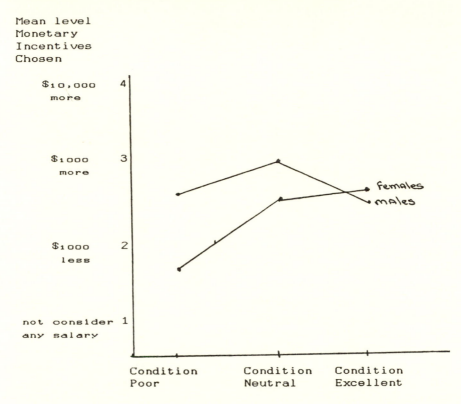

DISCUSSION

Although this study did not support the idea that internal/external locus of control would have an influence on an individual's reaction to monetary incentives, it did help to support the idea that there is a significant difference in the way males and females react to the same monetary incentives. Of particular interest were the responses to the first scenario, in which an individual's ability to perform the job was combined with extremely poor work conditions. The females were unlikely to accept this type of job at any salary. A score of 1 was seen for 20 of the 30 female subjects; while the males were divided, with 7 having a score of 1, indicating they would not accept the job at any salary, and 7 having a score of 4, indicating they would accept the job for at least $10,000 more than the salary considered appropriate for it.

It seems possible that these reactions may be in some way connected to social expectations. This is seen in McLaren's study (1982), where the ambitions of women were found to be connected to powerlessness, self-blame, and alternative social institutions which have also, at different times, been used to define the female's place in society. Likewise, Gilligan (1988) found gender differences in moral orientations that support society's view of females as the caregivers and males as the protectors.

Money motivation seems to be a complex topic consisting of many variables. The more that is learned about it, the more complex the topic seems to become. In the past, theories have dealt with the environmental influence on attitudes and performance (Katzell & Thompson, 1990; Vroom & Deci, 1970), but it seems as if more effort needs to be spent investigating individual differences. Salary has an ambiguous quality which allows it to be viewed not only as a control mechanism but also as a source of information about an individual's performance (Salancik, 1975). It becomes more complex as more variables are explored (feelings of competence, task difficulty and variety, self-determination) and found to have an influence on intrinsic motivation (Pritchard, Campbell, & Campbell, 1977) or to produce an increase of motivation in one situation while producing a decrease of motivation in another (Pinder, 1976).

In considering these facts about the variables that influence motivation, it is likely that there are many intrinsic needs that affect how an individual reacts to monetary incentives that are not related in any way to his locus of control. In general, the interactions of different variables may be so individualized that it will always be difficult to generalize results from motivational studies and apply these results in the workplace.

The other factor that needs to be considered is how needs and attitudes of society change over time. Not too far in the past, credit was not a common commodity. Today it may be taken for granted by many people. The subjects in this study seemed to relate credit only slightly to money and salary. The statement equating credit and money correlated with the subjects' views of credit ($r = .4756$, $p = .001$) but showed no correlation with their view of money. Property, which most people obtain by credit, showed no significant correlation with credit, although it did correlate with money ($r = .6311$, $p = .001$) and salary ($r = .3921$, $p = .01$).

Education level seems also to relate to how the subjects viewed certain situations. The more education a subject had, the less likely he or she was to view money and credit as being the same. However, the higher the education level, the more likely the subject was to view community status as being related to income.

These are only an indication of attitudes that may be of value to explore within the area of money motivation. Society is faced daily with changing organizational structures (Katzell & Thompson, 1990). This brings a need to develop new sources of commitment for employees. Our fast-moving technology will continue to cause changes that will affect motivational policies in the workplace and lead to new areas of motivational research.

REFERENCES

Atkinson, J. W., & Raynor, J. O. (1978). *Personality, motivation and achievement*. New York: Halsted.

Earn, B. M. (1982). Intrinsic motivation as a function of extrinsic financial rewards and subjects' locus of control. *Journal of Personality 50(3)*: 360–71.

Gellerman, S. W. (1963). *Motivation and productivity*. New York: Vail-Ballou.

Gilligan, C. (1988). Two moral orientations: gender differences and similarities. *Merrill-Palmer Quarterly 34(3)*: 223–37.

Katzell, R. A. & Thompson, D. E. (1990). Work motivation: theory and practice. *American Psychologist 45(2)*: 144–53.

Lawler, E. (1971). *Pay and organizational effectiveness: A psychological view*. New York: McGraw-Hill.

McClelland, D. C. (1961). *The achieving society*. New York: Van Nostrand.

McLaren, A. T. (1982). Ambition and accounts: a study of working-class women in adult education. *Psychiatry 45(3)*: 235–46.

Opsahl, R. L., & Dunnette, M. D. (1966). The role of financial compensation in industrial motivation. *Psychological Bulletin 66*: 94–118.

Pinder, C. C. (1976). Additivity versus nonadditivity of intrinsic and extrinsic incentives: implications for work motivation, performance, and attitudes. *Journal of Applied Psychology 61(6)*: 693–700.

Pritchard, R. D., Campbell, K. M., & Campbell, D. J. (1977). Effects of extrinsic financial rewards on intrinsic motivation. *Journal of Applied Psychology 62(8)*: 9–15.

Reeve, J., Olson, B., & Cole, S. (1987). Intrinsic motivation in competition: the intervening role of four individual differences following objective competence information. *Journal of Research in Personality 21(2)*: 148–70.

Ross, I. C., & Zander, A. (1957). Need satisfactions and employee turnover. *Personnel Psychology 10*: 327–38.

Rotter, J. B. (1966). Generalized expectancies for internal versus external control of reinforcement. *Psychological Monographs 80* (1 Whole No. 609).

Salancik, G. R. (1975). Interaction effects of performance and money on self perception of intrinsic motivation. *Organizational Behavior and Human Performance 13(3):* 339–51.

Vroom, V. H. & Deci, E. L. (Eds.). (1970). *Management and motivation*. New York: Penguin.

6

Drugs and Money

DAVID T. COURTWRIGHT

Drugs and money are the yin and yang of the most lucrative industry in the world. International revenues from the sale of illicit drugs have been estimated as high as a half trillion dollars a year, or more than twice the value of all U.S. currency in circulation. A more conservative assessment by the Treasury Department places worldwide sales at $300 billion a year, including $110 billion generated in the United States—equivalent to 2 percent of the gross national product. Only about 20 percent of this money is said to represent the cost of the drugs. The rest is dealers' profit.[1]

Illicit drugs, which are either manufactured from widely available chemicals or processed from crops grown and harvested by peasant labor, are not intrinsically expensive. The high prices they command are a function of their controlled or prohibited status. Consider the prices of coffee, tobacco, and commercial grade marijuana (i.e., ordinary marijuana, not sinsemilla) during a single randomly chosen year, 1984. Coffee spot market prices ranged from $1.35 to $1.60 a pound; tobacco farm prices averaged $1.81 a pound; and wholesale marijuana sold for $400 to $600 a pound. It was no harder to produce marijuana than to produce coffee or tobacco. The difference was risk, in the form of arrest, imprisonment, forfeiture of assets, and possible assault or murder by customers and rival traffickers. A lower-level dealer who sells a pound of marijuana in quarter-pound units will typically settle for a 40 percent profit. If he sells the same pound in one-ounce units, he will take a 60 percent profit. Dealing in ounces instead of quarter pounds means sixteen rather than four separate sales. Because the latter course entails greater risk of detection, the dealer compensates by charging a higher price.[2]

Trafficking in narcotics and stimulants is even more profitable than trafficking in marijuana. Heroin and cocaine are more potent, more euphorigenic, and, pound for pound, much more valuable. Again using 1984 for purposes of comparison, cocaine then sold wholesale for between $40,000 and $50,000 per kilogram, or roughly $18,000 to $23,000 a pound. Heroin sold for $100,000 to $350,000 per kilogram, or $45,000 to $160,000 a pound (Lyman 9, 13). Large-scale cocaine smuggling into the United States developed in the 1970s when it occurred to Carlos Lehder and other enterprising criminals that the small airplanes used to ferry marijuana shipments from Colombia could earn much more carrying cocaine.

Cocaine has other black-market advantages. Like heroin, it can be easily adulterated after it enters the country. Dealers can double or triple their profits simply by doubling or tripling the bulk of their product. In an illicit market there is no third party to assure quality control. The addictiveness of cocaine and heroin further enhance their profitability. Addicts must consume larger and larger amounts to achieve the same effect and must have the drug to avoid withdrawal symptoms. Because their demand for drugs is constantly increasing and relatively inflexible, their addiction plays directly into the dealers' hands.

The failure to slow, much less to quash, the illicit drug traffic is due to the compactness of drugs and the large sums of money they generate. Historically, international prohibition efforts have been most successful when their targets have been large and readily detectable. Think of efforts to stop piracy, or slave trading, or the illegal killing of whales. These were, and are, made simpler by the fact that it is difficult to conceal a pirate ship, or a slaver, or a rogue whaling vessel. Not so with drugs, where a fortune's worth can be stuffed into a duffel bag.

The drug enforcement problem is compounded by the fact that mid- and higher-level traffickers routinely set aside portions of their profits to purchase various forms of protection. *Pace* Lord Acton, money corrupts, but drug money corrupts absolutely. Traffickers have bought police and politicians, banks and intelligence networks, sometimes entire governments and guerrilla armies. Those whom they cannot purchase they can evade or outrun. Big operators can easily spend hundreds of dollars on sleek Cessnas and Learjets, and tens of thousands more to outfit them with computerized navigation systems and auxiliary fuel tanks. They have at their disposal the best and latest smuggling technology that money can buy.

All of this is by way of introduction, and a brief one at that. Much more could be said about the political and economic consequences of drug money. However, the deeper and more interesting relationship between drugs and money, and the real subject of this chapter, is a paradox. The paradox is that money, the indispensable motivator and protector of drug dealers, is simultaneously their greatest curse. The money that dealers realize from selling drugs is quite commonly the source of their downfall, either at the hands of the police or of criminal rivals.

LOWER-LEVEL TRAFFICKING

Consider the lower-level dealers at the retail end of the drug business. Media impressions to the contrary, they do not realize thousands of dollars every day, nor do they all drive a Mercedes. Peter Reuter, who has studied the microeconomics of drug dealing in the District of Columbia, reports that most young men who sell drugs do so on a part-time basis; many also hold legitimate jobs. The attraction of dealing is that they can earn about $30 an hour, versus $7 an hour for most noncriminal jobs. But dealing is also risky. For every year spent selling drugs on a regular basis, a dealer can expect to serve 2.25 months in prison. He also has a 1 in 14 chance of serious injury and a 1 in 71 chance of death (Reuter et al. *passim*).

Those who discount the risks and plunge into dealing full-time will, of course, make the most money. They will also spend the most money, and therein lies the rub. Dealers flush with cash tend to spend extravagantly. A surprisingly high percentage of their earnings goes for clothing and accessories. The aforementioned D.C. dealers spent an average of $463 a month on clothing, versus only $277 for housing and $181 for food (Reuter et al. 70). The clothes that they and other dealers purchase often include flashy items like silk shirts, Gucci leather sneakers, tailored Italian trousers, Rolex watches, and gold chains. Conspicuous consumption is just that: conspicuous. Costly apparel and free spending alert the police and attract the notice of other criminals.

Because they are likely to have money and drugs, as well as expensive clothes and jewelry, dealers are prime targets for robbery and burglary. More is at stake then the simple loss of property, for if a dealer loses a consignment of drugs or the money to pay for them, his creditors are apt to exact payment in blood. One New York City dealer who "messed up the money" (i.e., failed to pay his supplier) was beaten with iron pipes, then dragged to the curb and placed so that his feet extended into the street. The supplier then drove a car over his legs, crippling him for life (Johnson et al. 175). Dealers protect themselves against this kind of calamity by buying automatic or semiautomatic guns and shooting anyone who attempts to rip them off. This is the reason why drug trafficking is so violent: it is a business in which everyone is armed to the teeth and justifiably paranoid.

Many teenagers begin by selling, but not necessarily using, drugs. The attraction is the money, not the high. The young dealers have nothing but contempt for their addicted customers. Before long, however, they begin experimenting with and then regularly using their own product. Because they have plenty of cash and ready access to supplies, their use often escalates to a very high level. To have a "dealer's habit" is to have a large or expensive habit. It is also to be on a treadmill. The addicted dealer has to keep dealing because it is virtually the only way to get the money and drugs he needs. Yet the larger his habit, the less his suppliers are likely to trust him. If he becomes desperate, and tries to cheat or steal from his supplier or another dealer, he is likely to end up with a bullet in his head.

HIGHER-LEVEL TRAFFICKING

Violence is a constant risk for higher-level dealers as well. To protect themselves they resort to the age-old expedient of private armies. Their ample profits permit them to purchase the services of bodyguards and enforcers. Yet their profits simultaneously make them vulnerable, particularly to law enforcement efforts. Big dealers have the same visibility problems as small dealers, only worse, because of the larger sums involved.

Money, which we are accustomed to thinking of in abstract terms, has a physical presence. As cash payments (originally made in five-, ten-, and twenty-dollar bills) are passed back up the distribution system, a great deal of currency accumulates—not only in total amount, but in weight and volume as well. Each bill weighs one gram. A million dollars in twenties weighs 50,000 grams, or over 100 pounds. That's *five times* as much as a million dollars' worth of heroin weighs, if the wholesale price is $50,000 a pound. Cash in large quantities is also voluminous. A million dollars in tightly bound stacks of fifties occupies just under a cubic foot; in stacks of twenties, well over two cubic feet. Large cash seizures, involving several millions of dollars, cover entire desktops with deep piles of money.[3]

In an age of credit cards and muggers, few ordinary people routinely carry or transport substantial amounts of cash. Anyone who does is automatically suspect. Air security personnel, for example, are instructed to look for any crew members with unusually large amounts of money, as a possible sign that they (and the aircraft they fly or service) are involved in smuggling drugs (U.S. Treasury Department 4).

If cash in quantity invites trouble, the obvious thing to do is get rid of it. There are basically four ways to go about this. Traffickers can spend the money, hide it, deposit it in a bank, or smuggle it out of the country. Each approach has its advantages and drawbacks. None is risk-free.

When higher-level traffickers or their agents dispose of money by spending it, they usually purchase small, legitimate businesses or personal property for which there is a ready cash market, such as gold coins, jewelry, bullion, communications equipment, boats, and expensive cars. A dealer who owns $100,000 worth of gold and jewelry is not necessarily being ostentatious, for this is the sort of asset that can be quickly converted back to cash, should the need arise. Small businesses are not as easy to dispose of, but they are useful for other reasons. The Bandidos, a motorcycle gang active in Arkansas and other south central states, used the proceeds from sales of marijuana and methamphetamine to buy a string of after-hours nightclubs. The clubs doubled as fronts for the gang's drug and prostitution businesses, and provided a means for laundering money (U.S. Department of Justice 42).

The disadvantage of using cash to purchase small businesses or valuable personal property is that such transactions may be noticed or reported. One suspected Idaho trafficker, who had no legal employment, openly spent more than $400,000 during a four-year period. He was convicted of tax evasion and sentenced to prison (U.S. Department of Justice 41).

Since 1985 merchants have been required to report cash sales of more than $10,000 to the IRS. There are various ways to skirt this requirement. Merchants can put fictitious names on receipts; or accept payments in multiple cashier's checks, each in an amount less than $10,000; or they can sell merchandise not listed on inventories checked by IRS agents. Evasions of this sort are widespread. IRS investigations in Florida in 1989 found that more than a third of car dealerships and 60 percent of other businesses such as horse farms and boat dealerships were not reporting all cash sales in excess of $10,000. A 1990 GAO investigation using undercover agents in nine cities found even higher levels of noncompliance nationwide (Saelens B1, B4). However, the fact that *many* merchants will wink at large cash transactions does not mean that they can *all* be counted on to bend or break the law. The dealer who wants to convert cash to property must trust the merchant's discretion, and any violation of that trust can trigger a chain of events culminating in investigation, arrest, and federal or state prosecution.

One alternative, which has the virtue of simplicity, is to hide the money. There is always the hole in the backyard, the shoe box in the closet. But money thus concealed is not necessarily safe. Dealer's premises are tempting, if dangerous, targets for thieves. Burglars are sometimes able to score thousands of dollars by breaking into dealers' apartments (Johnson 67). One former Harlem heroin dealer coped with this sort of problem by renting a safety deposit box at the 100th Street branch of the Chemical Bank. He simply took his surplus cash and put it in the box, which was locked in the bank's vault (Courtwright, Joseph, and Des Jarlais 157).

Most of us put our surplus cash in bank accounts, not safety deposit boxes, for reasons of both convenience and interest. But banks, like merchants, are required to report all cash transactions of $10,000 or more, again creating the problem of a suspicious paper trail. One response has been the use of "smurfs," or hired couriers who make a series of transactions under the $10,000 limit. A smurf might visit several different banks to purchase cashier's checks or money orders in amounts of less than $10,000, which are then delivered to third parties who deposit them in a bank account, all without triggering the reporting requirements of the Bank Secrecy Act (Cooper 42).

The principal disadvantage of "smurfing," aside from the fact that it is illegal under the 1986 Money Laundering Control Act, is that it is inconvenient and time-consuming. It takes more than 100 smurfing operations to deposit a million dollars, and a million dollars may be only a fraction of the sum that a big-time trafficker needs to launder. The alternative, and the way in which most drug profits are currently handled, is to ship the cash abroad and deposit it in places like the Bahamas or Panama or Colombia, where bank and government officials are rather more accommodating. One infamous bank, the Bank of Credit and Commerce International, specialized in serving criminals and drug traffickers, among them General Manuel Noriega. On the day it was closed the BCCI had over 900 million dollars, most of it illegitimate (U.S. Senate, *BCCI Affair* 39–40).

Once the traffickers have shipped their profits out of the country and deposited them in a foreign bank, they can, if necessary, be wired back into the United States, or to a dummy corporation, or for that matter anywhere else. Every business day one trillion U.S. dollars are wired throughout the world, a sum that dwarfs and, by its sheer volume, conceals even very large electronic transfers of drug money (U.S. Senate, *Drug Money Laundering, Banks, and Foreign Policy* 22, 26). The catch is that the bundles of money have to be concealed and shipped out of the country, just as the drugs must be shipped in. The risks and complications associated with smuggling are thus doubled. Sometimes they are more than doubled, for the accumulated cash can be heavier and bulkier than the drugs that were purchased with it. Drug money is usually flown out, often through return trips by the same pilots who smuggled the drugs. It can also be secreted in appliances and other export products, everything from Pampers boxes to Monopoly games, the latter with the play money removed to provide extra space (Blau 17). But even ingenious smugglers can be tripped up. A two-way, drug-and-money smuggling operation necessarily increases the odds of detection.

All money laundering operations, whether domestic or foreign, entail another weakness: they create witnesses and potential informants. Drug trafficking organizations, small as well as large, typically employ specialists to launder their money (U.S. Department of Justice 17). Because the activities of the launderers are both illegal and detectable, they may themselves be arrested and persuaded to serve as informants or testify against their employers. Salvatore Amendolito was a crooked Italian financier who began smurfing for the Mafia in 1980, then moved up to big-time, offshore laundering operations. Arrested by the FBI in 1983, he became an informer and subsequently a key witness in the celebrated Pizza Connection case, which proved to be the largest drug-and-Mafia trial in American history, and resulted in the conviction of eighteen defendants (Alexander *passim*).

Law enforcement officials frankly acknowledge that their most important cases now involve money rather than drugs, as higher-level traffickers almost never handle the drugs themselves. The chief limitation to this approach is a lack of investigators and prosecutorial resources: laundering cases tend to be drawn-out and enormously complicated. In Los Angeles—next to Miami, the most important money laundering city in the United States—the U.S. attorney's office has given up prosecuting drug money cases involving less than a certain amount, reported to be $500,000 (Leen et al. 1A, 25A; Cole 13). Mere smurfs have little to fear in L.A. Here, incidentally, is another paradox surrounding the drug traffic: the more successful the government is at prosecuting dealers, the more overloaded the criminal justice system becomes. At some point, which most large American cities have already reached, lesser crimes are simply, if unofficially, ignored.

When Scrooge beheld Marley's ghost, he saw a specter bound about the waist with a lengthy chain of cash-boxes, keys, padlocks, ledgers, deeds, and heavy purses wrought of steel. Dickens intended this chain as a metaphor for the self-enslavement of greedy men, but it strikes me as an equally apt symbol for the self-endangerment of drug dealers. The astonishing profits they earn also bring them endless trouble—trouble in the form of robbers and rip-off artists, of suspicious squares and inquiring feds, of indictments brought and proved on the basis of monetary and financial evidence. Perhaps this is fitting. Insofar as drug money brings destruction to its recipients as well as to society, it serves as an instrument of ironic justice.

NOTES

1. Half trillion: U.S. Senate, *Drugs, Law Enforcement, and Foreign Policy* 8; 300 billion: U.S. Senate, *Drug Money Laundering, Banks and Foreign Policy* 3–4.

2. Tabacco: U.S. Department of Commerce 660; coffee: Coffee, Sugar, & Cocoa Exchange 8; marijuana: Lyman 5–6.

3. For example, the photographs on Blau 19 or opposite p. 179 of Rice.

REFERENCES

Alexander, Shana. *The Pizza Connection: Lawyers, Money, Drugs, Mafia*. New York: Weidenfeld & Nicolson, 1988.

Blau, Charles W. "Role of the Narcotic and Dangerous Drug Section in the Federal Government's Fight Against Drug Trafficking." *Drug Enforcement* 11 (Summer 1984): 16–20.

Coffee, Sugar, & Cocoa Exchange, Inc. *1984 Statistical Abstract*. New York: Coffee, Sugar & Cocoa Exchange, Inc., 1985.

Cole, Benjamin Mark. "Bank Deposits Getting High on Drug Money Flooding L.A.'s Underground Economy." *Los Angeles Business Journal* 3 June 1991: 13.

Cooper, Mary H. *The Business of Drugs*. Washington, D.C.: Congressional Quarterly Inc., 1990.

Courtwright, David T., Herman Joseph, and Don Des Jarlais. *Addicts Who Survived: An Oral History of Narcotic Use in America, 1923–1965*. Knoxville: University of Tennessee Press, 1989.

Johnson, Bruce D., et al. *Taking Care of Business: The Economics of Crime by Heroin Abusers*. Lexington, Mass.: Lexington Books, 1985.

Leen, Jeff, et al. "Miami Awash in Cocaine Cash." *Miami Herald* 11 February 1990: 1A, 25A.

Lyman, Michael D. *Gangland: Drug Trafficking by Organized Criminals*. Springfield, Ill.: Charles C. Thomas, 1989.

Reuter, Peter, et al. *Money from Crime: A Study of the Economics of Drug Dealing in Washington, D.C.* Santa Monica: The RAND Corporation, 1990.

Rice, Berkeley. *Trafficking: The Boom and Bust of the Air America Cocaine Ring*. New York: Charles Scribner's Sons, 1989.

Saelens, Dave. "Lax Reporting of Cash Sales Benefits Drug Dealers." *Florida Times-Union* 27 January 1991: B1, B4.

U.S. Department of Commerce. Bureau of the Census. *Statistical Abstract of the United States, 1990*. Washington, D.C.: Government Printing Office, 1990.

U.S. Department of Justice. Office of the Attorney General. *Drug Trafficking: A Report to The President of the United States*. Washington, D.C.: Government Printing Office, 1989.

U.S. Department of the Treasury. Customs Service. *Air Carrier Security Manual*. Washington, D.C.: Government Printing Office, 1989.

U.S. Senate. Committee on Foreign Relations. Subcommittee on Terrorism, Narcotics, and International Operations. *The BCCI Affair*. 3 vols. Senate Hearings 102–350, 102nd Congress, 1st session. Washington, D.C.: Government Printing Office, 1992.

———. *Drug Money Laundering, Banks and Foreign Policy*. Senate Report 101–104, 101st Congress, 2nd session. Washington, D.C.: Government Printing Office, 1990.

———. *Drugs, Law Enforcement, and Foreign Policy*. Senate report 100–165, 100th Congress, 2nd session. Washington, D.C.: Government Printing Office, 1989.

Part II

Money and History

7

Images of Majesty: Money as Propaganda in Elizabethan England

CLIFTON W. POTTER, JR.

At a time when it was not considered proper for a woman to seek a career in the theater, Elizabeth I was the greatest actress of her day, or perhaps any age, because her stage was the world. Thus, if perchance, some courtier had sought to amuse the queen by reciting Jaques' immortal lines from scene 7 of act 2 in Shakespeare's satirical hit of 1599, *As You Like It*, she no doubt would have smiled and silently agreed that

> All the world's a stage
> And all the men and women merely players,
> They have their exits and their entrances,
> And one man in his time plays many parts, . . .

Elizabeth played many parts during her long lifetime from that of the shy, forgotten princess who moved like a shadow across the final troubled years of her father's reign to the bright hope of the Protestant cause who bided her time as her Roman Catholic sister lay dying; but her greatest role was that of the emblem of an England reborn like a phoenix from the ashes of religious controversy. The transformation of this young woman of twenty-five, who ascended England's throne in 1558, into Gloriana four decades later was no mere accident, but a carefully planned and executed scheme designed to help heal the nation's wounds while giving the people a symbol of national greatness. The use of poetry, drama, and song to accomplish this end is well-known, but the artist's brush and pen, the sculptor's chisel, and the engraver's tools also served to make the image of the queen more familiar to her subjects than that of any monarch before her time. Of particular importance was the seemingly endless shower of gold and silver coins that poured from the Royal Mint bearing the visage of the queen and proclaiming her titles to all and sundry. The wealthy might commission portraits of Elizabeth I, but even a pauper might wear a coin of his sovereign round his neck to drive away the evils that beset him on all sides. The coins of Elizabeth were everywhere, a ready medium of exchange, but also a very subtle form of propaganda.

When Elizabeth I ascended the throne on 17 November 1558, public confidence in England's coinage was very low both at home and abroad. Gold coins had long ago disappeared from circulation either to be melted illegally by speculators or to be hoarded by citizens fearful of England's ultimate economic collapse. The silver coins which still passed were for the most part debased and essentially worth only a fraction of their declared value. The counterfeit pieces and foreign coins that were used in everyday commerce were often preferred by the average citizen to the legal tender of the realm. This situation was due to a number of factors, some beyond the control of the government; but there were others which might have been manipulated to England's advantage by Elizabeth's father, brother, and sister.

Henry VIII was a very extravagant man, who in a reign of almost forty years squandered several fortunes, including his inheritance from his father, Henry VII, and much of the wealth gained from the confiscation of the property of the Roman Catholic church in England, as well as the regular annual revenues accruing from a number of sources. Admittedly King Henry was a victim, like his fellow sovereigns, of the inflationary spiral which affected all of the European economies in the sixteenth century. The influx of gold and silver from the Spanish colonies in the New World forced down the price of bullion, causing the relative purchasing power of the various monies in circulation to fall. To those living on fixed incomes these changes proved financially devastating, while those whose assets were more fluid were able to profit from these fluctuations. Henry VIII reacted to the inflation by debasing the coinage instead of maintaining its integrity. While he left the gold coins untouched, he repeatedly ordered that the fineness of the silver circulating medium be reduced by alloying the bullion with base metals like zinc, copper, and lead. Thus the weight of the coins was maintained and the actual number of pieces in circulation was increased while the intrinsic value of England's money was reduced. The public reacted by hoarding gold coins and any silver pieces which predated the debasement. By the time of Henry's death in 1547 English money was avoided by the foreign exchanges and regarded as worthless by international bankers.

The government of Edward VI and later that of Mary I attempted unsuccessfully to deal with the crisis. Admittedly neither monarch was on the throne long enough to establish a policy and insist on a strict adherence to it, but it is also true that their advisers were at a loss to know what to do (Sutherland 149). It is only with the accession of Elizabeth I that a remedy was proposed and adopted with the complete support of the sovereign. Among those that advised the queen in the matter of monetary reform was Sir Thomas Gresham, whose ideas on "good money" and "bad money" have achieved the status of law in the popular mind (Feaveraryear 78). Ever cautious, Elizabeth I began the process of slowly restoring the public's confidence in its coinage by initially making no changes in the fineness of the coins being struck by the Mint, only in the design. Thus the coiners were able to use the blanks prepared for Mary to strike the first coins of Elizabeth. The obverse design was based on the same pattern used for the official coronation portrait, and it remained basically unchanged until the end of her reign. Elizabeth's initial departure from current practice at the Mint was to order the striking of gold coins for the first time in years. The psychological effect on the employees of the Mint as well as the general public was immediate and positive (Craig 118). The number of coins struck was small, but their reappearance in the coffers of the merchants and the purses of shoppers seemed a sure indication that the economic situation was bound to improve, and hopefully in the near future. Having begun to lay a foundation for public support, Elizabeth began to build upon it.

In 1560, on the advice of her Privy Council, Elizabeth I ordered that the entire circulating medium with only a few exceptions be withdrawn and recoined. Since the purchase of large quantities of silver on the open market would prove prohibitive, it was decided that the bulk of the bullion required for this mammoth project would come from the debased coins still in circulation. They would remain legal tender, but at reduced values, while they were systematically removed and replaced by coins struck in the standard originally established in 1485 by the queen's grandfather Henry VII. The final plan for the devaluation of the debased coins was kept a secret until the government was ready to implement its replacement plan. First, all of the statutes which dealt with the exportation of bullion were strictly enforced lest speculators, discovering the intentions of Elizabeth's government, seek to make a profit from exporting debased coins to the Continent.

In August 1560 government agents, posing as ordinary citizens satisfying a wager, simultaneously examined every butcher's till in London and counted the coins, taking special note of the denominations they found there. These data were used to fix the redemption value of the denominations then in circulation (Feaveraryear 83). The intentions of the government were outlined in a proclamation which was issued without any warning whatsoever on 27 September 1560. Prices were frozen and the values of the debased coins were lowered. A study of the fate of most of the shillings struck during the reign of Edward VI provides an excellent example of the operation of the plan which the government evolved for dealing with the devalued coins. Normally worth 12 pence, some shillings were devalued to 4½ pence, while others were reduced to 2¼ pence. The latter coins actually contained 4 pence worth of silver; thus when they were redeemed at the Mint for new coins of the proper weight, the government really made a profit of 1¾ pence per shilling. In this manner the bullion needed for the recoinage was cleverly garnered without cost to the Exchequer (Craig 118, Feaveraryear 79). Since these debased shillings comprised a large proportion of the coins then in circulation, an easy and inexpensive method was devised to denote their relative values. Shillings worth 4½ pence had a portcullis stamped in front of the king's head, while those worth 2¼ pence had a greyhound in the same spot. For a modest fee the Mint provided punches to communities to expedite the stamping process.

The extra facilities to house the increased operations at the Mint had already been completed at the Tower of London before the proclamation was issued, but the intended function of the so-called Upper Mint remained a secret until the news of the recoinage was made public. New coins were ready for immediate redemption, and on September 29 a second proclamation was published offering 3 pence for every £1 of debased coins presented at the Mint. This generous benefit was originally offered for four months, but the response of the public was so enthusiastic that it was extended until the following August. So many debased pieces were presented during the first days of the program that the supply of new coins was quickly exhausted and the staff was hard-pressed to maintain its schedule for the recoinage. To squelch rumors that the program was in trouble the government actually purchased silver bullion abroad at considerable expense to increase production (Craig 118).

A German firm, David Wollstat and Company, had been hired to carry out the melting and refining of the debased coins, but problems developed almost as soon as they commenced their work. In ever-increasing numbers the foreign workers started to sicken and die of metal poisoning. They were aspirating large quantities of lead and zinc released by the smelting process. Numerous remedies were tried by the physicians summoned to treat them, including drinking milk from a human skull, but the deaths continued throughout the period of the recoinage (Craig 121). To quiet the fears of those already employed and to attract new workers, salaries at the Mint were raised in December 1560, and the queen herself came to strike some new coins by her own hand in February 1561. By the time of her visit the staff had reduced from twenty to eight days the period of time needed to recoin base pieces into good. The positive response of the general public was overwhelming, and by the end of 1561 it was almost impossible to pass a debased shilling regardless of its counterstamp.

Despite the several attempts by the enemies of the queen to undermine the public's confidence in the recoinage, the effort was completed by mid-1562, and in September of that year the "Upper Mint" was closed and the staff reduced to its normal size. The number of coins in circulation was three times what it had been a decade earlier, and most of them were in the new standard. For a brief period a few pieces dating from the reigns of Edward VI and Mary I were allowed to continue in circulation, but the bulk of the circulating medium bore the visage of Elizabeth I, a circumstance which the queen exploited to her advantage. The royal profile found on the obverse of all but the tiniest denominations was produced like all other portraits of the queen according to a carefully developed formula.

With one or two exceptions the representations of Elizabeth I that survive were not done from life; they are images of an ideal of majesty which the queen fostered as a means to instill not merely loyalty to the Crown, but a reverence for it. In a very subtle manner she used the coinage of the realm to aid her in this crucial endeavor. Over four decades she barely aged on the obverse of her coins, in fact toward the end of her reign she grew younger. Elizabeth the Queen slowly was transformed into Gloriana, the national icon.

The arts as practiced in England during the reign of Elizabeth were only indirectly influenced by trends on the Continent. The lack of funds which the Crown could devote to patronage is often cited as the primary reason why the queen preferred native artists to foreigners, but it is also true that the exclusive promotion of Englishmen gave Elizabeth a control over them and their artistic creations which would have been impossible with alien craftsman. Thus a style peculiar to England, and particularly in the graphic arts, evolved during the last half of the sixteenth century with the enthusiastic support of the queen and her court (Strong, *Icon* 1). Described as neo-medieval, it was characterized by the use of brilliant colors and the almost total absence of chiaroscuro. Thus Elizabethan artists seemed to reject the techniques of the Renaissance in favor of those employed by an earlier generation of painters. Artists also relied on numerous symbols to enhance their work as well as to convey subliminal messages in the manner employed by their artistic forebears. In particular this reliance on symbolism is found in the production of medals and coins because the use of a metaphorical color scheme was impossible.

In 1558 those noble and wealthy families hopeful of continued royal favor sought to add a portrait of the new sovereign to their accumulation of paintings; in fact in most cases the visage of Elizabeth I became the focal point of each collection. Paintings were just becoming the vogue as a wall covering, and the demand for royal portraits became almost overwhelming (Strong, *Portraits* 7–8, 23). Many of the works executed during the early years of the reign were of inferior quality, and thus the government sought to find an effective method of controlling the production of royal portraits. The absence of a large number of foreign artists was certainly advantageous, but it was not an adequate control since a host of native painters were working at a feverish pace without supervision or reference to royal instructions to supply the market.

In 1563 a proclamation was prepared but never issued, which laid down the guidelines which artists were to follow when reproducing the royal image. The queen chose instead to regulate such creations through the company of Painter-Stainers, which she incorporated for that purpose (Auerbach 110). Every member of this guild who wished to exercise his right to portray Elizabeth in any medium he chose was required to do so according to the rules and regulations approved by the queen. There were those, however, who ignored these prohibitions, and in 1596 by order of the Privy Council all portraits of Elizabeth which did not meet her standards were destroyed (Strong, *Portraits* 5–6). The pattern books by which the artists worked have not survived, but their existence can be surmised by the presence of certain elements of design found in the portraits produced simultaneously by artists scattered throughout the country. Favorite pieces of jewelry, certain fabrics, particular symbolic backgrounds, and items of clothing appear over and over again in portraits produced at opposite ends of England. At times certain elements in a pattern had to be altered to suit the medium. Thus the ornamental ruff worn by the queen in her coronation portrait is absent in the obverse design of her coins because its retention would have obscured her face in profile.

In the reign of Elizabeth it became the fashion to wear a portrait of the queen around one's neck. For the wealthy and the powerful these representations of Elizabeth were a pledge of loyalty, but for ordinary folk they were often a charm against evil (Farquhar 128). In the reign of Henry VIII the painted miniature had become the rage, and the queen's favorite painter, Nicholas Hilliard, developed it as an art form which closely resembled the icons of Byzantium. Also extremely popular as adornments were carved cameos of Elizabeth, along with numerous medals struck to commemorate important events in her reign. For the average citizen a coin with a hole carefully drilled near the upper rim of the obverse served the same purpose as the courtier's miniature on its gold chain or bright ribbon.

In either case, the coins of Elizabeth I were produced either by the hammer or the screw press. The former method was of ancient origin and carefully protected by the guild of moneyers. Most of the steps were performed by hand and the final product, while perhaps the best of its kind, was decidedly inferior to the machine-made coins produced on the Continent. From 1561 to 1572 the queen permitted Eloye Mestrell, a Protestant refugee who had been employed at the Paris mint, to produce coins of superior quality using the latest machinery available. Unfortunately, pressure from the guild of moneyers forced an end to his experiment. Although Mestrell was fired, his coins continued to circulate into the next century, wearing far better than the hand-produced pieces (Porteous 180–81).

Exclusive of the experiment with machine-made or milled money, the coinage of Elizabeth I may be divided into three periods on the basis either of the fineness of the bullion, or of the denominations produced. From 1558 until 1560 the standard of fineness established by Mary I was retained. From 1560 until 1583 the emphasis in production was on the minor coins needed to facilitate everyday commerce. Larger denominations dominated the production at the Mint from 1583 until the queen's death in 1603. Throughout the period the basic portrait of Elizabeth remained unchanged. Men who were in their prime when Good Queen Bess rode to her coronation grew old and stooped, but the portrait of their sovereign was ever that of the young girl they cheered on her way to the Abbey. Her costume might change from simple dress to elaborate gown to armor, but the face remained the same. The silver crowns and half crowns of 1601 and 1602 revealed a woman no longer a girl, but nonetheless still youthful. This convention was not the result of mere feminine vanity, but an attempt to reflect the same spirit that animated the poets and painters who portrayed their sovereign as the youthful embodiment of the age that bears her name. Even in death she would remain for them a maiden enthroned in heaven as she was upon the gold sovereigns struck during her long reign.

Elizabeth lived on in the hearts of her subjects long after 1603. When the novelty of being ruled by a king quickly began to pall during the early years of the reign of James I, the English embroidered the myth of the Virgin Queen until she became a cult figure. Every time they reached into their purses to make the simplest transaction her face was before them. Elizabethan pieces made up the bulk of many coin hoards hidden in the 1640s at the time of the Civil War (Challis 230–31). Chipped and worn though they might have been, these thin pieces of gold and silver reminded another generation born long after her death that the England of Elizabeth was a land blessed by peace and prosperity. The faded legends still proclaimed that she was "A ROSE WITHOUT THORNS," and that "BY THE LORD THIS WAS DONE AND IT IS MARVELOUS TO OUR EYES." Perhaps the myth of that halcyon age still haunts us all.

REFERENCES

Auerbach, Erna. *Tudor Artists*. London, 1954.
Challis, C. E. *Tudor Coinage*. Manchester, 1978.
Craig, Sir John. *The Mint*. Cambridge, 1953.

Farquhar, Helen. "Portraiture of Our Tudor Monarchs on Their Coins and Medals," *British Numismatic Journal*. Vol. IV. London, 1908.

Feaveraryear, Sir Albert. *The Pound Sterling*. Oxford, 1963.

Linecar, H.W.A. *British Coin Design and Designers*. London, 1977.

Porteous, John. *Coins in History*. New York, 1969.

Seaby, Peter. *The Story of the English Coinage*. London, 1952.

Shakespeare, William. *Major Plays and the Sonnets*. G. B. Harrison, ed. New York, 1948.

Strong, Roy. *The English Icon: Elizabethan and Jacobean Portraiture*. New Haven, 1969.

————. *Portraits of Queen Elizabeth I*. Oxford, 1963.

Sutherland, C.H.V. *English Coinage, 600–1900*. Oxford, 1973.

8

"There Is No More Money Here": Money Famine and Tax Revolt in Early Modern France

Thomas M. Luckett

Among the greatest challenges to his economic policies that Jean-Baptiste Colbert had to confront in his lengthy career as royal minister of finance was the so-called Stamped-Paper Revolt of 1675 (E.S.B. et al.; Garlan & Nières; Mousnier, *Fureurs paysannes* 123–56). Oddly, the revolt was confined to precisely the region of France that seemed to have benefited most from those very policies: the western provinces that carried on the lucrative trade with Africa and the Americas. Only here did cities or countryside refuse to pay the excise taxes he had created to fund the Dutch War—a war, moreover, whose manifest purpose was to drive the Dutch from the sea and thus establish the commercial hegemony of France's Atlantic ports. Colbert could only be astonished by the ingratitude of the westerners. Already in December 1673, when the estates of Brittany had requested the revocation of his new stamped-paper tax, Colbert had sent off a harsh letter to the duke of Chaulnes, royal governor of the province, in which he stressed this paradox. Both Languedoc and Provence had already accepted this tax, he pointed out, so why not Brittany?

I do not doubt that you profit from everything His Majesty has done since the last Estates, and which he continues to do every day to protect and increase the commerce of this province, by keeping the Mediterranean free and swept of all corsairs; from the powerful fleets of vessels in Cádiz that uphold the commerce of Saint-Malo and of all other cities of Brittany, and that escort the vessels to their ports; from other fleets in the islands of America that keep the vessels of Nantes safe, and that convoy them on their voyages and when they return; and in a word by an infinity of other payments that His Majesty makes in order to draw money into this province, whence it flows into the others of his Kingdom. (Depping 1: 534)

An even greater paradox was discovered by the duke of Chaulnes himself when he was called upon to crush the Breton revolt in the summer of 1675. Despite everything Colbert believed he had done to draw bullion into France's seaports, Brittany was suffering from an apparent shortage of money that made the new taxes impossible to pay. 'We have just learned of the bankruptcy of one of the greatest bankers of Vannes," wrote Chaulnes, "which will cause the ruin of many people. . . . It is certain that there is hardly any money left in Brittany. We do not believe that there is a million [livres] in trade" (Depping 3: 259). At about the same time Colbert received a letter from François d'Argouges, president of the Parlement of Rennes, in which he pleaded, "Permit me to point out to you that there is no more money here, and that in the last twenty-four hours we have had two large bankruptcies, which will be followed by those of all who are involved in business if you do not have the graciousness to postpone for some time the payment [of taxes]—I mean for a month or six weeks" (Depping 3: 261 n.). Another Breton authority made it clear to Colbert that this shortage of money was the primary cause of the revolt. "What raises tempers this year against the edicts," he wrote, "and especially against the stamped paper, is that it is certain that specie is lacking in this province, and that this edict clearly draws money out while the people suffer greatly from penury" (Pillorget 125–26).

At one level, then, the Stamped-Paper Revolt is not hard to explain. What easier way to provoke a rebellion than to impose taxes requiring people to pay money that they simply do not have? Yet at a deeper level it becomes problematical. The famous "bullionist" policies of Colbert, as implied in his letter to Chaulnes, aimed to benefit crown revenues by drawing bullion into the country, thus increasing the pool of money from which taxes were to be paid. Yet after more than a decade of such bullionism, the port cities where money should now have been entering France were the only region to experience a shortage of money severe enough to make taxes uncollectible.

To explore this paradox, I need to begin with a few general observations based on my own current research into the function of commercial credit under the old regime. First, the monetary crisis in Brittany was anything but unique. Known to contemporaries as *une disette d'argent*— literally a "money shortage" or "money famine"—this sort of event disrupted France's commercial economy every few years. During the half century preceding the Revolution of 1789 (a period for which quantitative evidence is far more plentiful) the city of Paris endured a dozen money famines, most of which also affected the other financial centers of the kingdom. Like that of 1675 these money shortages tended to occur in moments of low bread prices, and were thus clearly not the result of grain famine (Meyer 2: 849). Lasting typically three or four months, occasionally longer, the money famine was a scourge for great merchants and small shopkeepers alike, for it threatened even the most prosperous business owners with illiquidity and poor sales, and raised the prospect of default, imprisonment, and bankruptcy.

My second observation concerns the nature of money itself in early modern France. When contemporaries used the word *money* they meant nothing other than the specie that royal edicts defined as legal tender. Apart from brief experiments in paper currency, the money supply was thus understood as the country's stock of minted coin. Yet by the middle seventeenth century, currency constituted only a small part of the circulating medium of exchange. Most sales of merchandise between business owners were made on credit and gave rise to the creation of written promises of payment at some future date. The two most important types of these IOUs were the promissory note (*billet de commerce*) used for transactions within a given city, and the bill of exchange (*lettre de change*) that made possible payments across geographic distances without the physical transport of specie.

The circulation of commercial paper as a medium of exchange dates properly from the 1620s, when both types of IOU first became negotiable (Lévy-Bruhl 103). By the practice of endorsement, it became possible for a businessperson to receive an IOU as payment in one transaction, then sign it over to another party in an unrelated transaction. In this way it could change hands ten or fifteen times before it came due, and even when it was finally presented for payment to the original debtor, he could often simply clear it by signing over another credit from his own portfolio. Thus Pierre de Boisguilbert did not greatly exaggerate when he wrote that in times of prosperity money "does not form the tenth part, nor even the fiftieth part" of all payments (2: 889). "It is then that people say ridiculously that money abounds, because this substance that is so precious in times of shortage becomes absolutely unwanted in times of abundance, its storage being unprofitable, unlike that of other goods, on which one can make a fortune" (2: 966).

Nevertheless, as its name implies, the money famine was *experienced* by economic actors as a generalized lack of currency in circulation. The retailer suddenly found it difficult to persuade any of his customers to pay in cash, or even to buy on credit at reasonably short term. Within established networks of credit, creditors found it impossible to collect on paper that had come due. Since they now needed such payments to service their own debts, they in turn were forced to write to their creditors and ask for extended term. Where cash could be borrowed the rate of interest rose sharply above its usual level, but more often such loans were impossible to find at any price. The crisis had an absurd quality. There seemed to have been no loss of property, everyone's assets were more than enough to cover his obligations, yet everyone was penniless and the threat of imprisonment and ruin was suddenly all too real: "The scarcity of money, various bankruptcies, and the large number of bad investments continue still at the Place de Change" (Michon 287). "Money, which is the soul of commerce, has never been so scarce" (Luckett 134). "Besides which, money is extremely scarce in this city" (Luckett 134). "Money is of an unbelievable scarcity, and no money can be got for paper" (Cornette 112).

Such statements as these crop up constantly in the commercial letters written in times of money famine. By their implication that the money supply was the crucial variable determining credit costs, they represent a popular mercantilism that probably inspired the literary mercantilism so well-known to historians of economic thought. For businesspeople who conceived the crisis in these terms, one great question imposed itself: *where had the money gone?* The answers proposed to this question testify to the creative imagination of the commercial mind. Coin had been melted down to make silver plate and gold cloth. It had been exported to England and Spain, even though a favorable exchange rate made it cheaper to transfer funds by bill of exchange. Worse yet, the nation's coin had been hidden away by speculators whose design was to drive up the interest rate and profit from the people's misery.

Pierre de Boisguilbert was one of the few economists of the old regime to point out the fallacy in this line of thought. In a series of polemical works for which Louis XIV finally condemned him to internal exile, Boisguilbert explained that the money famine was caused not by a fall in the supply of money, but by a sharp rise in the demand for money. "They do not reflect," he wrote of his compatriots, "that there are two things that make a substance scarce, the first being its shortage, and the second the sudden multiplicity of those who need it. Money suffers this kind of scarcity for the second cause, and they have the blindness to put the blame on the first" (2: 675).

To state the point rather differently, the causes of money famine were psychological rather than monetary. Occurring generally in a period of prosperity and expansion, the crisis began as a financial panic. "A momentary alarm," wrote the economist Turgot, "the event of a few bankruptcies, rumors of war, can spread a general fear that suddenly raises the price of all negotiations of money" (286). Suddenly businesspeople feared that the IOUs in their portfolios would not be paid when they came due, and that their own creditors would be prepared to prosecute. In desperation they tried to increase their cash reserves as the only possible safeguard against debtors' prison. Ironically, as debts were called in and purchases ground to a halt, as interest rates soared and prices plummeted, these fears proved self-fulfilling.

In this way [wrote Boisguilbert] all revenues of industry cease altogether, and money, which only forms so much revenue insofar as it moves, not leaving tight fists, stops entirely its ordinary course. This paralyzes the country in all its members, and renders a state miserable amid an abundance of all sorts of goods. (2: 619)

To return at last to Brittany, the financial panic that lay at the origin of the revolt seems to have begun shortly after July 1674, when the Dutch admiral de Ruyter succeeded in closing the transatlantic trade routes to French merchant shipping. Over the previous decade, due to the development of trade in sugar and slaves, France's Atlantic ports had undergone an astonishing economic expansion (Mims 236, 245, 263, 280). The number of private French ships going to the sugar islands had grown from just four in 1662 to 131 in 1674. The rise in trade also brought important industrial development to western France as sugar refineries were established in Nantes, La Rochelle, Bordeaux, and other coastal cities. While most of this investment until 1668 was channeled through the West Indies Company, thereafter the sugar trade was opened to private commerce, and by 1674 was entirely in private hands. This bull market necessarily expanded the volume of circulating credit and consequently raised levels of individual indebtedness in proportion to cash reserves. Brittany, therefore, was already poised for a crash when the Dutch War cut off the trade routes in the autumn of 1674. By late the following spring every merchant's worst nightmare had become a reality, for as each failed business ruined its principal creditors, bankruptcy spread through the province by chain reaction (E.S.B. et al. 79–80).

But the primary importance of this episode lies in the evidence it provides that money famine could provoke a certain type of tax revolt. The Breton Revolt began as a distinctly *urban* uprising, drawing its partisans from the merchants and artisans of major Breton towns, while the peasantry responded only belatedly in western Brittany, and elsewhere not at all. For urban business owners large and small, taxes that were merely burdensome in times of commercial expansion had been rendered unpayable, and thus intolerable, by the money famine. A single example, however, does not constitute a pattern. What other revolts in French history seem to be tied to this type of financial crisis?

From 1647 to 1649, Paris endured a prolonged money famine severe enough to drag down the royal fiscal system along with the commercial economy. The finance minister, who, given the "scarcity of money," was unable either to raise taxes or borrow, issued a partial default in July 1648 that reduced government annuities by nearly two thirds. Royal bankruptcy, however, only exacerbated the financial crisis by ruining state creditors and multiplying the number of business failures (Bonney 203–7; Braudel 1: 417; Moote 156–57). "This shortage is not confined to the king," commented prime minister Jules Mazarin. "No individual however rich could have found a thousand écus to borrow, since no one wants to let go of his money" (3: 194).

At this precise juncture Parisian shopkeepers revolted against royal taxation in the famous "Days of Barricades" of August 26 to 28, an insurrection that marks the beginning of the abortive revolution known as the Fronde (Bonney 207–8; Moote 151–52; Bourgeon 122–42; Mousnier, "Quelques raisons"). The *mazarinades*, or antigovernment pamphlets, that flourished over the following year complained bitterly of the money famine. "The merchant charged with debts has no more customers," wrote one pamphleteer; Mazarin's greed has caused France's gold coin to "faint away" (Carrier 2, no. 43: 10). Another pamphleteer claimed to have interviewed a large number of merchants who could not restock their shops because their debtors had not paid them in months, and who lived in fear of prison and bankruptcy. "Poverty, beggary, or lack of money are such contagious diseases this year," reflected the author, "that from popular they have become, so to speak, royal" (Carrier 2, no. 35: 3).

My third example is not literally a revolt but a related event that in many ways foreshadows the pre-Revolution of 1787. After Louis XIV died on 1 September 1715, the news of his death was greeted across France with bonfires and popular celebrations. "The people, ruined, impoverished, desperate, rendered thanks to God with scandalous rejoicing," commented the duke of Saint-Simon, while Marie-Jeanne d'Aumale indicated that the revelers "hoped to see immediately diminished the multitude of taxes" created by Louis to fund the War of the Spanish Succession (Saint-Simon 28: 378; Aumale 2: 356). The celebrations were greatest at Paris, where crowds gathered in the plain before the Saint-Denis Basilica to await the royal burial. "Every manner of food and refreshments was sold there," wrote Charles-Pinot Duclos, "and one saw on every side the people dance, sing, drink, and abandon themselves to scandalous joy, while some had the indignity to vomit insults when they saw the hearse pass by with the body" (498).

This symbolic revolt against the king and his extraordinary taxes, like the earlier literal revolts, occurred in the midst of a particularly severe financial crisis (Lüthy 1: 256–57). In Paris the number of bankruptcies in 1715 rose fourfold over the previous year, and in Marseille sevenfold (Luckett 221; Carrière 2: 1056). The short-term rate of interest, which usually stood at about 5 percent, now rose to fifty (Law 3: 6–7). In Lyon the crisis was vividly described by Léonard Michon, a barrister with that city's Bureau of Finance. As early as May he wrote of the "scarcity of money in spite of the devaluation of the currency, the poor sales of merchandise, the insolvency of business people in Paris, various large bankruptcies in Marseille, Rouen, Paris as well as in this city," and his journal continues to talk of the money famine until April the following year (287). Caused in large part by the virtual bankruptcy of the royal fiscal system, this money famine—to use the language of the day—"discredited" the aging monarch in the last months of his reign.

It is time for me to confess that the preceding discussion has had a hidden agenda. These three events drawn from the era of Louis XIV reveal an intriguing pattern. Under certain circumstances, prolonged money famine could provoke various forms of urban revolt in which the royal fiscal system—due both to its bankruptcy and its attempts to impose extraordinary taxes—became the focus of popular anger. If this generalization is accurate, it informs the history of the pre-Revolution, for the lengthiest money famine of the eighteenth century began in December 1786 and lasted nearly two years.

Initiated by the "Affair of the Altered Bills of Exchange," a criminal scandal that temporarily undermined confidence in the Parisian credit market, this new financial panic was exploited by the radical press and helped to "discredit" the efforts of the Calonne ministry to resolve the government's deficit crisis (Bouchary 3: 60–65). Dismissed on April 8, the unfortunate Calonne emigrated to England but was not so quickly forgotten. In September and October Paris witnessed a series of carnivalesque riots at the Place Dauphine and the Pont Neuf that were strangely reminiscent of 1715. Bonfires were lit and fireworks set off. Calonne himself was hanged in effigy and speakers harangued the crowd with denunciations of his financial policies, now held to be responsible for the high rate of interest and catastrophic shortage of money (Bachaumont et al. 36: 87, 90–92, 96; Rudé 28–30).

There is no need here to insist that a great fiscal crisis finally destroyed the old regime, or that the problem of the royal debt was at the center of the constitutional transformations of 1789. But the character of the money famine helps to explain why, from the start, ordinary people would have felt so directly concerned by the possibility of a royal default. In a pamphlet published immediately before the riots at the Place Dauphine, the future revolutionary leader Jacques-Pierre Brissot warned that in the event of such a default, "private bankruptcies would multiply. . . . From that point on, no more private good faith, no more credit, and by consequence no more commerce, no more industry, and no more agriculture" (8).

The great irony of this story is that social revolution is hardly the way to restore confidence to a credit market. In Avignon on 28 August 1789, the Englishman Arthur Young tried to make just this point to a group of French travelers, "but," as he tells us, "in vain."

I asked, if the union of a rusty firelock and a *bourgeois* made a soldier? I asked them, in which of their wars they had wanted men? I demanded, whether they had ever felt any other want than that of money? And whether the conversion of a million of men, into the bearers of muskets, would [make] money more plentiful? I asked, if personal service was not a tax? And whether paying the tax of the service of a million of men increased their faculties of paying other and more useful taxes? I begged them to inform me, if the regeneration of the kingdom, which had put arms into the hands of a million of mob, had rendered industry more productive, internal peace more secure, confidence more enlarged, or credit more stable? (1: 364–65)

REFERENCES

Aumale, Marie-Jeanne d'. *Souvenirs de Madame de Maintenon*, ed. Gabriel-Paul-Othenin de Cléron, comte d'Haussonville and Gabriel Hanitaux. Paris: Calmann-Lévy, 1902–4, 3 vols.

Bachaumont, Louis Petit de, et al. *Mémoires secrets pour servir à l'histoire de la république des lettres en France*. London: Adamson, 1777–89, 36 vols.

Boisguilbert, Pierre le Pesant de. *Pierre de Boisguilbert, ou la naissance de l'économie politique*, ed. Alfred Sauvy, et al. Paris: I.N.E.D., 1966, 2 vols.

Bonney, Richard. *The King's Debts: Finance and Politics in France, 1589–1661*. Oxford: Clarendon, 1981.

Bouchary, Jean. *Les Manieurs d'argent à Paris à la fin du XVIIIᵉ siècle*. Paris: Rivière, 1939–43, 3 vols.

Bourgeon, Jean-Louis. "L'Ile de la Cité pendant la Fronde: Structure sociale," *Paris et Ile-de-France, Mémoires*, 13 (1962); 23–142.

Braudel, Fernand. *Civilisation matérielle, économie et capitalisme, XVᵉ au XVIIIᵉ siècle*. Paris: Armand Colin, 1979, 3 vols.

Brissot, Jacques-Pierre. *Point de Banqueroute, ou lettre à un créancier de l'Etat sur l'impossibilité de la banqueroute nationale et sur les moyens de ramener le crédit et la paix*. London: n.p., 1787.

Carrier, Hubert, ed. *La Fronde: Contestation démocratique et misère paysanne*, 52 mazarinades. Paris: E.D.H.I.S., 1982, 2 vols.

Carrière, Charles. *Négociants marseillais au XVIIIᵉ siècle*. Marseille: Institut historique de Provence, 1973, 2 vols.

Cornette, Joël. *Un Révolutionnaire ordinaire: Benoît Lacombe, 1759–1815*. Paris: Champ Vallon, 1986.

Depping, Georg B., ed. *Correspondance administrative sous le règne de Louis XIV*. Paris: Imprimerie nationale, 1850–55, 4 vols.

Duclos, Charles-Pinot. "Mémoires sécrets sur les règnes de Louix XIV et de Louis XV," *Nouvelle collection des mémoires pour servir à l'historie de France*, ed. Joseph-François Michaud and Jean-Joseph-François Poujoulat. Paris: Guyot, 1839), ser. 3, 10: 429–630.

E.S.B., Arthur de la Borderie, and Boris Porchnev. *Les Bonnets rouges, les historiens et l'histoire*. Paris: Union générale d'èditions, 1975.

Garlan, Yvon, and Claude Nières. *Les Révoltes bretonnes de 1675: Papier timbré et bonnets rouges*. Paris: Editions sociales, 1975.

Law, John. *Œuvres complètes*, ed. Paul Harsin. Paris: Sirey, 1934, 3 vols.

Lévy-Bruhl, Henri. *Histoire de la lettre de change en France aux XVIIe et XVIIIe siècles.* Paris: Sirey, 1933.

Luckett, Thomas M. "Credit and Commercial Society in France, 1740–1789," Ph.D., Princeton University, 1992.

Lüthy, Herbert. *La Banque protestante en France de la révocation de l'Edit de Nantes à la Révolution.* Paris: S.E.V.P.E.N., 1959–61, 2 vols.

Mazarin, Jules. *Lettres du Cardinal Mazarin pendant son ministère,* ed. Pierre-Adolphe Chéruel. Paris: Imprimerie nationale, 1872–1906, 9 vols.

Meyer, Jean. *La Noblesse bretonne au XVIIIe siècle.* Paris: S.E.V.P.E.N., 1966, 2 vols.

Michon, Léonard. "Journal de Lyon" (ms. at Musée historique de Lyon), 1 (1715–17).

Mims, Stewart L. *Colbert's West India Policy.* New Haven: Yale University Press, 1912.

Moote, A. Lloyd. *The Revolt of the Judges: The Parlement of Paris and the Fronde, 1643–1652.* Princeton: Princeton University Press, 1971.

Mousnier, Roland. *Fureurs paysannes: Les Paysans dans les révoltes du XVIIe siècle (France, Russie, Chine).* Paris: Calmann-Lévy, 1967.

———. "Quelques raisons de la Fronde: Les Causes des journées révolutionnaires parisiennes de 1648," *Dix-septième siècle,* 2–3 (1949); 33–78.

Pillorget, René. "Les Problèmes monétaires français de 1602 à 1689," *Dix-septième siècle,* 70–71 (1966); 107–30.

Rudé, George. *The Crowd in the French Revolution.* Oxford: Oxford University Press, 1959.

Saint-Simon, Louis de Rouvroi, duc de. *Mémoires de Saint-Simon,* ed. Arthur-André-Gabriel-Michel de Boislisle. Paris: Hachette, 1916, 41 vols.

Turgot, Anne-Robert Jacques. *Ecrits économiques,* ed. Bernard Cazes. Paris: Calmann-Lévy, 1970.

Young, Arthur. *Travels during the Years 1787, 1788 and 1789.* Dublin: Cross, 1793, 2 vols.

9

A Discriminating Taste for Money: An Examination of the New York Antebellum Banking Market

ANDREW ECONOMOPOULOS

Any increase in bank failures raises questions concerning the safety of the money supply and the stability of the banking system. In the face of crisis, some argue that reform is needed—in particular, the elimination of deposit insurance.[1] They contend that federal deposit insurance eliminates the incentive of depositors to monitor their banking institutions. When they are not accountable to depositors, banking institutions may take unwarranted risks. However, in the absence of federal deposit insurance depositors would be induced to keep track of the creditworthiness of their banking institutions. Since their deposits would be uninsured, depositors would now discriminate among the various banks, choosing the bank that was safe and sound. Thus, discriminating between banks would induce the banking institutions to respond to the depositors' concerns for safety and soundness.

What is critical to the reformist arguments is that depositors effectively discriminate between "good" banks and "bad" banks.[2] In order to determine whether depositors can and do discriminate, it is important to examine them in an uninsured environment such as the antebellum banking market. During the antebellum period there was no FDIC, there were fewer regulations, frequent failures, and significant distinction between individual banks and bank liabilities.

Two recent studies of this period suggest that bank creditors did discriminate among issuers of money. Rolnick and Weber showed that in the free banking era people held bank notes on the basis of their expected value; they did not attempt to explain the motives of bank depositors and the possible substitution of one type of liability for another. Economopoulos presented evidence that free bank depositors may have been able to discriminate between poorly managed and competently managed free banks, though no explanation is given as to how these depositors were able to discriminate between banks.

In this study, we examine the New York antebellum banking market. The New York banking market was selected in this preliminary investigation because it provides a good cross section of different banking institutions operating in what has been called one of the most successful antebellum banking markets. If the New York antebellum depositor was able to discriminate among the various banks, surely depositors today could also do the same.

The paper proceeds as follows. In the first section, an overview of the New York antebellum banking market is given. This section gives the market environment of bank creditors during this period. In the second section, the theory of banknote discrimination in a free banking market is examined through the model of banknote demand and supply. In the final section, the evidence will be presented. The results indicate that even in a "sound" banking system, the bank creditor had a discriminating taste for money.

THE NEW YORK ANTEBELLUM BANKING MARKET, 1829–63

Prior to the enactment of the National Currency Act of 1863, the issuance of money was primarily regulated by the individual states. Each state allowed banks to issue money in the form of currency or demand deposits according to the prescribed regulations. The individual bank was personally liable for currency issued, and hence the term *banknote* was used to denote the currency component of money.

Two types of banks existed under the New York State banking system: the incorporated bank and the free bank. Prior to 1829 incorporated banks were individually chartered by the legislature. Consequently, the restrictions imposed on banks varied from one bank to another. This form of incorporation gave way in 1829 to a general banking law according to which charters issued were approved by the legislature, but banks operated under a uniform code. In 1838, the legislature relinquished control of licensing charters for a system of free entry while maintaining a uniform code. Two types of free banks were allowed by law: the "individual banker" and the "association." The individual banker was the sole proprietor of the institution, while the association consisted of a group of stockholders. Both types of free banks were subject to the same regulations, except for the minimum capital requirement—individual bankers were required to have at least $50,000 in equity and associations were required to have $100,000.

In general, both incorporated and free banks operated under similar regulatory codes; many were designed to limit debt, to protect the bank creditor, and to restrict lending practices.[3] One group of provisions focused on the safety of the banknote holder. Three provisions applied to both the incorporated bank and the free bank:

1. Par redemption of banknotes. A bank was required to redeem its banknote into specie upon demand. Failure to honor the request would result in the forfeiture of banking privileges.

2. Extended stockholder liability. A stockholder was personally liable for debts of the bank equal to his share in the corporation.[4]

3. First lien rights. Banknote holders had first lien rights to all the bank's assets.[5]

Yet, there were some subtle regulatory provisions that may have influenced a bank creditor's choices. Banks that were incorporated between 1829 and 1838 were commonly called "safety fund" banks because they were required to pay up to 3 percent of their capital into an insurance fund. In case of insolvency, the state would draw upon the fund to pay off note holders. Although free banks were not required to participate in the insurance program, free banks were required to set up a secondary redemption fund of government securities and real estate mortgages with the state. Printed on each banknote was the type of asset used to back it. The amount of outstanding circulating notes could not exceed the lesser of the fund's par or market value.[6] When the fund's market value fell below the outstanding issue, the banks were required to call in banknotes or increase the pool of securities. There was no limit to the amount of banknotes issued by the free bank, whereas the incorporated banks were limited to three times the bank's capital.[7]

The insurance protection provided by these funds did not necessarily guarantee that they were circulating at face value. Typically, banknotes from outside New York City circulated within the city at a discount. The discount was usually determined by the distance from the redemption center and the riskiness of the bank's asset portfolio. However, the maximum discount allowed by law was 0.5 percent prior to 1851 and 0.25 percent after 1851. To offset redemption costs to New York City banks, the law also included a provision requiring New York "country" banks to set up agencies in New York City, typically a New York City bank, for the redemption of their notes.

The depositors of both the free and incorporated banks did not receive the protection that the banknote holder did. Some have suggested that the nature of the banknote and deposit as a medium of exchange may have been the reason why state legislatures did not enact provisions protecting the depositor. Laughlin, the spokesman for the conventional view, states that[8] the noteholder is usually an involuntary, and the depositor a voluntary creditor of the bank. The use of the deposit always implies recourse to the bank in order to give it payment; while no proof, no indorsement, no identification in establishing its right to move in the world of exchange. The depositor selects his own bank and takes the risk implied in the voluntary choice. . . . Consequently, the reasons for the guaranty [first lien rights] of the notes are obvious; while they would have no application to the guaranty of the deposits. (Laughlin 86)

Not only do Laughlin's remarks justify the first lien provision for note holders, but they also imply that note holders were more likely to be nondiscriminators of banknotes than depositors.

The regulations governing earning assets were generally the same for both the free and the incorporated bank. The bank was to "carry on the business of banking, by discounting bills, notes and other evidences of debt . . . by buying and selling . . . bills of exchange, in the manner specified in their articles of association . . . by loaning money on real and personal security" (Cleaveland and Hutchinson 95). What distinguished a free bank's asset portfolio from an incorporated bank's asset portfolio was the assets held in reserve for banknote redemption. Free banks were required to hold as reserves either New York State bonds, U.S. bonds, or mortgages on unencumbered real estate. New York and U.S. bonds were generally considered "AAA" quality while the mortgages were regarded by some as "junk" quality. In the comptroller's report of 1849, the comptroller offered his opinion on the quality of mortgages: "All the experience of this department shows that mortgages are not the best security for this purpose [i.e., backing banknotes. . . . Capitalists are cautious about purchasing mortgages], and the consequence is that they have sometimes sold for less than 20% on the amount secured by them" (Fillmore 682). It appears that the legislature did not share the comptroller's concern, for they never repealed this provision.

For the individual on the street (or merchant), information was available to help discriminate among the issuers. One of the cheapest forms of information concerning an individual was the banknote itself. The law required all banks to print their name on the banknote and for all free banks to print the type of security held as reserves. Immediately, the individual would know whether the banknote was issued by an incorporated bank or a free bank association. They would also know who issued the banknote and, in general, the type of assets held by the bank.

More costly information was also available to the individual. Both the incorporated and free bank were required to publish their balance sheets in the local newspaper each quarter. Other sources of information available on a monthly basis were *Thompson's Banknote Reporter* and *Banker's Magazine*. *Thompson's Banknote Reporter* contained the current discount rate on banknotes of banks across the country and counterfeit banknote issue, and *Banker's Magazine* reviewed the current state of the market. Thus, it is clear that the public could easily discriminate among the different issuers of money. It is unclear why they chose a particular portfolio of money. An investigation into the bank creditor's money portfolio choice is reviewed in the next section.

DEMAND AND SUPPLY OF BANKNOTES

Demand for Banknotes

Demand for a bank's banknote depends on the general market demand for currency as well as the risk-related characteristics of the individual bank. A bank creditor would be indifferent, indiscriminate, between banknotes of different banks if all banks were equivalent in risk. In such a case, individuals would randomly redeem banknotes without considering the issuer. Holding one bank's banknote would have no greater benefit than holding another's. Under the assumption of equivalence, the demand for a bank's currency would then depend on market structure and general economic activity. However, if banks differed in risk, then bank creditors would demand the bank's currency according to the relative risk of the individual bank's issue and would discriminate among banks by using safe banknotes or refusing to accept risky banknotes.

For the individual, assessing the relative risk of New York banks could be a costly proposition; the individual would have to weigh the marginal benefits of gathering information on the banks against the marginal costs. For the New York banknote holders, there were over four hundred banks to assess. Although it would appear that the cost of assessment would have been prohibitive, the individual was able to discriminate among the different types of issuers. Two important pieces of information were free to all note holders—the type of issuer (incorporated or free) and the reserves backing the banknote. As noted earlier, printed on each free bank banknote was the type of asset backing the note. Thus, the individual could discriminate on the basis of the composition of the bank's asset portfolio and type of institution.

Larger note holders, such as brokers, merchants, and banks, could gather other sources of information in assessing the risk of the issuer. Brokers and merchants could review the quarterly financial reports as well as monthly financial publications. Both sources would provide the individual information on capital adequacy of the various issuers, market opinions, and so on. Bankers also had a strong interest in monitoring and assessing the risk of other banks. Each "country" bank (all banks exclusive of those located in Albany and New York City) was required to have a redemption agent in Albany or New York City. It was crucial for these agents that the issuing bank be of sound character. Furthermore, a nonagent bank would normally exchange its own banknotes for another bank's banknotes. Since bankers were aware of daily market conditions, one would expect that they would be discriminating among the issuers.

Thus, at any point in time, the taste for holding a particular bank's banknote would depend on the perceived risk of the bank. Perceived risk can be observed through several pieces of financial and institutional information: specie reserves, the level of capital contributed by the stockholders, mortgage portfolio as a percentage of total earning assets, the management of the bank, and the type of banking institution:

$$BN_i^d = (SPR, CAP, MORT, MAN, TYPE), \qquad (1)$$
$$+ \quad + \quad - \quad ? \quad ?$$

where the expected sign is given below each variable.

If the public discriminated among note issuers, one would expect that these variables would influence the public's willingness to hold bank i's banknotes. The larger bank i's specie reserve (SPR), the higher the demand for bank i's banknotes *ceteris paribus*. Higher specie reserves would indicate a higher degree of liquidity and lower risk. The banknote holder would also view the stockholder's contribution (CAP) to the firm as a form of insurance. Higher capital levels would be associated with an increase in the willingness to hold bank i's banknotes. The riskiness of bank i's banknotes can also be estimated by the reserves backing the banknote. If the public agreed with the comptroller that mortgages were more risky than government securities, then we would expect that the higher the mortgage-asset ratio, the lower the willingness to hold banknotes of bank i.

The last two variables in the demand relationship, management and institutional type, may indicate whether institutional factors were considered by the public. Better management of the asset portfolio would provide greater security to the bank creditor and should increase the public's willingness to hold the bank's liabilities. Since better management is qualitative rather than quantitative, a proxy for management expertise is necessary. If expertise is a function of experience, than it can be said that the longer the bank has been in existence, the greater the expertise and the lower the risk. However, we would expect diminishing marginal gains from experience.

Whether the public would demand more banknotes as managerial expertise increases is uncertain. Typically you would expect that the age of the institution (i.e., lower risk) would increase the public's willingness to hold the bank's banknotes, but at a decreasing rate. However, if the public is to choose between holding a newly formed bank's banknotes or having a deposit at the bank, the results could be reversed. The risk-averse public would choose the medium of exchange that would have the lowest relative risk, *ceteris paribus*. Since banknote holders had first lien rights to the assets of the bank, the public would be more likely to prefer banknotes over deposits of a newly formed bank. As the bank management become more "seasoned," the public would be more willing to adjust their money portfolios from banknotes to deposits. Thus, the age of the bank (AGE) should show managerial expertise, but whether more banknotes would be held by the public is left to the evidence.

We may also find that the public may discriminate among the types of issuers. Charter, free, and individual bankers were governed by slightly different regulations. Did the public view the secondary reserve of the free banker as additional security? Did the public view the banknote of a sole proprietor (individual banker) to be more risky than the free bank association or incorporated bank?

Supply of Banknotes

Although the public may have had a preference for a particular bank's banknote, for different levels of risk, the bank may not have been willing to supply the amount of banknotes desired by the public. The antebellum banks had two main sources of funds: banknotes and deposits. The willingness of the antebellum bank to supply banknotes would depend on the relative costs of the two sources. The bank's profits would be maximized when the marginal cost of funds of attracting one more dollar of a liability would be equal across all sources of funds. Thus, the supply of banknotes would depend upon the costs associated with the issue of banknotes as well as deposits.

Two additional inputs were necessary for banknote issue: equity and specie. For any business entity, the level of equity would provide the basis of debt acquisition. This basic principle would also apply to an individual antebellum bank. For the antebellum bank, as the level of equity increased, the bank would be able to expand the level of liabilities. The expansion of liabilities, however, was limited by the amount of specie held by the bank as reserves. Although the New York banks were not required to hold a fixed percentage of liabilities in specie, banks would need to hold reserves for the redemption of the liabilities.

Thus, at any point in time the supply of banknotes would depend on the availability of the inputs (specie and equity), the relative price of substitutes (deposits), and the degree of competition (note issue of other banks):

$$BN_i^s = (SPR, CAP, DEP, BNC). \qquad (2)$$
$$+ \quad + \quad - \quad -$$

Higher specie and capital would provide the basis of banknote expansion, whereas higher levels of deposits would reduce the bank's willingness to issue banknotes. Also included in the supply relationship is the degree of competition. A more competitive market would lower an individual bank's ability to issue banknotes.

EMPIRICAL

Data and Variables

New York antebellum bank data came from quarterly reports made to the comptroller. A cross section of New York country banks was taken from the 1 October 1856 and 1857 reports. Country banks were located outside of New York City and Albany. The selection of country banks was made to minimize any distortions that may have been created by New York City and Albany being major money centers. All of the incorporated and individual banks that reported in both periods were included in the sample. A random sample of free bank associations was taken. An equal number of associations were selected from the group of banks that issued banknotes backed solely by bonds, and from the group of banks that issued banknotes backed by mortgages and bonds.

The years 1856 and 1857 were selected so that we could test the response of banknote holders under the severest of market conditions. In mid-October of 1857 New York banks suspended the payment of specie to bank creditors. Some economists suggested that the panic started in mid-August when the Ohio Life Insurance Company, located in New York City, closed its doors to the public.[9] A banknote holder between August and October would have profited the most by discriminating among the issuers. In order to account for the seasonality of banknote issue, data were collected from the 1 October 1856 report.

The quarterly reports of the comptroller contained balance sheet information on all banks: specie, loans, bonds, mortgages, other assets, banknotes, deposits, other liabilities, and equity. From this information, a measure of banknote competition was constructed (BNC). BNC equaled the total banknotes issued by competing banks in the county where the sample bank was located and issued by banks in contiguous counties. The comptroller was also required to report the portfolio of secondary reserves held as security for free banknote issue. From this information a measure of portfolio risk was developed. If the comptroller's report on the "junk" quality of the mortgages was indicative of public perception, then the ratio of mortgages to total asset should provide an index of relative risk among the banks.

Model and Results

The two-stage least squares technique was used to estimate the structural equations (1) and (2) for banks operating on 1 October 1857.

$$BN_i^d = (SPEC, CAP, MORT, AGE, AGESQ, CHARTER, IND), \quad (1')$$
$$ + \quad + \quad - \quad ? \quad ? \quad ? \quad ?$$

$$BN_i^s = (SPEC, CAP, DEP, BNC). \quad (2')$$
$$ + \quad + \quad - \quad -$$

The model estimates banknotes (BN) and specie (SPEC) simultaneously.[10] CAP, DEP, and MORT are variables denoting capital, deposits, and the mortgage-asset ratio for bank i. AGE is the proxy for managerial expertise of bank i; AGESQ shows whether the public assigns diminishing marginal risk to managerial expertise. CHARTER and IND are dummy variables that take on the value of 1 for a bank that is incorporated or a bank that is an individual bank, and zero otherwise. BNC is the regional measure for banknote competition.

The two-stage procedure is also applied to structural equations (1') and (2') for banks that operated between October 1856 and October 1857, except that this model examines the change in banknotes as a function of the independent variables.

$$DBN_i^d = (SPEC, CAP, MORT, AGE, AGESQ, CHARTER, IND, BNLAG), \quad (1'')$$
$$ - \quad - \quad + \quad ? \quad ? \quad ? \quad ? \quad ?$$

$$DBN_i^s = (SPEC, CAP, DEP, BNC). \quad (2'')$$
$$ - \quad - \quad - \quad -$$

The expected signs of the coefficients are given below. Given that this period of time was one of considerable economic uncertainty and stress, the banks that would show the smallest change in demand would be those that were financially strong. Thus, higher levels of specie and capital would result in a smaller change in banknote demand, whereas a higher percentage of mortgages to total assets would show a higher change in banknote demand. Included in the model is banknotes issued last period by each bank (BNLAG). This variable is added to the model in order to account for the relative size of the note issue of each bank.

Demand for Banknotes—October 1857

The results of the second stage of the procedures show that banknote holders discriminated among the issuers. The demand equation shows note holders strongly prefer banknotes of charter banks over those of free banks. With all independent variables held constant, the public would be willing to hold almost twice as many banknotes of charter banks as of free banks—$55,845 more. Although the results also suggest that note holders prefer a free bank association to an individual free bank, the difference is not statistically significant.

The findings also point to the public's discriminating on the basis of the level of bank capital. For every $100 increase in bank capital, the public would be willing to hold $29 in banknotes. However, the public does not seem to be influenced by the level of specie reserves held by the bank. This suggests that the public may have limited current information on the liquidity risk of the bank, whereas they key on the solvency risk of the institution.

The results of the management expertise variable (AGE) shows that the public is less willing to hold banknotes of a bank as the bank grows older. If age is an accurate measure of managerial experience, we would expect the public to be willing to hold more subordinate debt of a bank. Since banknote holders reviewed first lien rights to the assets, deposits of the bank were subordinate to banknotes. The results suggest that the public view banknotes to be less risky than their alternative medium of exchange, deposits. It also suggests the public is willing to hold more deposits as managerial expertise improves.[11]

Surprisingly, the mortgage–total asset ratio did not influence the public's demand for banknotes. The comptroller insisted that mortgages were high-risk security for banknotes, yet the public showed no apprehension in holding notes of those banks.

Change in Banknote Demand—October 1856 to 1857

We also find that the public did not discriminate among the various type of institutions during financial stress. Although the incorporated banks showed a larger decline in banknote demand relative to free banks, the change is statistically insignificant. In fact, the positive and significant intercept term of $22,848 indicates that banknote demand would have actually increased over the period if there were no other influential factors. One possible explanation for this result could again be tied to the public's demand for deposits relative to banknotes. During periods of uncertainty, the public may have been reallocating their money holdings from deposits to currency.

The reallocation hypothesis is further supported by the significant coefficient on the level of banknotes issued last period. Banks with a large banknote issue prior to the period of financial stress showed a smaller change in the demand for their banknotes. From our banknote demand analysis, banks that had a large banknote issue also issued fewer deposits. Thus, we would expect that the reallocation did not affect these banks as hard during the period of financial stress.

It appears that the public also view the well-established banking institutions much more highly than recent entrants. The public increased their banknote demand of banks at an increasing rate for more experienced institutions. For the average-aged institution of 12.1 years, the bank would expect an increase in banknote demand of approximately $8,000.

One interesting result does stand out: during this period of uncertainty, the public did not rely upon the financial strength information to discriminate among the institutions. All of the variables that would indicate financial strength were insignificant. Thus, the public appeared to discriminate among issuers based on general, historical characteristics rather than current "rational" information.

CONCLUSION

The New York antebellum banking market provided an excellent case study of the public's taste for money. An individual in this market could potentially see banknotes issued from over four hundred banking institutions, regulated under three different codes, and managed by stockholders with various degrees of expertise. Some have called this system of money creation chaotic and far too lenient: banknote holders would be subject to fraud and abuse by overzealous, unscrupulous bankers. The evidence, however, paints a different picture. The public discriminated among the banknote issuers, choosing those banks that were better managed, and having a higher level of insurance (capital stock) than their competitors. The public, however, showed little concern for the type of security used by the bank, and it appears that the comptroller's concerns about mortgage-backed banknotes was not shared by the public.

The evidence also suggests that the public may have discriminated among the alternative media of exchange issued by a particular bank: banknotes were generally preferred by the public over the subordinate deposits. In times of financial stress, the public showed movement to the "reliable." Older, experienced banks saw an increased demand for their banknotes relative to the inexperienced bank.

The evidence of the antebellum market has important implications concerning the banking reform debate going on today. Reformists who suggest that deposit insurance should be reduced to cover only the small depositor may be offering good advice. Like the antebellum depositors, if large depositors were uninsured in today's banking system, they too would no doubt keep a close eye on the creditworthiness of the banking institutions. Closer scrutiny by the public would, in turn, induce banks to have a greater concern for the safety and soundness of their investments. Banks with a proven track record and large commitment of capital from stockholders would gain significant benefits.

NOTES

1. Theoretical arguments are given by Jacklin and Bhattacharya, Wallace, and Kareken and Wallace. Charles T. Calstrom surveyed the literature and concluded that the recent failures are "at least partly the result of the incentive structure created by deposit insurance" (3).

2. Diamond and Dybvig, Gorton, and Friedman and Schwartz suggest that in a deregulated environment depositors do not necessarily react to economic information concerning their bank, nor do they discriminate among banks.

3. See Miller (171–85) or Green (102–6) for a detailed discussion on antebellum banking policy.

4. In 1854, the New York legislature enacted a bill that made the individual banker liable for *all* debts of the bank (Cleaveland 203).

5. The laws stated that first lien rights to banks incorporated after 1829 (known as the "safety fund" banks) applied to *all* bank creditors. It appears from courts records and subsequent legislation that the intent of the legislation was to give the rights *only* to banknote holders.

6. A free bank would receive banknotes equal to the mortgage value as long as the mortgage value did not exceed two fifths of the land's market value. The total amount of mortgages held as reserve could not exceed half of the banknotes issued.

7. The limitation of three times the capital applied to all debts of the bank.

8. Although Laughlin was directing his comment toward the relationship during the national banking period, and not the antebellum period, the statement was relevant to the antebellum relationship. Dunbar also held this position.

9. Many economists have examined the causes of the panic. The Ohio Life theory was espoused by J. S. Gibbon, who was closest to the event (343–63).

10. The model suggests that the level of capital is also determined simultaneously with specie and banknotes. However, if we assume that the bank adjusts its level of capital from banknote demand more slowly (i.e., a long-run adjustment) than specie, we can assume that capital is exogenous in the short run.

11. To verify this assertion, a two-stage least-square regression model was tested on deposit demand. The model, similar to the banknote model, showed that the level of deposits increased with age but at a decreasing rate.

REFERENCES

Calstrom, Charles T. "Bank Runs, Deposit Insurance, and Bank Regulation, Part II." *Economic Commentary*, Federal Reserve Bank of Cleveland (15 February 1989).

Cleaveland, John, and G. S. Hutchinson. *The Banking System of the State of New York*. New York: Arno Press, 1980.

Diamond, Douglas W., and Phillip H. Dybvig. "Bank Runs, Deposit Insurance, and Liquidity." *Journal of Political Economy* (June 1983), 401–19.

Dunbar, Charles F. *The Theory and History of Banking*. New York: G. P. Putnam's Sons, 1891.

Economopoulos, Andrew J. "Free Bank Failures of New York and Wisconsin: A Portfolio Analysis." *Explorations in Economic History* (September 1990), 421–41.

Fillmore, Millard. "Banking System of New York." *Banker's Magazine* (3 May 1849), 678+.

Friedman, Milton, and Anna J. Schwartz. *A Monetary History of the United States, 1867–1960*. New York: Princeton University Press, 1963.

Gorton, Gary. "Bank Suspensions of Convertibility." *Journal of Monetary Economics* (March 1988), 177–93.

Green, George D. *Financing and Economic Development in the Old South: Louisiana Banking 1804–1861*. Stanford, Calif.: Stanford University Press, 1972.

Jacklin, Charles J., and Sudipto Bhattacharya. "Distinguishing Panics and Information-based Bank Runs: Welfare and Policy Implications." *Journal of Political Economy* (June 1988), 568–89.

Kareken, John H., and Neil Wallace. "Deposit Insurance and Bank Regulation: A Partial Equilibrium Exposition." *Journal of Business* (July 1978), 413–38.

Laughlin, John L. *Banking Progress*. New York: Charles Scribner's Sons, 1920.

Miller, Harry E. *Banking Theories in the United States before 1860*. Cambridge: Harvard University Press, 1927.

Rolnick, Arthur J., and Warren E. Weber. "Explaining the Demand for Bank Notes." *Journal of Monetary Economics* (January 1988), 47–71.

Wallace, Neil. "Another Attempt to Explain an Illiquid Banking System: The Diamond and Dybvig Model with Sequential Service Taken Seriously." *Quarterly Review*, Federal Reserve Bank of Minneapolis (Fall 1988), 3–16.

Part III

Money and Russian and American Literature

10

Money in Alexander Pushkin's "The Queen of Spades"

ANDREI ANIKIN

"The Queen of Spades" is a story of some twenty-five pages written in 1833 and published in 1834 in Ossip Senkovsky's newly founded magazine *Biblioteka dlia chtenia* (*Library for Reading*). It is a specimen of "Petersburg prose" and is a precursor of some of the best works by Nicolai Gogol and Feodor Dostoyevsky. Its peculiar feature is that it combines a very realistic motif of a man's thirst for money with some romantic and fantastic elements.

Money meant much for Pushkin, as for many poets. The reflection of the theme of money in his works is particularly original and unusual. An inquisitive researcher of Pushkin's creations and an outstanding poet himself, Vladimir Khodasevich wrote in the early 1920s: "Money played a great role in his life. Much space is devoted to this subject in his letters. The theme of money often enters his literary works" (91).

Though money and its different aspects were prominent in literature at a very early date, at least since the Renaissance in Western Europe, it became a *persona dramatis* in works of art in the bourgeois era. Since the development of a capitalist commercial society in Russia lagged behind Western Europe, money as an important subject in literature arose a century or more later. Actually, it was Dostoyevsky who introduced it on a grand scale thirty or forty years after Pushkin.

But during Pushkin's short life span (1799–1837) the status of money and economic phenomena connected with it were changing considerably. Two aspects of this process would seem to have been of special importance in Pushkin's life and work: the commercialization of literature (sale of literary works by writers) and the process of mortgaging of estates and serfs by landlords. Both of these aspects concerned Pushkin personally to a very high degree and both found a vivid reflection in his works.

As early as 1824 Pushkin wrote an extensive poem in the form of a dialogue between Poet and Bookseller. As Boris Tomashevsky observed, the author is as it were split between the two interlocutors. Poet is the "former" Pushkin, a young romantic and idealist who regards the meanness of life from the summit of pure art. Bookseller is not only a personification of the world of money and commerce but at the same time Pushkin himself, who has become more mature, practical, and cynical. The proverbial words "there is no sale of inspiration but a manuscript can be sold" are put into Bookseller's mouth but these words could have been pronounced by Pushkin himself. We can find proof of this in a French letter Pushkin wrote at about the same time from Odessa to one of his friends.[1] In English: "I have already overcome my repugnance to writing and selling my verses for a living—the greatest step has been taken. Though I still write only under the capricious prompting of inspiration, I regard my verses, once written, as nothing but merchandise at so much per piece" (*Letters* 158). By this time Pushkin had successfully sold his early romantic poem "The Fountain of Bakhchisarai," inspired to some extent by George Gordon Byron. The Bookseller's generalization on the role of money in the new commercial age belongs undoubtedly to Pushkin as well: "Our age is a tradesman, in this iron age there can be no freedom without money."[2] Note here the epithet "iron" applied to the word "age." This "iron age" as a characteristic of the era of money and capital was used repeatedly by Pushkin later.

A curious fact is that a year earlier, Lord Byron published *The Age of Bronze*, in which there are remarkable passages with strong social and even economic aspects. He denounced the greed of big British landlords and said a few scathing words about the international bankers of London, who were, in his view, all Jewish:

> All states, all things, all sovereigns they control
> And waft a loan "from Indus to the pole." (ch. XV)

I do not imply that Pushkin could have seen Byron's poem and that he somehow associated his iron age with Byron's age of Bronze which rather reflected the military coloring of the first quarter of the nineteenth-century with its long succession of wars, revolts, and revolutions. Still, this selection of words by the two poets seems remarkable.

One more aspect of Pushkin's life is important for a better understanding of the theme of money in "The Queen of Spades." Soon after his marriage to Natalia Goncharova early in 1831, Pushkin found himself in financial difficulties. He had practically no income from his small estate and didn't earn enough through his literary work or in the form of salary as the imperial historiographer. Shortly before this marriage, which didn't bring him any dowry, he mortgaged the small estate with about two hundred male serfs (and about the same number of females) and received a long-term loan of 40,000 rubles (at the time approximately eight thousand dollars). This money was spent very quickly for financing the lavish marriage ceremonies and the new way of life appropriate for the family of a nobleman close to the court. In 1832 Pushkin made a futile attempt to get a new, smaller loan on a second mortgage. This was denied because the acreage of arable land in the mortgaged estate was found to be insufficient.

So the theme of sudden enrichment as a way of solving acute financial problems entered Pushkin's mind, letters, and works. In "Table Talk" (notes with the English title given by Pushkin himself) he tells the story of an acquaintance, Durov by name, who was obsessed with the idea of getting one hundred thousand rubles. The story was told with brilliant humor. Durov enumerates and discusses different ways of reaching his goal. Among them: "His last project was to coax this money out of the English by playing upon their national vanity and relying on their love for oddities. He intended to address them with the following speech: 'Gentlemen, the English! I have made a bet of ten thousand rubles that you will not refuse to lend me a hundred thousand. Gentlemen, the English! Save me from this loss which I now face because I hoped for your magnanimity known all over the world.' Durov asked me to take up his case with the British ambassador and demanded my word of honor that I do not make use of his project myself."[3]

Another method is suggested in a real (or imaginary) talk with Durov by Pushkin himself: to apply to Rothschild. Probably the Rothschilds of Paris, not of London, are meant here.

This reference to the family of the "king of bankers" is quite remarkable, particularly because their name later came to occupy a prominent place in Dostoyevsky's works. The young hero of the novel *Adolescent* is obsessed with the "Rothschild idea"—to get hold of a million rubles and thus acquire power over people.

Characteristically, the same one hundred thousand rubles appear at least twice in Pushkin's letters as the sum which could cut the knots of his troubled life. He would like to find a creditor who could lend him this sum but remarks melancholically in one of his letters that in Russia this is impossible (*Letters* 695, 712). Though Pushkin's reference to the poor development of credit in Russia is very pertinent, it is fairly difficult to guess what security he could offer for such a loan; he had practically no property free of mortgage. Later he managed to get a much smaller loan from the state treasury, pledging his salary.

The subject of money in Pushkin's letters and works is closely connected with the idea of freedom. Poverty (in terms of the relevant social status) makes a man dependent and constrained. For poet like himself this dependence means first of all restriction on creative liberty. In the new commercial world money is the only power able to give a poet a significant degree of creative liberty. Money is not so much an end but a means—this is one of the tenets of Pushkin's practical philosophy. One of the best English-language works on Pushkin, by John Bayley, contains an interesting analysis of this subject based on Pushkin's later work—the so-called little tragedy *The Covetous Knight* (213ff.).[4]

An aspect of Pushkin's life and work which is indispensable for analyzing "The Queen of Spades" is his lifelong interest in gambling, particularly with card games. He was a passionate gambler before his marriage and a more moderate one in his later years. Sometimes he won and lost large sums. In a letter dated during the spring of 1829 he mentions having lost about twenty thousand rubles in a card game. In a number of works preceding "The Queen of Spades," a card game plays a certain role or is at least mentioned. The quarrel at the game table is an important episode of the short story "The Shot," written in 1830. So when Pushkin chose the card game as a central point of his new work he could deal with it professionally.

The hero of "The Queen of Spades" is a young officer, Hermann by name. The name sounds not quite Russian and he was actually "the son of a German who settled in Russia and left him some small capital sum. Being firmly convinced that it was essential for him to make certain of his independence, Hermann did not touch even the interest of his income but lived on his pay, denying himself the slightest extravagance" (Pushkin 162–63).[5] The German minority was quite noticeable in the Petersburg population and was in some respects fairly influential. Many "specialists"—engineers, doctors, architects, teachers—were of German descent. The most successful of them could join the Russian nobility by way of university education, high rank in the civil or military service, or award of an order. Pushkin knew quite a number of such "Russian Germans" by name and personally. One could suppose that Hermann from "The Queen of Spades" might have belonged to such a family.[6]

To create a contrast with the later rise of Hermann's maniacal urge to achieve quick enrichment, Pushkin first emphasized his "German" qualities which he must have inherited from his father and grandfather. When he first learns the "anecdote of the three cards" (the story of the old lady who knew the secret of the three reliably winning cards), he says to himself: "No, economy, moderation and hard work are my three winning cards. With them I can treble my capital—increase it sevenfold and obtain for myself leisure and independence" (Pushkin 163).

Hermann is citing here the classical bourgeois virtues which could be called the pillars of the "Protestant ethic." But this ethic was not very appropriate in the society which he entered by the right of his nobility and position as an officer of the privileged troops stationed permanently in the capital. We meet him for the first time in the company of young

noblemen, high-life playboys, who are addicted to gambling. The anecdote of the three cards is told by Count Paul Tomsky, descendant of an
old aristocratic family. The story starts in a high-style gambling house and
finds its end there.

On the one hand, Hermann differs fundamentally from these profligate
playboys. As we saw, he declared accumulation as his aim. But accumulation is a slow, tedious, and sometimes uncertain process. If he left his
capital of forty-seven thousand rubles on deposit with the bank, he could
receive approximately 5 percent annual interest. For reasons both of lack
of investment outlets and of his social status Hermann could not hope
to invest it in a more venturesome way for higher return and capital
appreciation.

The capital Hermann inherited from his father was a substantial sum
of money (more than nine thousand dollars at the then rate of exchange).
But as compared to the wealth of many aristocratic families, his was fairly
modest. Hermann evidently did not possess any lands or serfs, which
were the basis of the wealth of such families. At the prevailing deposit
rate of interest Hermann would have had to wait many years to treble
his capital and had no chance to see it magnified sevenfold.

Now we see the contradictory nature of Hermann's personality. On the
one hand he is a bourgeois type of saver and investor. On the other,
being intrinsically impatient, passionate, and adventurous, he is drawn
by circumstances to the ''noble'' way of making money in an aristocratic
gambling house. This duality of Hermann's nature and behavior is clearly
visible in the scene in which he pleads with the old countess (Tomsky's
grandmother) to reveal to him the secret of the three cards: ''For whom
would you keep your secret? For your grandsons? They are rich enough:
they don't appreciate the value of money. Your three cards would not
help a spendthrift. A man who does not take care of his inheritance will
be a beggar though all the demons of the world were at his command. I
am not a spendthrift: I know the value of money. Your three cards would
not be wasted on me'' (Pushkin 170–71).

Hermann tries to contrast himself with the old lady's progeny both
personally and socially. He emphasizes that he does not belong to the
spendthrift nobility unable to use money in its proper way—as capital.
We can only try to guess how Hermann would deal with his money if he
won the three rounds with the three winning cards, which he later mys-
teriously learned from the ghost of the countess.

I am sure that most people know the plot of ''The Queen of Spades''
more from Peter Tchaikovsky's great opera than from Pushkin's story.
But the opera differs in some important aspects from the story. In the
latter, Lisa, a young ward of the countess, falls in love with Hermann but
her love is unrequited. Hermann cynically exploits her love as a way to
penetrate the house and to force the old lady to reveal to him the secret.

Tchaikovsky and his librettist probably regarded this Hermann as too trite and prosaic and forced him tragically to tear himself between his passionate love for Lisa (who in the opera is the countess's granddaughter) and his mad obsession with money. Tchaikovsky's music gave an artistic life of great intensity to this Hermann.

Both in the story and in the opera Hermann involuntarily kills the old woman. She dies of fear and old age when he threatens her with a pistol. After the apparition of her ghost, who tells him the secret on condition that he marry the poor girl (he seems to ignore this condition), Hermann decided to try the revealed secret in the gambling house. Pushkin describes this house as a sort of partnership operated by a manager (Tchekalinsky) who also acts as faro bank keeper. Hermann makes a stake of forty-seven thousand rubles, which attracts general excitement and interest because the sum is unusually high. The first magic card wins. Hermann has a drink of lemonade and goes home. Next night he starts the game with ninety-four thousand rubles and wins again. The third night he evidently risks the enormous sum of one-hundred-eighty-eight thousand rubles (then about thirty-eight thousand dollars—of 1830s purchasing power!). But instead of an ace, which Hermann needs in order to win, he suddenly sees the queen of spades, who seems to smile at him wryly. He is struck by a mysterious likeness of the queen of spades and the old countess. Adding a special "Conclusion" to the story, Pushkin writes: "Hermann went out of his mind. He is now in room number 7 of the Obuhov Hospital. He returns no answers to questions put to him but mutters over and over, with incredible rapidity: "Three, seven, ace! Three, seven, ace!" (Pushkin 183).

The scenes of the three rounds of the game are very interesting from the point of view of the subject of money. When Hermann declared his intention to make a stake of forty-seven thousand, the faro bank keeper could not permit him to do it without presenting cash. "Hermann took a bank-note from his pocket and handed it to Tschekalinsky, who after a cursory glance placed it on Hermann's card" (Pushkin 181). This banknote was probably in fact a deposit receipt written to bearer. There were no private banks in Russia at that time and practically no payments by means of transfers of bank money were possible. But the state-owned savings banks could issue such receipts against deposits. They could serve as means of payment and could fulfill this function in the particular situation of a gambling house.

Pushkin writes that Tchekalinsky paid Hermann the sum won in banknotes. I do not think they were in this case deposit receipts of the same sort. It is hardly imaginable that he kept such significant sums of money in this form, since usual stakes (as he mentions) never exceeded 275 rubles. So he probably needed money in smaller denominations. This money must have been the so-called assignants, or assignations (*assignazia*), a special type of paper money the issue of which was started in the 1760s. At first they were redeemable in silver rubles at par (approximately eighteen grams of silver per ruble), but fairly soon the redemption ceased and the assignants depreciated to the level of about 0.27 silver rubles. At this level they were stabilized, in the 1830s. The highest denomination of the assignants was two-hundred rubles. The assignant ruble was the actual monetary unit and practically all prices were cited in assignants. The second night Tchekalinsky paid Hermann ninety-four thousand rubles. Counting such a huge sum must have taken quite a time, but Pushkin omits these details to achieve the effect of extreme concentration of action.

"The Queen of Spades" was an immediate success, which cannot be said about Pushkin's other works in prose. One of the reasons for this success was probably the fact that it touched on sensitive strings in the mentality of the Petersburg public: the growing role of money and monetary wealth in people's minds and lives.

NOTES

1. To Alexander I. Kaznacheev, beginning June 1824. Quite a number of Pushkin's letters were written in French. One of the last letters, also in French, sent one month before Pushkin's sudden death (he was killed in a duel) and addressed to the French ambassador, Baron A. G. Barante, contains a short analysis of the commercialization of literature in Russia and of the newly passed copyright law (*Letters* 809–10).

2. There seems to exist no translation in verse of the "Talk of Bookseller and Poet." I have translated the cited excerpts in prose.

3. My own translation. The word *speech* is written in English by Pushkin.

4. The theme of money occupies a central place in the play. It is also in a curious way connected with English literature. When publishing it in 1836 Pushkin gave the play the subtitle *Scenes from Chenstone's Tragicomedy The Covetous Knight*. The title of the "tragicomedy" was written in English. The incorrect Russian transcription of the name stands for the English poet William Shenstone (1714–63). It was a mystery, since no work like this was ever discovered in Shenstone's not very voluminous literary legacy. But there exists a long poem by Shenstone entitled "Economy" in which some motifs similar to Pushkin's play can be found. So the problem of the relation of Pushkin to Shenstone remains unresolved. In the literature in English dealing with this subject an outstanding contribution is an article by R. A. Gregg (*Comparative Literature*, 1965, N 2).

5. This seems to be a standard translation (by Rosemary Edmonds).

6. By the way, Hermann is a family name, not a first name, as the American author John Thomas Shaw thinks. This strange mistake destroys the very foundation of some of his reasoning in an otherwise useful article (117–18).

REFERENCES

Bayley, John. *Pushkin: A Comparative Commentary*. London: Cambridge University Press, 1971.

Byron, George Gordon. *The Age of Bronze*.

Gregg, R. A. "Pushkin and Shenstone: The Case Reopened." *Comparative Literature*, 1963, N 2.

Khodasevich, Vladimir F. *Poeticheskoye khosiaystvo Pushkina (Pushkin's Poetical Economy)*, Leningrad: Priboi, 1924.

Letters of Alexander Pushkin. Translated and edited by J. Thomas Shaw. Madison: University of Wisconsin Press, 1967.

Pushkin, Alexander S. *The Queen of Spades*. Harmondsworth, Middlesex: Penguin Books, 1962.

Shaw, J. Thomas. "The Conclusion of Pushkin's 'Queen of Spades.' " *Studies in Russian and Polish Literature in Honour of W. Lednicki*. Ed. by Zb. Folejewski. The Hague: Mouton, 1962.

Tomashevsky, Boris L. *Pushkin*. Vol. 2, Moscow: Academy of Sciences Press, 1961.

11

Health Is Capital: Henry James' *The Wings of the Dove*

Joann P. Krieg

So thoroughly did an obsession with economic power drive the national interests of late nineteenth-century America that it extended into areas of the arts and sciences. Medical science, especially, seeking an increased professionalism via the newly formed American Medical Association, pursued institutionalization by allying itself with the power of corporate wealth. One highly influential figure in the advancement of the medical community at the time was John Shaw Billings, who blatantly combined the interests of medicine with those of business in his dictum, "Health is not merely analogous to capital, *it is capital*, the value of which to a certain extent may be expressed in coin" (Smillie 1). It was a sentiment that had the ring of truth to a people schooled in the Franklinian notion that "time is money," and Billings' pronouncement sounds in the background of many a biography and fictional work of the period, especially in the work of Henry James.

In large part, the pronounced monetary theme of so many of James' works reveals his fascination with the fictive exploration of the exercise of power (Dietrickson 155). By far the most extraordinary use of the theme appears in *The Wings of the Dove*, however, where the metaphoric interchange of disease and money becomes the medium for the author's self-emancipation from a tyrannous, family-bred equation of health with wealth. The emancipation was practical as well as psychological, for by changing his publication mode for *Wings* James freed himself of an earlier economic dependency, while in the writing of the novel he came to terms with the ghost of a young female cousin whose death years before had left him burdened with a great psychic debt. The linking of the monetary theme to the novel's tubercular heroine also suggests James' acceptance of the idea reflected, obliquely, in much of nineteenth-century American literature, that the widespread appearance of tuberculosis in America was to some degree a sign of the human enervation which sustained the nation's economy. In New England, where Puritan influences still were felt, the economic underpinning of the disease was intuited (one can hardly say perceived, so veiled are the references) as a sign of a conflict between matter and spirit. But because he was James—for whom the idea of power was an overriding concern—the most compelling aspect of *Wings* is unrelated to such metaphysics and is, rather, the linking of health and wealth to a secondary theme, the power to shape the lives of others.

Written in 1902, *The Wings of the Dove* belongs to James' "major phase," that is, to the final stage of his long career as a novelist and writer of short stories. But the term refers to more than mere chronology or periodicity; it signifies his achievement of a mastery of the art of writing fiction that few others have reached. At this point in his career James exhibits complete freedom in his art, by which he allows his imagination to shape and develop every idea and every word, drawing from each the fullest possible meaning. In these final works his sentences are long and convoluted, finely spun webs that mirror the intricate action of the plots they describe. As William Dean Howells facetiously pointed out, there are a great many words in these Jamesian masterpieces. Howells' "complaint" brings to mind the possibly apocryphal anecdote of a similar quibble raised by Mozart's royal patron, that the composer had employed too many notes in writing one of his operas. That kind of Mozartean artistic profligacy, apparent in James' final works, is the economic basis upon which the present study of *Wings* will ultimately rest.

The determining factor in the development of James' final stage, during which he wrote four novels, was the author's conscious decision to abandon plans to serialize his work in literary magazines. Immediately, then, *The Wings of the Dove* fell under the influence of a new kind of literary economy: it would not bring its author the surety of payment that serialization promised, but, released from the spatial constraints imposed by that medium, the author was free to invest as much of his art as he wished in its creation.

James chose to invest this economic and artistic freedom in a story he had long wanted to tell, though for the time its subject matter was questionable. As he says in the preface to the 1909 New York edition, "[T]here are subjects and subjects, and this one seemed particularly to bristle" (James v). The subject, of dubious propriety, "involved, to begin with, the placing in the strongest light a person infirm and ill—a case sure to prove difficult and to require much handling" (James vi). James was conscious of the disgust and repulsion that disease aroused in the minds of many but nevertheless endowed his heroine with great wealth as well as disease. The combination is not surprising for, as we shall see, the idea of health as something that could be invested or even wasted had an uncommon hold on James' thinking.

The Wings of the Dove is one of James' explorations of the international theme of the behavior of Americans abroad. Within that thematic frame are his stories of the American "girl" encountering European mores, *Daisy Miller*, *The Portrait of a Lady*, *The Golden Bowl*, and *The Wings of the Dove*. The heroine of *Wings* is Milly Theale, a young American woman who is the last surviving member of a prominent New York family, described as a "luxuriant tribe . . . of free-living ancestors" (James 111) from whom Milly has inherited extraordinary wealth. From the point at which her illness is revealed—she suffers from a disease that, though unnamed, is symptomatic of tuberculosis—the connection between the disease and the victim's economic status is implied. Her hinted-at tuberculosis appears even to be part of Milly's weighty inheritance, since James refers to her wealth as "the mass of money so piled on the girl's back" (James 106). Despite this, she is "a young person with the world before her" (a deliberate echoing of Milton's *Paradise Lost*), a "princess," in the eyes of her New England friend, Susan Stringham, and "the potential heiress of all the ages" (James 109).

Advised by her doctor to seek a change of scene, Milly heads for Europe with Mrs. Stringham, who is a writer of short stories for "the best magazines" (an interesting grace note from James, who had so recently renounced the role). Our first real view of Milly comes through the eyes of her companion, an older woman who is much concerned for the heiress's well-being. As she gazes on Milly, Mrs. Stringham contemplates the young woman's princesslike quality, which she fancies to be a weight upon her friend's head, and concludes that this quality, which so makes the difference between Milly and herself, is all the result of having money. Though, to her friend's eyes, Milly is the least vulgar person one could imagine, everything about her reveals the quality her money is able to purchase: "She couldn't have lost it if she had tried—that was what it was to be really rich. It had to be *the* thing you were," Mrs. Stringham comments privately (James 121).

When Milly sits contemplating the Alpine scene spread before her, the impression made on Mrs. Stringham is that of someone surveying "the kingdoms of the earth"; "Was she choosing among them or did she want them all?" (James 124). The question of "allness" comes to the fore in the first conversation between the two women to which we are privy. Milly has raised the subject of her illness, the exact nature of which remains a mystery to her, in an effort to learn if her doctor has imparted some knowledge of it to Mrs. Stringham. Her companion expresses concern that she should speak of it:

"Are you in trouble—in pain?"
"Not the least bit. But I sometimes wonder—!"

"Yes"—she pressed: "wonder what?"

"Well, if I shall have much of it."

Mrs. Stringham stared—"Much of what? Not of pain?"

"Of everything. Of everything I have."

. . . "You 'have' everything; so that when you say 'much' of it—"

"I only mean," the girl broke in, "shall I have it for long? That is if I *have* got it."

. . . "If you've got an ailment?"

"Ah *that*—like almost nobody else."

"Then for how long?" (James 130–31)

This entire exchange is quoted to point up its deliberate ambiguity, which leaves the reader uncertain as to precisely what is being spoken of, whether pain, disease, or money. The only certainty established, though with the referent still vague, is that the young American princess "has it all." As James later makes clear, however, to Milly's mind there is still a deficiency in her life, for she has not yet experienced love.

When the two women journey to London to visit with an old friend of Susan's, Milly enters a world for which she is wholly unfit. Though she becomes the object of attention and admiration within the English upper-class circle to which her hostess introduces her, she also becomes the target of an elaborate and base plan. Included in the circle of friends is a young couple who are in love but financially unable to marry, and who therefore keep their affections secret. The young woman in this pair, Kate Croy, becomes Milly's intimate friend; after learning two things—one, that Milly became acquainted with Merton Densher, the man Kate wishes to marry, during his stay in America, and two, that Milly is gravely ill— she sets in motion a plan. The design of Kate's plan is that Densher shall pretend to be in love with Milly, shall in fact marry her and become her heir, which will open the way to their future. The plan proceeds toward seeming success until another intimate of the circle, Lord Mark, proposes marriage to Milly. Since she can afford the luxury of refusing an English nobleman in the hope of marrying for love, Milly declines. Rebuffed, and suspicious that Milly intends to marry Densher, Lord Mark reveals to her his knowledge of the long-standing relationship Densher has maintained with Kate. At this Milly "turns her face to the wall" and, a short time after, dies. In a grand gesture that affirms not only her noble qualities but also the increasing aura of sanctity engendered by her illness, Milly leaves her fortune to Densher. Shamed by the gesture, Densher refused to allow himself and Kate to profit from Milly's death; he will marry Kate without the money or not at all. When he tells Kate they shall marry, but "as we were," she turns toward the door with the final word: "We shall never be again as we were!"

Readers familiar with the novel will no doubt rebel at this truncated plot summary, which conveys nothing of the finely wrought and tenuous narrative lines on which James has constructed his story. In truth, no reduction of a James plot can ever do justice to the work since the author's style is so singularly his; further, I have made no attempt to suggest the extent to which a number of the characters, beyond Kate and her lover, conspire for various reasons of their own in the deception of Milly Theale. The plot is here reduced to its essentials in order to focus attention on the interplay James develops between Milly's money and her illness, and on the sense of guilt that overshadows the ending, destroying all possibility of a future together for Kate and Densher.

Though the matter of Milly's wealth is a constant source of comment in the book, her illness is referred to only by its symptoms and by subtle hints, such as her American doctor's instructions to seek a change of scene. The London doctor she consults, Sir Luke Strett, never offers any diagnosis, nor does he prescribe any treatment beyond advising her to escape the London winter, to worry about nothing, and "to live." Mrs. Stringham quotes Sir Luke as having said of Milly's case, that "it *isn't* a case," which he later explains as not "*the* case" Milly had supposed, though he admits his examination revealed "something else" (James 245, 6). The "something else" is never clearly identified, but it would seem from all appearance that tuberculosis is what James has in mind.

For critics, the question of what illness is being referred to is settled by James' frank admission, in *Notes of a Son and Brother*, of the enormous effect on him of the death in 1870 of his young cousin, Minny Temple, from consumption. In 1892 his sister Alice died of breast cancer, which, from the descriptions of her death, had no doubt spread to her lung. It is possible that James had this in mind, that it is cancer that Milly Theale fears when she consults the London doctor and that, on examination, he finds is not "*the* case" but rather "something else"—consumption far enough advanced that there is nothing he can do but advise his young patient "to live," meaning, though he will not say it, to enjoy what life remains to her. For Milly there is but one thing for which she must still live, to know love.

Perhaps it was because Milly was the fictional representation of James' cousin Minny that he could not bring himself to name the disease, that he could only hint at it. As he points out in his preface, it was not the first time he had introduced into his novels a character who is terminally ill. Ralph Touchett in *The Portrait of a Lady* dies of a chronic lung disease, but Ralph is a secondary character in that novel. Still, the similarity between Ralph and Milly extends beyond their illness, for both are wealthy Americans involved with European schemers, and both arrive, in the course of their illness, at an understanding of the proper uses of wealth. Ralph leaves his money to the heroine of the novel, who is his cousin, and thereby enables her to fulfill her aspirations to independence. Milly leaves her money to Merton Densher, making possible for him a life of his own, with or without Kate Croy.

Milly Theale differs from Ralph Touchett, however, in that she shares more of Minny Temple's character, as James described it in a letter he wrote to his brother William only a short time after their cousin's death. There James admits that his grief at Minny's death is tempered by the awareness that "her character may be almost literally said to have been without practical application to life." Minny was, he says, "the helpless victim and toy of her own intelligence. . . . She was restless . . . she was helpless . . . she was unpractical. . . . But what strikes me above all is how great and rare a benefit her life has been to those with whom she was associated" (Edel 223–34). Milly Theale, American "princess" and heiress, possesses all of Minny Temple's qualities as James describes them here, including the benefit to others gained from her life. That James considered himself to be chief beneficiary of Minny's life, and death, is, at its base, the economic point on which his fictional equation of disease and wealth turns.

The family of Henry James was extremely gifted intellectually, but there existed among its members a peculiarly emotional bond of mind and body which was strengthened by a belief in a shared fund of health comparable to the inherited wealth which sustained them all. Just as Henry's extended tour of Europe as a youth affected his brother William's plans by drawing off a larger share of the family funds, so too Henry's health at any given time was seen as a withdrawal from the family's joint deposit of health. The idea derived from the nineteenth-century belief in "neurasthenia," or nervous exhaustion, propounded by such figures in the new science of neurology as George M. Beard. According to this theory, nervous exhaustion occurred from too great a drain on the finite amount of energy deposited in the human nervous system. It is possible to see, in this peculiar notion (which is not all that peculiar given the care monied people of the time took with investments and all things economic), something of Emerson's theory of compensation, though in a skewed fashion. Emerson had struggled through personal disasters of illness and death toward an understanding of life as made up of polarities balanced by some law of nature, which brought to each individual life equal amounts of good and evil. One of his earliest articulations of this belief occurred in early manhood after his near blindness was corrected; undoubtedly the experience had taught him something of the compensatory nature of human sensory perception: "The whole of what we know is a system of compensations," he wrote. "Every defect in one manner is made up in another. Every suffering is rewarded; every sacrifice is made up; every debt is paid" (Rusk 115). In his literary theory Emerson also revealed a belief in this compensation extended to the plane of energy and power and broadened beyond individual resource, as in "The Poet," when he describes "a great public power" from which the intellectual man draws energy beyond "his privacy of power as an individual man" (Whicher 233).

The James family simply enlarged the Emersonian idea to include a shared, and finite, fund of health from which its members drew, so that when one member of the family was ill the illness was looked upon as a sort of deposit in the family bank from which the other members were drawing the benefit (Strouse 111). With this in mind, we can return to the letter James wrote to his brother at the time of his cousin's death and understand him when he speaks of "the gradual change and reversal of our relations: I slowly crawling from weakness and inaction and suffering [James had experienced an attack of typhus while traveling abroad] into strength and hope: she sinking out of brightness and youth into decline and death" (Edel 224). Like Ralph Touchett, the TB sufferer in *The Portrait of a Lady* who gives up his inheritance to make possible his cousin's chance at life, Minny Temple, to James' mind, had sacrificed her health for his.

This thought burned in James' consciousness for years; as he says in the preface to *Wings*, "I can scarce remember the time when the situation on which this long-drawn fiction mainly rests was not vividly present to me," the situation being that of Minny's illness and death (James v). Having long projected "a certain sort of young American as more the 'heir of all the ages' than any other young person whatever," he writes, "here was a chance to confer on some such figure a supremely touching value" (James ix). His use of the word *value*, a word with decidedly economic connotations, cannot be ignored despite whatever other meaning it is meant to convey when applied to the young American. For one thing, it is exactly the word Milly uses when the full realization of her position comes to her: "wouldn't her value, for the man who should marry her, be precisely in the ravage of her disease? *She* mightn't last, but her money would" (James 267). While such calculation could never be attached to the Emerson marriage, James, whose father was acquainted with Ralph Waldo Emerson, knew full well that Emerson's writing career had been made possible by the small fortune he inherited at his first wife's death from tuberculosis. The opportunity James now has to confer "value" on the image of Minny, whose death, like that of Ellen Emerson, seemed to him to have made possible his own career, coincides with his decision to free himself from the tyranny of literary magazines. It is as if his freedom to do so is another part of his inheritance from Minny, part of the family store of health/wealth on which he continues to draw.

As might be expected, especially from so highly principled a mind as that of Henry James, there was a sense of guilt at having benefited from Minny's deposit of healthful energy in the family fund. The guilt comes through in the preface, where James cannot resist the suggestion that his heroine contributes to her own betrayal. Though in Milly Theale James created a perfect dove of innocence, he seems, in the preface, to dwell on her culpability in the plot by which she is undone. Once having decided on Milly as fulfilling the dovelike role, he tells us that his business was to watch, "as the fond parent watches a child perched, for its first riding-lesson, in the saddle," but knowing that "a creature with her security hanging so by a hair, couldn't but fall somehow into some abysmal trap" (James ix). This of course echoes James' letter to William in which he spoke of the inevitability, had she lived, of Minny's downfall. But in the preface the inevitability of Milly's fall does not entirely absolve her, in James's mind, of all guilt. He refers to her as one of the Rhine maidens, and may have had in mind Wagner's *Das Rheingold*, in which the Rhine maidens who guard the golden ring set in motion a great economic disaster by their sexual provocations. Milly's existence would create yet another kind of havoc, James decides, "very much that whirlpool movement of the waters produced by the sinking of a big vessel or the failure of a great business" (James x). Despite these "communities of doom," he claims to have seen the disaster "much more prepared *for* my vessel of sensibility than by her—the work of other hands (though with her own imbrued too, after all, in the measure of their never not being, in some direction, generous and extravagant, and thereby provoking)" (James x). Try as he may, James cannot seem to eschew the economic imagery, nor can he view Milly as entirely innocent and must point out her culpability, even if parenthetically.

In retrospect James sees his heroine provoking, even tempting others, by her great wealth and her desire to have it "all," into "promoting her illusion" that her love for Merton Densher is returned. Of these others James is also keenly aware (no doubt having felt some kinship to them) and justifies having delayed his heroine's appearance until, using two books of the first volume to accomplish it, he had set the stage for the intrigue to come: "If one had seen that her stricken state was but half her case, the correlative half being the state of others as affected by her . . . then I was free to choose, as it were, the half with which I should begin" (James x).

"Then I was free to choose" becomes the operative phrase, by which we are made aware that there is a great deal about this book that speaks of James' own sense of having been drawn into Milly's orbit. Only for him it is more truly Minny Temple's orbit, the circumference of which was formed, as James says of her image so long held in memory, "to make the wary adventurer walk round and round it" (James v). That image, rooted in the memory of his cousin's death, gave rise to a subject matter, illness, which, he claims, had "a charm that invited and mystified . . . it might have a great deal to give, but would probably ask for equal services in return, and would collect this debt to the last shilling" (James v). It is not possible to miss the connection in James' mind between this mysterious and tempting subject matter of ill health, and money. It would appear, however, that his use of tuberculosis as a metaphor for the economic freedom which Milly becomes acutely conscious of only when it is threatened, is in some way related to his own expanded artistic economy, a kind of full-blown literary consciousness, the luxury of which may have been strongly reminiscent of the impracticality of the real Milly, Minny Temple.

Having scorned the role of a Susan Stringham and turned his back on the well-playing periodicals, James claims to have known a freedom in writing *Wings of the Dove* that allowed him to choose at every point what he most wished to do. As the text bears witness, what he most wished was to compose in a manner that might be termed spendthrift in its discursiveness. (Indeed, in letters to William Dean Howells written at the time James refers repeatedly to the subject of word limitations and speaks of his fears that *Wings* is too long.) Against those who might complain at this and at the novel's resulting length, James defends himself by admitting that he expects "attention of perusal" from his readers, adding: "The enjoyment of a work of art, the acceptance of an irresistible illusion, constituting, to my sense, our highest experience of 'luxury,' is not greatest, by my consequent measure, when the work asks for as little attention as possible" (James xxi). Clearly the connection between health and wealth established within the novel extends to the benefit of artistic freedom James feels he has gained by at last committing to art the tribute to his cousin he had long wished to make, even though it required that he "look so straight in the face and so closely to cross-question that idea of making one's protagonist 'sick'" (James vi). Whatever it was about Minny that fascinated him while at the same time making him wholly uneasy as to her ability to get through life without encountering, even provoking, the kind of disaster he invents for Milly Theale, had to do with the fact that Minny's character was "without practical application to life." The risk he took in exercising his creative freedom with such a character was that it might, at the least, be equally without practical application to art.

The critical attention to this text has been wide, and there has been no attempt made here to add to it with a detailed *explication*, especially since the intent is to concentrate on James' use of illness and money in the working out of plot. In that regard the conjunction of great wealth with disease seems not only to follow other economically based references in James' works, but to equate the power of wealth with another kind of power, the often manipulative power of ill health to shape the lives of others in lieu of one's own. It is interesting to note that though most critics have not taken Milly Theale to task in the way that James does in his preface, one who has finds her "doomed as much by her own psychology [which makes her unable to cope with life] as by her illness" (Fowler 86). In subjecting his text to his own scrutiny at the time of preparing the New York edition, James noted the "indirection" with which he had treated the subject of Milly's illness. His style "resorts for relief," he admits, "whenever it can, to some kinder, some merciful indirection: all as if to approach her circuitously, deal with her at second hand, as an unspotted princess is ever dealt with; the pressure all round her kept easy for her, the sounds, the movements regulated, the forms and ambiguities made charming" (James xxii). The charm with which James masks the forms and ambiguities of illness (the ambiguity revealing itself even by the need to clear his princess of clinical associations to tuberculosis by claiming she is "unspotted") is the employment of his art in such a way as to give free rein to the indirection of metaphor, and thus assert his own economic and artistic freedom. Health may, indeed, have been capital in the James family, but in *The Wings of the Dove* the author repaid his young cousin's deposit of health with the valued coin of genius.

REFERENCES

Dietrickson, Jan W. *The Image of Money in the American Novel of the Gilded Age*. New York: Humanities Press, 1969.

Edel, Leon, ed. *Henry James' Letters*. Vol. 1, 1843–1875. Cambridge, Mass.: Harvard University Press, 1974.

Fowler, Virginia C. *Henry James; American Girl: The Embroidery in the Canvas*. Madison: University of Wisconsin Press, 1984.

James, Henry. *The Wings of the Dove*. New York: Charles Scribner's Sons, 1909.

Rusk, Ralph L. *The Life of Ralph Waldo Emerson*. New York: Charles Scribner's Sons, 1949.

Smillie, Wilson G. *Public Health, Its Promise for the Future*. New York: Arno Press, 1976.

Strouse, Jean. *Alice James, A Biography*. Boston: Houghton Mifflin, 1980.

Whicher, Stephen E., ed. *Selections from Ralph Waldo Emerson*. Boston: Houghton Mifflin, 1959.

12

Giving Williams Some Credit: Money and Language in *Paterson*, Book Four, Part II

John Ulrich

> Credit, or belief, involves the very ground of aesthetic experience, and the same medium that seems to confer belief in fiduciary money (banknotes) and in scriptural money (created by the process of book-keeping) also seems to confer it in literature. That medium is writing.
> —Marc Shell, *Money, Language, and Thought*, 7

> credit : the gist
> —William Carlos Williams, *Paterson*, 184

The formal history of money, its progression from minted coin to paper money and electronic transaction, has been met at each point of change with suspicion and resistance. As Marc Shell observers, this suspicion centered around what was thought to be a disruption in "the relationship between substance and sign" (7), between the value seemingly inherent in some forms of matter (like gold) and the inscription or sign of that value. This focus on the nature of the symbol turned the debate into a matter that concerned "not only money, but also aesthetics" (Shell 6). For at least one aesthetic practitioner of the first half of the twentieth century, though, the shift to a credit-based economy deserved suspicion not because credit seemed to create something out of nothing, but because the creative power of credit itself—its liberating potential—was "stalled in money," withheld from the community by the narrow, profit-minded interests of a few.

In search of a theoretical ground compatible with both his socially reformist ideals and, ultimately, his aesthetics, William Carlos Williams turned toward the Social Credit theory of the British economist C. H.

Douglas. During the 1930s in the United States, Social Credit theorists identified the crux of America's economic crisis as a problem of credit directed toward production rather than consumption.[1] Social Credit theory explains that credit, when controlled primarily by banks, creates a gulf between the price of a product and the purchasing power of the community (*SCP* 13–14). Social Credit would reform this process of creating money by refocusing credit on the consumers' buying power, rather than on production; thus, "Social Credit proposes to eliminate the evils which are inherent in our present system of creating money, by transferring the control of the community's credit from the banks to the community itself" (*SCP* 16).

Williams' own interest in Social Credit theory has been well documented.[2] In general, literary critics have regarded Williams' interest in economic theory with disdain, attributing that interest solely to the influence of Ezra Pound.[3] Writing two years after the publication of Book Four of *Paterson*, for example, Guy Davenport asserted that Williams' thoughts on money, credit, and usury are all derived from Pound, especially in Part II of Book Four, where "most of the ideas are Pound's, appear in *The Cantos*, and can best be understood by reading Pound's *Six Money Pamphlets*" (189).[4] Although *Paterson* does indeed incorporate some of Pound's ideas, including portions of Pound's correspondence with Williams, *Paterson* offers us much more than a mere reiteration of Social Creditism (or Poundism), for it is here that Williams articulates a visionary relationship between credit and money, an articulation that hinges on credit's medium—on writing. And because that medium is also his own, Williams will align his vision of credit with the project of writing itself, with what he regards as the liberating aesthetics of discovery and invention.

In the second section of *Paterson*, Book Four, Williams offers the following definitions of credit and money:

> What is credit? the Parthenon
>
> What is money? the gold entrusted to Phideas for the statue of Pallas
>   Athena, that he "put aside" for private purposes
>
>   —the gold, in short, that Phideas stole
>   You can't steal credit : the Parthenon   (183)

Here the opposition between credit and money is drawn along public and private axes. In its metaphorical equation with the Parthenon (a temple of Athena), credit is represented as the social, an ideal made manifest in a gathering place for the community in honor of Wisdom. Money, on the other hand, is represented as anything *but* the social; money is gold, matter, a commodity, appropriated and privatized by individuals. While the very materiality of gold allows it to be stolen and hoarded, credit, inasmuch as it exists *figuratively* (as belief, in Shell's sense), cannot be stolen or privatized.

Williams soon adds a further dimension to this opposition of money to credit, one of temporality:

> Money : small time
> reciprocal action relic
> precedent to stream-lined
> turbine : credit   (184)

Williams' configuration here represents money as "preceding" credit, as the embryonic rudiment of a later evolved form. This evolution of money into credit is also echoed in the casting of the lines. Williams does not repeat the silent equivalence of "money (colon) reciprocal action relic" with "credit (colon) stream-lined turbine," but instead inverts the latter, so the temporal reading of the lines mimics the evolutionary process, from money to credit. But money here is a "relic"; it is not simply the "seed" of credit, so to speak, but has been *superseded by* credit. Further, the "reciprocal action" of money recalls Marx's general formula for capital (M-C-M'), in which money circulates reciprocally, returning to the capitalist in a greater quantity, after passing through commodities in the process of buying and selling (Marx 149–53). Whereas money generates only itself (a closed, static system), credit, as "a stream-lined turbine," generates energy at top efficiency (an open, propelling system). Thus credit outstrips money through its modernity (stream-lined) and its productive capacity (as a turbine). Credit moves forward; money moves in circles.

Even though Williams privileges credit throughout his text, the phenomenon of money receives, in many ways, a much more elaborate articulation than the concept of credit. In Part II of Book Four, in fact, money receives a twofold analogical characterization: money as joke ("MONEY : JOKE" [181]) and money as uranium ("money : uranium" [181]). Just as a joke delivers its effect through language, as a trope, money effects its power, its status as money, through language, as inscription. Thus any attack on money would have to proceed at the level of writing:

> Money : Joke
> could be wiped out
> at stroke
> of pen
> and was when

> gold and pound were
> devalued   (184)[5]

Marx too points to the legislative history of monetary inscription (a history of "strokes of pens," if you will) as revealing the arbitrary relationship between inscription and commodity (metal), between "money-name" and weight (Marx 102–3).[6] Williams' rhyming of "joke" and "stroke" here solidifies this connection between money and the medium which confers its value—writing. Although reified and fetishized, money is thus a joke in the sense that it is really nothing, nothing more than written language, and therefore readily modified, rewritten. And yet money here is in another sense *not* a joke, not a laughable matter ("—do you joke when a man is dying/of a brain tumor?" [181]); money is a "crime / under the circumstances" (181), the circumstances of everyday poverty.

Williams' focus on the creative possibilities latent in money, especially in the sense that money has the potential to be "re-written," receives a further elaboration in Williams' metaphorical equivalence of money and uranium, an association which ascribes a natural elemental process of decay (albeit a special one) to money. Just as uranium decays into radium on its ways to becoming lead, money, if its developmental potential were left "unblocked," would lead to credit. Thus:

> Money: Uranium (bound to be lead)
> throws out the fire
> —the radium's the credit—the wind in
> the trees, the hurricane in the
> palm trees, the tornado that lifts
> oceans .   (181)

Money, as uranium, is "bound to be lead" in the sense that it will inevitably proceed through a natural process to another elemental end, but also in the sense that it is tied up, confined, and may thus be guided along some path (natural or not) to some (perhaps social) end. Williams here associates radium/credit with a natural movement, the wind, in its most powerful and dramatic manifestation—as hurricane or tornado. Significantly, for Williams this power can be directed toward the progressive rather than the destructive ("Trade winds that broached a continent / drive the ship forward" [181]). The movement of the wind, of uranium and credit, moves objects, propels them forward, recalling Williams' earlier association of credit with a modern engine of productivity, the "stream-lined turbine." Thus the special "nature" of the elemental process of uranium decay lies in the fact that it can be harnessed by humans toward a social application, since this natural movement of radium, its emission of gamma rays and alpha particles, has a *curative* as well as progressive function, as a means of treating cancer.

In terms of political economy, Williams identifies cancer as usury, to be cured, eradicated, by "a remedy of a lot" (185), by credit:

> Release the Gamma rays that cure the cancer
> . the cancer, usury. Let credit
> out . out from between the bars
> before the bank windows   (182)

The sense here that credit remains "imprisoned" within banks is made explicit in its description as being "stalled in money" (182). The productive, progressive, curative movement of radium and credit is here opposed (blocked) by the stasis of money. Williams identifies this stasis as a source of economic oppression: "Money sequestered enriches avarice, makes / poverty: the direct cause of disaster" (181). The accumulation of money in one place, its hoarding into the accounts of corporate monopolies, private capitalists, and misers (like Phideas), and away from the community, has the societal effect of mass economic destruction.

In these passages, Williams takes up the Social Credit viewpoint of poverty explicitly, a viewpoint that expresses the most disturbing contradiction in American society as "poverty in the midst of plenty" (*SCP* 8). Williams recognizes this contradiction most readily in his own profession, as a physician:

> Take up the individual misfortune
> by buffering it into the locality—not
> penalize him with surgeon's fees
> and accessories at an advance over the
> market price for
>
> > > > "hospital income"   (181)

Williams here invokes his reform as an imperative for the localization of credit within the community, rather than in private institutions and individuals. Toward the end of Part II, Williams reiterates this need for localization in the form of a proposal appropriated from Ezra Pound:

> > > > > > Will you consider
> > a remedy of a lot:
> > > > i.e. LOCAL control of purchasing
> > > > power
> > > > > > > > ? ?   (185)[7]

Even so, Williams' metaphoric connection between credit and radium is not limited to the Social Credit notion that credit, "imprisoned" by

banks, must be relocalized or re-leased to the community. That notion is
exceeded by a further connection between radium/credit and dissonance,
through the association of dissonance with writing and knowledge:

> A dissonance
> in the valence of Uranium
> led to the discovery
>
> Dissonance
> (if you are interested)
> leads to discovery   (175)

Williams here proceeds from a specific instance of dissonance, an inconsistency in the valence of uranium (which leads to the discovery of radium), to a more general contextualization of dissonance which leads
not to "a discovery" but "to discovery" itself (Sankey 179). Further, the
context of dissonance in this generalization, I would argue, is Williams'
own art, his writing, which expresses a formal dissonance (in the mon-
tage of poetry and prose, of original poetry and "found" writings like
letters, case histories, and advertisements that compose the poem *Paterson*), and also a thematic dissonance (of which money-as-joke and
money-as-uranium is but one example).[8] By contextualizing his poetry
this way, Williams also ironizes the denotative meaning of dissonance, as
discordant sound. The harmonics of lines like "Money : Joke / could be
wiped out / at stroke / of pen / and was when / gold and pound were /
devalued," resonate, of course, with close rhymes. The irony in this instance is itself a dissonant form, an inconsistency between the denotation
of dissonance and its aural context.

Shortly after this general contextualization, Williams connects uranium,
and consequently its dissonance, with the central trope of *Paterson*:
"Uranium, the complex atom, breaking / down, a city in itself" (177).
Paterson, both man and city, is here concretely connected to uranium,
an element in the process of decay, but one which also yields radium,
which for Williams is "LUMINOUS!" (176). This association of light with
radium (through its Latin root meaning *ray*, but also because it literally
causes x-ray plates to glow) is later linked firmly to credit, the "radiant
gist" (185), that which brings light and hope to American society ("Difference between squalor of spreading slums / and splendor of renaissance cities" [185]). Thus radium/credit again exhibits its "curative"
powers:

> But there may issue, a contaminant,
> some other metal radioactive
> a dissonance, unless the table lie,
> may cure the cancer .   (178)

This cancer is not only of the physical body, but also of the social body. The appearance of the word *cure* here recalls the name of radium's discoverer, Marie Curie, pregnant at the moment of discovery, embodying the process of generation (gestation yields an infant) and knowledge (uranium yields radium).[9] As Carol Donley has noted, however, Marie Curie was not pregnant at the time of her discovery; the simultaneity of her pregnancy and her discovery as asserted in *Paterson* is Williams' invention (Donley 9). While Donley explains this instance of poetic license as an attempt on Williams' part to link Curie to the Virgin Mary (and there is evidence of this elsewhere in Book Four), Williams also establishes Curie here as a metaphorical site for the convergence of several terms—generation, productivity, knowledge—each of which will be reinscribed into the broader metaphorics of the term *credit*.

Thus Williams brings us to the "essence" of Book Four, Part II.

> Uranium : basic thought—leadward
> Fractured : radium : credit
> Curie: woman (of no importance) genius : radium
>
> THE GIST
>
> credit : the gist   (184)

This passage, near the end of Part II, recaps the significant terms of this section—uranium, radium, Curie, and credit—with the notable exception of money, which we might expect to appear on the other side of uranium's colon. Instead, Williams gives us "basic thought—leadward." Thus the importance of money-as-uranium is not in its status as money, but rather in its movement, a process of decay, fracture, fragmentation, and dispersal (just as the very lines are fragmented and dispersed), a movement from the private to the social. Credit, as the new elemental form of money, is here equated with a new term, "the gist." Credit is the essence, the belief in community, the rewritten word of money, rewritten in the name of the social. Although some commentators have read the opening lines of Book Four, Part III—"Haven't you forgot your virgin purposes, / the language?" (186)—as a repudiation of the attention to money and credit at the end of Part II, Williams has not forgotten "the language" at all, as his foregrounding of the power of inscription in this section indicates.[10] Credit, in fact, informs the essence of Williams' "language" of this section of *Paterson*, and of his "dissonant" writing project as a whole. Williams' art is, therefore, itself a form of credit, "the radiant gist against all that / scants our lives" (185). And just as his work credits the social and the community, our reading (and this one), in turn, credits Williams.

NOTES

1. *The Social Credit Proposals* 11. This pamphlet (hereafter cited in the text as *SCP*), published by the New Economics Group of New York in the early 1930s, concisely summarizes the Social Credit position on American economic reform. For more detailed presentations of Social Credit theory, see Douglas's *Economic Democracy* (1920) and *Social Credit* (124, rev. 1933).

2. See, especially, Weaver 103–14, and Whittemore 259–64. During the 1930s, Williams contributed to Gorham Munson's journal *New Democracy* (which Mariani describes as a "Social Credit bi-weekly" [348]), and invited Munson to speak on Social Credit at a meeting of the Polytopics Club (Mariani 137). Munson himself invited Williams "to speak as an artist in defense of Social Credit" at the University of Virginia, an invitation which Williams gladly accepted (Mariani 395).

3. See Conarroe 117 for a brief account of a few typical objections. Conarroe himself describes Book Four, Part II, as "the least successful poetic unit in the book. The ideas are unconvincing, the tone often offensive, and the treatment of themes distractingly repetitious" (127–28).

4. More recent commentators have recognized that the relation between Pound's interest in Social Credit and Williams' own forays into economic reform theory is rather more complex than Davenport and others have represented it. Jay Rogoff, for example, has written persuasively that *Paterson* "dissonantly counters Pound at the same time as it appears to harmonize with him" (40). See also Whittemore 287–90.

5. Rogoff reads this passage, convincingly, as also a "devaluing" of Ezra Pound (40).

6. See also Shell 19.

7. See MacGowan's note for the original source in Pound (Williams 292).

8. Thomas Pison, in an essay concerned primarily with Williams' "attack upon linear continuity" (332), has described *Paterson* as employing "a diction distinctly and deliberately dissonant, disharmonious, and discontinuous" (331).

9. See Sankey 179.

10. See, for example, Conarroe 128 and Rogoff 40.

REFERENCES

Conarroe, Joel. *William Carlos Williams' Paterson: Language and Landscape.* Philadelphia: University of Pennsylvania Press, 1970.

Davenport, Guy. "The Nuclear Venus: Dr. Williams' Attack upon Usury." *Perspective* 6 (Autumn 1953); 183–90.

Donley, Carol C. "Relativity and Radioactivity in William Carlos Williams' *Paterson.*" *William Carlos Williams Newsletter* 5.1 (1979): 6–11.

Douglas, C. H. *Economic Democracy.* New York: Harcourt, Brace and Howe, 1920.

———. *Social Credit.* New York: Norton, 1933.

Mariani, Paul. *William Carlos Williams: A New World Naked.* New York: McGraw-Hill, 1982.

Marx, Karl. *Capital: Volume I*. Trans. Samuel Moore and Edward Aveling. New York: International Publishers, 1967.

Pison, Thomas. "*Paterson*: The Discontinuous Universe of the Present." *The Centennial Review* 19.1 (Winter 1975): 325–37.

Rogoff, Jay. "Pound-Foolishness in *Paterson*." *Journal of Modern Literature* 14.1 (Summer 1987): 35–44.

Sankey, Benjamin. *Companion to William Carlos Williams' Paterson*. Berkeley: University of California Press, 1971.

Shell, Marc. *Money, Language, and Thought*. Los Angeles: University of California Press, 1982.

Social Credit Proposals: Economic Security with Freedom. New York: New Economics Group of New York, n.d.

Weaver, Mike. *William Carlos Williams: The American Background*. Cambridge: Cambridge University Press, 1971.

Whittemore, Reed. *William Carlos Williams: Poet from Jersey*. Boston: Houghton Mifflin, 1975.

Williams, William Carlos. *Paterson*. Rev. ed. prepared by Christopher MacGowan. New York: New Directions, 1992.

_____ Part IV

Money and French
Literature

13

The Ultimate Seduction: Money and French Theater

ALEX SZOGYI

The two greatest subjects of the French world are money and food, and food costs money. So, ultimately, money is the greatest subject. The critic Lionel Trilling once stated that money came into its own in the nineteenth-century French novel. We immediately think of Balzac, but it was long before in the world of theater. The greatest, last work of the French medieval theater is an anonymous play called *Maître Pathelin*, a work which depends on money and its power. A dastardly lawyer sets out to get cloth under false pretenses to clothe his wife and himself. The draper is told to come to his home in order to collect his monies. When the duped draper arrives, the lawyer, Pathelin, makes believe he is deathly ill, and his wife backs him up in his skullduggery. Meanwhile, the lawyer has a law case pending with a young shepherd who has killed and eaten many of his sheep. He wins the case for his shepherd. The technique he has used is to tell the shepherd to respond only with an imitation of the braying of the sheep. When it is time to collect his fee from the shepherd, the shepherd uses the same technique on him: Beeeeh! The moral, in French: *A trompeur, trompeur et demi*. The lawyer cheats the draper; the shepherd cheats the lawyer. We are all paid back eventually. Money is the sorest subject.

Molière, of course, bourgeois that he was, does not neglect the subject of money in his plays. In the classical period, money is not a major subject of interest. But Molière uses it most fascinatingly, not only in obvious plays such as *The Miser* or *The Bourgeois Gentilhomme*, but also in *Georges Dandin* and most especially in *The Misanthrope*, wherein all human relationships are measured in terms of money, a metaphoric exploration of the power of payment.

In *The Miser*, Harpagon is in love with his gold. When his gold cassette is stolen, he mourns. He believes he is always a victim of those who would separate him from his beloved money. When his daughter's lover steals her affection, he feels that he has stolen his cassette. When he finds it is his daughter whom he is losing, it is for him yet another misfortune. In *The Bourgeois Gentilhomme*, M. Jourdain is a culture vulture. He buys everything and will neglect nothing to be able to purchase wisdom. He takes lessons in all endeavors and revels in the knowledge that he is speaking prose. In *Georges Dandin*, our hero marries beyond his wildest dreams into a noble family. His money is useful to them and they would gladly steal everything he owns, while his diabolical wife, Angélique, does everything to discredit and dishonor him. He falls victim to her constant machinations and never fully realizes that he has made a terrible error by allying himself with nobility. In the long run, he is suicidal. Money has not bought him any joy. The most prodigious of the usages of the vocabulary of money occur in Molière's *The Misanthrope*. The characters understand that all human relationships are a matter of barter. Scratch my back and I shall scratch yours. Unfortunately, we are rarely rewarded as we should be. The final words of Molière's *Don Juan* are uttered by his servant, Sganarelle, who realizes that he has been badly paid for his endeavors. He screams for his wages: "Mes gages! Mes gages!" These very bourgeois sentiments were not appreciated in Molière's time and after the banning of the play, when Armande, Molière's prodigiously unfaithful wife, asked Corneille's brother Thomas to redo the play in verse, making it so much more anodyne, they cut all the troublesome moments of the play, including the last lament of Sganarelle.

To come back to *The Misanthrope*, the characters often feel that they have been badly rewarded for their generosity of spirit. Arsinoé claims that Célimène has lovers only because she is willing to sleep with them (Richard Wilbur's translation):

> From which it's plain that lovers nowadays
> Must be acquired in bold and shameless ways,
> And only pay one court for such reward
> As modesty and virtue can't afford.
> (Molière: *The Misanthrope*, Wilbur: act III, scene 5, p. 83)

Philinte reveals the way of the world: to give equally in a relationship, which is, in a sense, the reduction of human relationships to equal measures of payment:

> When someone greets us with a show of pleasure,
> It's not polite to give him equal measure,
> Return his love the best that we know how,

And trade him offer for offer, vow for vow.
(Wilbur: act 1, scene 1, p. 7)

Alceste refuses such indiscriminate equality. He condemns esteem without discrimination:

Esteem is founded on comparison:
To honor all men is to honor none.
Since you embrace this indiscriminate vice,
Your friendship comes at far too cheap a price.
(Wilbur: act 1, scene 1, p. 8)

The genius of Molière was to envision human relationships in a commercial vein.

The eighteenth century imitated Molière, but no writer had the proper temperament. The most impressive Molièresque play, entirely devoted to the machinations of those who would succeed in the world of money, is *Turcaret* by Lesage. It is a play of brilliance, wit, fun. It shows what everyone will do for money in a society ruled by it. Turcaret, our despised hero, is a man who has made a lot of money and wishes to invest it in a good love affair. He is surrounded by people who would gladly do him in and who finally find the way to do it. It is a play of intrigue and architecture in which the moneyed are always in danger.

Whereas love, passion, and possession were the main subjects of seventeenth-century French theater, eighteenth-century theater is receptive to the problems of money and freedom. In *Turcaret*, money and power are linked, for money openly buys temporary passion. The date of the play, 1707, shortly before the death of Louis XIV, is a time of ferment. Luxury and gambling satisfy a people bored with the times. The chevaliers, marquis, and vicomtes we encounter are all vaguely bankrupt and on the make. They work with their domestics in order to get hold of more and more money, which eludes them. They are no longer of the bourgeois class, they are the nouveaux riches of the time. The bourgeois are on the way up and everything is for sale, including reputations. Luxury is the grand goal. The nouveaux riches are often more powerful than the nobles, but the financiers are the heroes of the day. Samuel Bernard, the banker, was one of the models of Turcaret. (George Sand was also fascinated by him and wrote about him a century later in her play *Les Mississipiens*.) The demimonde of *Turcaret* is somewhere between the world of the bourgeoisie and that of the nobles, which we have already witnessed in *The Misanthrope*.

The characters in *Turcaret* incarnate social types. *Turcaret* is somewhat of a Turk. The French writers never treated the Turks well; they were the villains of Molière's plays as well, especially *Scapin*. Jews and Turks in classical farce are usurers, scoundrels, and pimps. Turcaret and his sister are, of course, Jewish. Frontin is one of the first of those who will inherit the earth through their effrontery; they function with their Lisettes, soubrettes who have all the astuteness to win the world with their wits. No one is any good. They are all out for themselves and everyone is out to fleece everyone else. By the end, the servants have triumphed. We are several steps away from the mentality of *The Marriage of Figaro*.

Marine, the Baroness's maid, accuses the Chevalier and his servant, Frontin, of feeding on her and spending all her money. "It is true that since your widowhood he was the first to offer you his love; and this sincere gesture has established him so well in your home that he disposes of your purse as if it were his own." The Chevalier is always complaining about losing all his money. (In Molière's work, money is still symbolic. Here it is just plain money. Amounts of money are specified and everyone tries to raise them.) The Chevalier is to be pitied, but Frontin can always raise the needed amount of money. The Baroness is more than willing to sacrifice a diamond ring worth a fortune which she has received from Turcaret—noblesse oblige and all for love. Marine accuses her of being an old bourgeoise. Like M. Jourdain of *The Bourgeois Gentilhomme*, Turcaret is willing to give the gift of a ring, and he will also happily include a love poem. It is as if Lesage had studied with Molière, but his Turcaret hasn't the wit of M. Jourdain. His notion of poetry hasn't the simple grace of the prose in *The Bourgeois Gentilhomme*:

> Receive this note, charming Phyllis,
> And be assured that my soul
> Will always cherish its eternal bliss,
> As three and three are always six.
> (*Turcaret*: act 1, scene 4)

Marine appreciates Turcaret for what he is—he has money, he is prodigal, believable, a man made to be handled by coquettes. Money is part and parcel of the most ordinary conversations. Frontin assures Marine that his word is his bond (as good as cashable money). Marine is afraid he has come to them to steal their money. The Baroness curses Marine because she worries about the source of their money. She wishes to see her only if she has an account to render. Lesage uses every possible financial pun and Frontin realizes that making a profit is the name of the game. Perhaps no other work of theater in France is as money-oriented, and M. Turcaret is the victim of all the young monetary studs. Frontin sums it all up at the end of the first act: "I admire the way the world goes! We fleece a coquette; the coquette eats a businessman; the businessman pillages others; this makes for a ricochet of double dealing which is just the most pleasant thing in the world" (*Turcaret*: act 1, scene 10).

When Turcaret accuses the Baroness of stealing his money, she is defiant—which is utter nerve. Turcaret knows he is their milk cow and no amount of protest will be of any avail. The Baroness understands that Frontin is a genius who will be making his fortune. The older members of the society will watch the younger ones climb to success. Frontin must work to have money every day: "But patience! After a time of fatigue and hard work, I will finally arrive at a state of ease. Then what satisfaction I shall have. What tranquility of mind! . . . All I will have to pacify will be my conscience" (*Turcaret*: act 2, scene 10).

Turcaret is attacked more and more, but the Baroness defends him: "Monsieur Turcaret is known in the world to be a good man and an honorable one." But the Marquis attacks him: "Yes, he is. He loves the goods of men and the honor of women" (*Turcaret*: act 3, scene 4). Little by little, all the elements of Turcaret's life come to Paris, a usurer and even his wife, who has fallen in love with the Marquis. Turcaret has so much influence that he even promises the Baroness a carriage. Before the end of the play, everyone is in danger, even the Baroness, whose husband the Baron de Porcandorf (shades of *Candide*!) has contracted some debts. Turcaret assumes all the debts. We even have the apparition of Turcaret's sister, Mme Jacob, who reveals that Turcaret has a wife who is alive and he is in no way a widower (*Turcaret*: act 4, scene 10). "He is an old madman who has always loved all women except his own." At the end, everyone is there, everyone is confronted, everyone has deceived everyone. Mme Turcaret would have been glad to stay in the provinces if Turcaret had paid her rent, as he had promised. The Baroness finally gets rid of the Chevalier . . . Frontin has gotten hold of all the money. He exults: "Now the reign of M. Turcaret has ended, mine shall begin" (*Turcaret*: act 5, scene 14). And so one reign has ended and the world belongs to the young usurpers.

The world of Balzac is essentially the authentic history of nineteenth-century life in France, and it is in Balzac's work, before the work of Zola, that we see the role of money in society. Balzac wished to be a playwright. He once promised to write the true story of Orgon and his wife, Elmire, in *Tartuffe*, revealing their conjugal life and problems, which Molière never did. He did, however, write one marvelous play which is still performed occasionally, though it has never been translated into English. *Mercadet ou le faiseur* is the story of a confidence man who is in danger of going bankrupt and how he saves his skin. He is a Robert Maxwell who didn't go wrong because Balzac didn't let him. It is also a fascinating work because the characters in the play all await a financier named Godeau who will solve all their problems when he returns from the Indies. They spend their time waiting for Godeau. This is surely one of the leading sources for the title of Beckett's celebrated play of our time. Balzac, the master of plot and in many senses the Dickens of France (as Dickens is the Balzac of England), gives us the complex world of finance—the endless social battles and secret scandals.

Mercadet, a man of genius pursued by his creditors, is probably an avatar of Balzac himself. His house in northern Paris is built on a slope; he can easily avoid his creditors by leaving from the downside and disappearing. (Balzac, too, had endless financial problems.) Balzac enters into the nitty-gritty immediately, for he makes financial problems live theatrically. Bredif attacks Mercadet. He is his proprietor and must have his money:

BREDIF: Mercadet, I'm out of my mind. You will listen to me. I rent you an apartment with eleven rooms, in the heart of Paris, rue de Grammont, and for only two thousand and five hundred francs! I lose three thousand francs every year on it. Fortunately, you owe me six months worth. Your furniture has been seized and I'll sell everything.

MERCADET: Selling my furniture! And you woke up so early this morning to do such a dastardly thing to one of your own?

BREDIF: You're not one of my own, M. Mercadet. You are riddled with debt and I owe nothing; I am in my house and you are my tenant.

MERCADET: Of course, equality is no more than a word! We will always be divided into two castes, the debtors and the creditors, so subtly named by the English. Well then, be French, dear, ever so dear, infinitely dear M. Bredif. Give me your hand?

BREDIF: I'd rather get my rent paid, my infinitely dear M. Mercadet.

MERCADET: Please, let's be serious, you are the only one of my creditors who possess a real pledge (security)! Eighteen months ago you seized my furniture which is worth fifteen thousand francs, and pay attention, I shall only owe you two years of rent in . . . four months.

BREDIF: And the interest of my capital, do I lose all that?

MERCADET: Try getting them in a court of law. I'll allow myself to be condemned.

BREDIF: I do not speculate. I live off my revenues. Really, where would I be if all my tenants would be like you. No, let's finish this.

MERCADET: How, my dear Bredif? I who have been living for eleven years in your house, would you put me out? You who know all my problems, you know that I'm the victim of confidence in Godeau . . .

BREDIF: Are you going to sing the story of the flight of your associate yet again; I know it by heart and your creditors know it, as well. And why badmouth Godeau; he was a man of energy, a gastronome, high liver, he lived with a delicious little creature. (Balzac, *Le Faiseur*, act 1)

Balzac pulls us into the plot so masterfully. Both Bredif and Mercadet are desperate men. Mercadet must marry off his daughter, Madame Bredif will dance at the wedding, and he will be paid the next morning! Bredif is inexorable and he will not relent. Bredif menaces Mercadet with bankruptcy but Mercadet accuses him of stealing.

BREDIF: I came to be paid, not to be insulted.

MERCADET: Men make debt worse than a crime. Crime gives you a shelter, debt puts you out on the street . . . The street, sir, is the street, I'm wrong to be so stubborn. I will renounce my rights.

BREDIF: That is to be able to keep bargaining.

MERCADET: What do you care, that's my whole life. (*Le Faiseur*, act 1)

As soon as one creditor goes, enter another. Balzac's rhythm is always inexorable in the theater as well as in the novel. In order to calm his next creditor, Goulard, Mercadet claims his daughter Julie will be marrying a millionaire. His wife tries to help him. Their daughter Julie is not a beauty and her father capitalizes on that, always making her feel terrible. Mercadet hopes she will understand that marriage is a contract, a moneyed contract. Mme Mercadet accuses her husband of bringing everything down to money, and Mercadet accuses her of not having produced a beautiful child. Mme Mercadet says she is better than that. She is a virtuous one. Father and mother interrogate their daughter and humiliate her because she thinks of love and not money. Her lover is younger than she and one day that will make a terrible difference. His name is Adolphe and he is sincere and she trusts him. Julie is sure of him. They will be poor but happy and have never spoken of money. Mercadet holds out another possibility, a young man of quality who really has money. Mme Mercadet begs her to marry money. She hopes for the return of Godeau. Just as bad as waiting for Napoleon to come back, says Mercadet. Enter another creditor, a usurer, who congratulates Mercadet for marrying his daughter off to a millionaire. He offers to save Mercadet by getting an even better husband for Julie. Other creditors arrive and even one of the old workers, who comes to borrow money. Mercadet shares his poverty with him and begs another creditor for enough money to make the marriage possible. Balzac perpetrates a large dose of sentimentality. The ratio of sentimentality to high drama is always a factor in the world of Balzac, as it was in the world of Dickens. Mercadet: "I don't need caresses or moral statements, I need money!" (*Le Faiseur*: act 1). He threatens to kill himself if his friend does not help him. Julie refuses the charity. She does not wish to humiliate her poor father. Verdelin agrees to try to get the money, touched by the daughter's dignity. Minard, Julie's love, enters and shows great devotion despite the father's disdain. Julie: "He loves

me as I love him!'' (*Le Faiseur*: act 1). Mercadet tries to discourage Minard by admitting his own poverty but he gets nowhere with the honest
young man. Mercadet finally capitulates before goodness. Minard tries to
give Julie up, for her own sake. They part, miserably unhappy. Julie decides to marry the rich M. de la Brive to save her father. Mercadet feels
that he is born again: "Courage, men of the banking world, the bourse
[stock market] and the bluff" (alliteration in *b*, *en français*) (*Le Faiseur*,
act 2).

Balzac, who always works ironically, leaves us to believe that Mercadet
will be saved by the goodness around him, despite his miserable nature
and his lack of concern for his daughter. The second part of *Mercadet*
exploits every possible irony. Mme Mercadet tells Julie that her husband
needs a daughter who will be useful to him. M. de la Brive is happy to
contemplate marriage with Julie because her father will surely be generous to him. De la Brive and Mercadet, two schemers, will succeed side
by side. The father will surely settle one hundred and fifty thousand
francs on his daughter. De la Brive loves mathematical ironies: "I've always said so: it's exactly when I'll be penniless that I shall become rich"
(*Le Faiseur*, act 2). De la Brive wishes to be a political figure. He needs
a woman for that endeavor, preferably an ugly one, which always moves
the people. De la Brive knows he will have to give to get: "Pass me the
butter, I'll give you the cheese!" (*Le Faiseur*, act 2). Minard confronts de
la Brive. He has only his love to give. Mercadet is cruel to Minard and
praises de la Brive, the hope of France. De la Brive agrees: he is, after
all, a socialist! Mercadet, a capitalist, will help found the socialism of
capitalism, a collective endeavor.

Mercadet places all his hopes on de la Brive, even though he senses
the young man may have only a little parcel of land. Mutual flattery makes
both confident since both of them feel they have saved one another. Only
the audience knows they are both deceived. When Julie and Mme Mercadet arrive, compliments abound. De la Brive has loved her for many a
month without really knowing her. Julie suggests to de la Brive that her
father is bankrupt. She soon finds out de la Brive is a total impostor so
theirs will be the marriage of two bankrupt people. De la Brive loses
hope for the marriage. Instead of being a socialist, he is to be a com-
munist! De la Brive is a modern Tartuffe. Mercadet wishes to keep using
de la Brive so that it looks as if he has money. They still await Godeau
and hope he will not disappoint them. Minard suddenly finds out his
mother left him a considerable amount of money. Julie and Mme Mercadet are infinitely touched as he gives the money to Mercadet. Julie:
"Thank you, Adolphe, it's so good to be good" (*Le Faiseur*, act 2). He
refuses the money but gives his daughter to Minard when her dowry is
sufficiently high, in a month.

Meanwhile, they must go have dinner and look as if they were financially well-off. Everyone talks about the arrival of Godeau. De la Brive arrives dressed as Godeau, with an accent. "One must learn how to do everything when one has learned nothing" (*Le Faiseur*, act 2). Godeau's false arrival gives everyone a high. There he is: he has been changed by peppers, poppies, and paprika. Mme Mercadet bursts everyone's bubble, denies de la Brive-Godeau, and accuses her husband of being less than what he should be. Mercadet has found the way to triumph, feels inspired, and insists that the gospel is always to be trusted: "If you live by the sword, you shall perish by the sword" (*Le Faiseur*, act 2). Everyone begins to sound brilliant. Some believe one and one are three, one and one are one when one is haggling, or five when one adds the interest. "Mathematics, as one can see, is an exact science" (*Le Faiseur*, act 2). Mercadet is ready to slit his throat in front of everyone. He admits that Godeau is a myth, a fable, a specter, an illusion, a phantasm. And at this juncture everyone cries out that Godeau has really arrived from Calcutta, with a fortune which is "incalcuttable." And Adolphe is his only son: he has been adopted and will be known henceforth as Adolphe Godeau. Julie hesitates to marry a very rich man. Mercadet goes off to meet the fabulous Godeau, followed by the others. Balzac's prodigiously amusing *Mercadet* is a modern financial fairy tale, a bit like the film *Wall Street*. Every conceivable irony abounds. The rich are poor and the poor become rich and love is rewarded. The evil are punished and the good go to Godeau.

The greatest naturalistic playwright of the nineteenth century is Henri Becque. He wrote one play, *La Parisienne*, that is as witty and bright as Oscar Wilde's *The Importance of Being Earnest*. The other, even more celebrated, is a play of money and influence, *Les Corbeaux* (*The Vultures*). It goes beyond slice-of-life to portray a world in which money talks. Zola and Becque were both criticized for making life seem ugly. But in 1872–73, this work went way beyond the *pièces bien faite* to incarnate the "unvarnished simplicity of real life." *Les Corbeaux* was seen at the time of its first production in 1882 to be a product of a naturalist campaign. Becque was to triumph eventually where Scribe, Sardou, Augier, Dumas, Labiche, Meilhac, and Halévy were the temporary winners. At its opening on 14 September 1882 the play seemed merely distasteful. It was considered excessively pessimistic, ugly, and sordid. Becque hardly seemed to care about his characters. But time changes all perspectives. Becque wished always to be remembered by this play, and we now can see its depth of understanding.

No genre seemed at first to suit it. Was it a *drame*, a *comédie dramatique*, a *comédie de moeurs*, a *tragédie bourgeoise*? It is all these things and more, belonging to a genre of transparent realism in which we may include Sedaine's *Le Philosophe sans le savoir*, another play of the eighteenth century. Molière, Diderot, and Beaumarchais wrote such plays, but somehow more abstractly. Social types are depicted. In *Les Corbeaux* we have real people who are not exactly types or typecast. Life, unarranged and unrehearsed, is free from obvious *coups de théâtre*. Scribe's *pièces bien faite* were an attempt to take abstract events and metamorphose them into plays of social significance. Becque purified all this in an attempt to arrive at a deep truth about life. He knew that literature was not reality but a product of a writer's reflection and skill in arrangement. Style and arrangement made it all possible. There was an attempt at natural speech, the exact limit between spoken and written language. He avoids the soliloquy, the *aparté*, and tirade, all artificial modes of speech, to catch the exact inflection of everyday intercourse. "The theatre is not a teaching device, it is a painting, a representation" (Introduction by S. I. Lockerbie, pp. 7–40). Becque remains a man of the 1850s, a modern Molière. Incident is less necessary to drama than tension.

Like Maupassant, he selects the crises of life, sharp states of the soul and the heart. The basic situation of the play about the Vigneron family is a heightened one. Vigneron's death, suddenly occurring at the end of the first act, takes place in a prepared context in which everything instantly combines to produce a crisis. His commercial affairs had reached a most precarious point. His daughter is about to be married. His two chief business associates are in consummate and flawless agreement to defraud the bereaved family. This is a concentration of circumstances with an intensity which is not always found in life, to prevent his crisis from reaching that degree of extremity and abstraction that it reaches in the classical theater. Instead of compression of detail that electrified from the start, Becque devotes a whole act to showing us the family life of the Vignerons while there is no cloud on the horizon. The characters do ordinary things, converse in ordinary tones. The play does not appear to go forward because it is Becque's first concern to establish completely particularized and credible characters. To this he sacrifices dramatic tautness and urgency. His intention is to create the illusion of life precisely by the gradualness of our introduction to characters presented as entirely ordinary, and to this extent the first act presents what Maupassant meant by life in its "normal state."

The rest of the play has consistently greater urgency but still not the rhythm of the classics because great amounts of time elapse between acts. The effect is not to suggest a sweeping catastrophe but a slow attrition of time, as one would find in a novel. The Vignerons are not the exalted characters of classical tragedy, but troubled, uncertain, limited people who are quite incapable of seeing through the designs of the "vultures" who surround them. The central idea of vultures closing in on weakening prey is beautifully conveyed. We have a steadily increasing sense of uneasiness. The dialogue is adjusted to express the dangers. Teissier remarks at the final curtain, "You are entirely surrounded by scoundrels, my child, since the death of your father. Let's go and find your family" (Becque, *Les Corbeaux*, act 4, scene 10). (All translations are my own.) This is a bitter irony since Teissier himself is one of the scoundrels he refers to. Yet the last word, "Let us go and find your family," indicates that one of the scoundrels has become a protector of the family. The public of Becque's day expected the play to end with the announcement of a marriage, but Becque rejected such a conventional climax. The ending is sober, controlled realism, life as it is, life going on as before, slightly less bleak than it was because Teissier has now married one of the daughters. A viable realistic play is the most difficult genre to make work. Becque's example is one of the very few that have ever survived.

Does money play a part? Yes, even in the very first scene, when Vigneron talks about eventually selling his factory of six hundred thousand francs in ten years for a million. Prospective husbands' salaries are given. Madame de Saint-Genis' son, Georges, has never had any debts. Dowries are discussed in detail. The jewels that are seen at parties are mentioned as being worth a specific sum. Madame Vigneron, after her husband's unexpected death, can think only of the money she has left. She is warned against those who will not help her by those who will never help her. She hasn't a friend left when she is in her moment of need. Madame de Saint-Genis: "I hope with all my heart, my dear Mme Vigneron, for you, to whom I wish no harm, and for your daughters who are really charming, that the inheritance of Monsieur Vigneron will go so smoothly, but in matters of business, nothing goes smoothly. What is simple is complicated, what is complicated is incomprehensible" (*Les Corbeaux*, act 2, scene 1). And she thus withdraws her son from any marriage with the Vigneron daughters. Madame Vigneron insists she has no debts, but Teissier says one must pay for any inheritance. Marie, the wisest daughter, knows instinctively she must help her mother and her sisters by being nice to this man of finance, Teissier. He will know how to help her. Marie senses they are ruined; she is the only member of the family who understands money and necessity. She chides her sister Blanche: "You are the most charming woman on earth, all heart and feelings: money doesn't exist for you. But, you see, money exists for others. It is found everywhere. In business, and we are in business, with M. Teissier. In marriage, as well, you'll learn that at your expense. Money must have its price, because so many troubles happen because of it and it makes for the most terrible resolutions" (*Les Corbeaux*, act 2, scene 5). These words are Becque's inheritance from Balzac: greed for money is universal in society and is almost always a destructive force.

Mme Vigneron suffers because Teissier has told her that all she will have left is fifty thousand francs. Bourdon, her notary friend, tells her that Teissier is not a bad man but brutal about the question of money.

Soon the family is drowned in financial details. As in Chekov's work, Teissier finally decides the factory must be sold: there is no way to hold on to the past and its possessions. Bourdon, the notary, tries to help but Teissier is always cleverer. Their only hope is that Teissier may marry their daughter. Marie wishes to keep her family together, but she is hostile to Teissier. Teissier is afraid of her as well since girls are unknown quantities. "You're all lambs before marriage and no one knows what you will become after" (*Les Corbeaux*: act 3, scene 3). She returns his money defiantly. Mme de Saint-Genis breaks Blanche's spirit. Things get worse and worse, and the famous mute scene of the play shows it all. The family takes their coffee and we see without a word, what the lack of money and the love it steals away does to them. Mme Vigneron finally bursts forth: "Oh, my children, if your father could see us!" (*Les Corbeaux*, act 4, scene 4). Bourdon counsels Marie, who still hesitates to marry Teissier. "Let us tackle the only important question, the question of money," states Bourdon, unequivocally. "You must know that love does not exist. I've never encountered it. Only business exists in this world; the one that presents itself to you today will never appear again. . . . For lack of money, young ladies remain old maids" (*Les Corbeaux*, act 4, scene 6). Marie consents to marry Teissier. Teissier pays off one of their major creditors, threatening him. He is now the family's protector, and so ends one of the most devastating plays in the history of the French theater.

We will speak of just one more, because it treats money in a new way. Jean Giraudoux is the greatest writer in the history of French theater since his imaginary worlds create fantasies which nourish us. *The Madwoman of Chaillot*, known the world over, shows us a certain Parisian type, the woman who lives forever for a love she once experienced and who stops time to live always in that moment. Paris is in danger. It could be taken possession of by a breed of confidence men who would end romance forever. The big businessmen rule with counterfeit notes. It is amazing that Giraudoux could have predicted the rule of money so accurately and long before the world was completely run by the moneyed hordes. He underscored the symbolic lack of meaning of all this monetary control.

The President: "The stock issue is going beautifully. Yesterday morning at ten o'clock we offered five hundred thousand shares to the general public. By 10:05 they were all snapped up at par. By 10:20, when the police finally arrived, our offices were a shambles. . . . Windows smashed—doors torn off their hinges. You never saw anything so beautiful in your life! And this morning our stock is being quoted over the counter at 124 with no sellers, and the orders are still pouring in.

The Baron: But in that case, what is the trouble?

The President: The trouble is, we have a tremendous capital, and not the slightest idea of what to do with it.

The Baron: You mean all these people are fighting to buy stock in a company that has no object?

The President: My dear Baron, do you imagine that when a subscriber buys a share of stock, he has any idea of getting behind a counter or digging a ditch? A stock certificate is not a tool, like a shovel, or commodity, like a pound of cheese. What we call a customer is not a share in a business but a view of the Elysian fields. A financier is a creative artist. Our function is to stimulate the imagination. We are poets. (*The Madwoman of Chaillot*, act 1)

From there to the realization that beneath Paris there are treasures of oil is a vintage Giraudoux conceit. Civilization is the enemy, both civilization and sentimentality: "Civilization gets in the way all the time. In the first place, it covers the earth with cities and towns which are damned awkward to dig up when you want to see what's underneath. It's not only the real-estate people—you can always do business with them—it's human sentimentality. How do you do business with that? In Paris everything conspires to put off the scent. Women, perfume, flowers, history" (*The Madwoman of Chaillot*, act 1, pp. 13–14). Oil is the lure but they have to get at it. The arrival of the Madwoman of Chaillot takes the onus off the commercialism. The beauty of the world is in danger and the Madwoman will try to defend it. "Let's forget about these horrible men. The world is beautiful. It's happy. That's how God made it. No man can change it" (*The Madwoman of Chaillot*, act 1, pp. 32–35). The world has, however, changed, and been corrupted. The Ragpicker states: "The people are not the same. The people are different. There's been an invasion. An infiltration. From another planet. The world is not beautiful anymore. It is not happy. . . . Every cabbage has its pimp." The Countess finds the oil at 21 rue de Chaillot. The madwomen decide to save their beloved city. "The world has gone out of its mind! Unless we do something, humanity is doomed" (*The Madwoman of Chaillot*, act 1, p. 36). Many philosophical stances are taken. The Ragpicker: "Everyone knows that the poor have no one but themselves to blame for their poverty. It's only just that they should suffer the consequences. But how is it the fault of the rich if they're rich?" (*The Madwoman of Chaillot*, act 2, p. 57). Money is defined and romanticized. The Ragpicker: "Of course, when you have no money, nobody trusts you, nobody believes you, nobody likes you. Because to have money is to be virtuous, honest, beautiful and witty. And to be without is to be ugly and boring and stupid and useless" (*The Madwoman of Chaillot*, act 2, p. 59). When the oil is found, the Ragpicker will conquer the world. The madwoman accepts the gold of the moneyed men and gets rid of them by letting them go to their deaths, as they believe they are descending into the oil well. The Countess pontificates: "Wickedness evaporates" (*The Madwoman of Chaillot*, pp. 69–72). The Countess asks to be informed the next time humanity is in danger. And now she must feed her cats.

We have seen that money plays various roles in French theater. In *Pathelin*, it is a means of living: one must cheat to get it. All human goods come from its possession, and the world is a jungle. In the work of Molière, money is somewhat symbolic; in *The Miser*, money and passion are equated. This is the first step toward Balzac's *Eugénie Grandet*. In *Don Juan*, money reveals that we are never paid properly for our services in the world. In *Georges Dandin*, we realize that money cannot buy rank, it can only be a service which is never appreciated. In *The Misanthrope*, all human relations are reduced to payment. I scratch your back, you scratch mine, and we are never sufficiently paid back. Only in the world of *The Bourgeois Gentilhomme* is money wonderful, since it allows M. Jourdain to pay for all his pleasures. It brings him rank, consideration, and even a loving fling from time to time. In *Turcaret*, money is the way of the world; scheming is its by-product and the cleverest triumphs. Money leads to rank and power. It is rank in all senses and everyone falls victim to its lure. In the world of *Mercadet*, Balzac shows us the panache of money. The world is always tottering on the brink of bankruptcy, moral and personal, and the answer is money. Money brings joy and fulfillment and brings out the ingenuity of man. In *Les Corbeaux*, money is the answer to survival. Money talks. Only money can save a family in jeopardy. Money dictates human relations. In the *Madwoman of Chaillot*, money corrupts and is the supreme danger. Its values must be suppressed so that romanticism and the sweet life can return. The world is in danger of being taken over by the excitement of making money. It is the ultimate seduction for those who have no romanticism in their souls.

NOTE

Since *Turcaret, Le Faiseur* and *Les Corbeaux* have never been translated into English, I have translated the passages quoted.

REFERENCES

Balzac, Honoré de. *Mercadet ou le faiseur*. Paris: L'Avant Scene, 1973.
Becque, Henry. *Les Corbeaux*. London: George G. Harrap, 1962.
Giraudoux, Jean. *The Madwoman of Chaillot*. Adapted by Maurice Valency. New York: Hill & Wang, 1958.

Lesage. *Turcaret*. Paris: Nouveaux Classiques Larousse, 1962.

Molière, Jean-Baptiste. *The Misanthrope*. Translated by Richard Wilbur. New York: Harcourt, Brace, 1954.

Sand, George. *Les Mississipiens*. 1840. Prologue (pp. 93–120) in *The George Sand Papers*. Translated by Alex Szogyi. New York: Hofstra University, AMS Press, 1978.

14

Molière's *Tartuffe*: Money and the Quest for the Unequivocal Sign

HELEN L. HARRISON

For an individual who seeks to decipher the codes of a complex world, the monetary sign may have a certain attraction. The good faith of participants in a bargain seems clear when money changes hands. While other signs, such as words or visual icons, are often obviously elusive and ambiguous, a coin can give the impression of being a signifier with a fixed signified. The actual buying power of a coin may change, but the coin itself conjures up the idea of a dollar or, in seventeenth-century France, the idea of the *livre tournois*.[1] A government decree assigns value to a coin or a bill, though the referent of the monetary sign, the goods or services which a given sum may purchase, remains virtual. When the coins in question contain precious metal, as they did in Molière's time, the bond between the value represented by the coin and the substance of the coin itself may appear less arbitrary than the link between linguistic sign and referent. Because coins apparently leave little room for misreading, money and signs which resemble money provide a sense of security for characters who, like the Orgon of Molière's *Tartuffe*, suffer from a lack of interpretive energy.[2]

Signs which are similar to money include those which an observer would be tempted to take at "face value," to accept without further interpretation. The person who believes in these signs may justify his passivity by invoking their concreteness and the authority which guarantees them. As Molière's text will demonstrate, moreover, anyone drawn to the moneylike quality of signs tends to use them to eliminate differences between dissimilar referents. Such an individual creates a currency which, like money, can make unlike items seem equivalent.[3] While all sign systems function by their ability to make such equations, blind faith in the sign as currency threatens to upset the balance of difference and identity upon which monetary and linguistic codes depend.[4] An excessive attachment to the monetary properties of signs can undermine the hierarchies which structure society and can, at the same time, destroy any distinction between truth and falsehood.

As Orgon's brother-in-law, Cléonte, suggests when he warns against confusing hypocrisy and devotion and valuing "la fausse monnaie," counterfeit, as good coinage (act 1, scene 5, 338), *Tartuffe* provides an excellent illustration both of the dangers of slothful interpretation and of the threats inherent in the monetary properties of signs. Monetary transactions and monetary metaphors draw the attention of Molière's spectators and readers to the ridiculous lengths to which Orgon, the host and dupe of the hypocrite, will go in order to avoid assigning multiple meanings to one sign. This determination to escape ambiguity will, at times, lead Orgon to accept unlikely readings while rejecting the more probable ones supplied by family and friends. To underline Orgon's stubborn preference for signs which resemble money, the text gives an ironic twist to the character's reading of the world: Orgon treats signs like money, but he refuses to recognize the part which riches play in his own relationship with Tartuffe.

While Tartuffe himself does not make an appearance on stage until the third act, readers and spectators discover in the opening scenes a few essential facts about the hypocrite and his host. Orgon is rich and Tartuffe is penniless. The other members of the household resent the sums which Tartuffe's false piety extracts from the master of the house. The hypocrite's ungodly motives in accepting Orgon's gifts are difficult not to decipher. If Orgon gives his daughter to Tartuffe, the hypocrite gains her dowry. A still larger fortune promises to come his way when Orgon flies into a rage, disowns his son, and signs all of his wealth over to his friend. Tartuffe is a parasite and a thief who degrades piety when he uses it as "métier et marchandise," as trade and merchandise (act 1, scene 5, 366). Unfortunately for Orgon and the members of his family, the parasite does indeed offer tempting wares—salvation, links to a higher social class, and a simple way of reading the world—which Orgon is willing to purchase with all his wealth.

However transparent Tartuffe's actions and motivations appear to the competent reader, the host has numerous reasons for not recognizing his guest's desire for riches. Orgon cannot read his guest accurately without denying signs which he has already accepted. Orgon privileges the concrete, the real. He believes that solid objects, Tartuffe's somber dress and the coins distributed to the poor, observe more credit than mere words, even words spoken by friends and family. As Suzanne Relyea has demonstrated, for this character, knowing is seeing (50). Orgon has seen in Tartuffe's demeanor the signs of saintliness and of a poverty which accompanies unworldliness. He has taken Tartuffe's charity toward other beggars as the result of religious zeal and, perhaps, as an action befitting a "gentilhomme," a man noble by birth who can be expected to practice, among other virtues, the liberality deemed typical of the Second Estate.[5] To choose another interpretation and to view Tartuffe's distribution of alms to beggars as a calculated attempt to gain additional alms for himself would, for Orgon, be impossible. Such an interpretation would appear to reconcile two opposites, generosity and greed.

As his inability to discern Tartuffe's love of money may suggest, Orgon's preference for the concrete and the monetary applies to the sign rather than to the referent. Other members of the household can identify money as one of the objects of Tartuffe's desire precisely because they can accept that a single sign may have different meanings. Orgon, at least since becoming the benefactor of Tartuffe, looks no further than the sign itself. He chooses to see signs not only as unequivocal but also as binding. The monetary transactions between patron and protégé cease to be a cause for speculation concerning Tartuffe's character and become, instead, a contract in which Orgon has confidence. Money has indeed changed hands between the two men, and the host therefore has no doubt that his pious guest will reward him.

Both the determination to bind one meaning to each sign and the faith in financial, or quasi-financial, contracts distort social and familial relations and change Orgon from a benign father into a tyrant. He not only strives to impose his reading of Tartuffe on wife and offspring but also seeks to subvert their own words in a way that works in his guest's favor. Financial metaphors are particularly open to such subversion, as we see when Orgon's daughter, Mariane, thanks her father for his love. Mariane uses a conventional expression of debt: "Je suis fort redevable à cet amour de père [I am much indebted to this fatherly love]" (act 2, scene 1, 434). Orgon agrees with this statement of gratitude: "C'est fort bien dit, ma fille; et pour le mériter, / Vous devez n'avoir soin que de me contenter [That is very well said, my daughter; and in order to deserve it (fatherly love), your one care must be to content me]" (act 2, scene 1, 435–36). Orgon fails to distinguish between possible meanings. Rather than understand the word *redevable* as polite acknowledgment of his affection, the father treats it as recognition of a financial or legal agreement. Thus, in his reply the verb *devoir*, though used as a modal which I have translated as *must* rather than as *to owe*, echoes *redevable*. As Orgon orders his daughter to wed Tartuffe, he continues to exploit the idea, first enunciated by Mariane herself, that she owes her father everything and must pay him as he demands: "Enfin, ma fille, il faut payer d'obéissance, / Et montrer pour mon choix entière déférence [Finally, my daughter, you must pay with obedience and show complete deference for my choice]" (act 2, scene 2, 577–78). Orgon places himself in the role of the creditor who determines what shall be paid when and with what interest.

As the above example suggests, what at first may appear as an overly submissive attitude toward certain types of signs rapidly becomes an attempt to use signs to guarantee one's own authority.[6] Orgon cannot or will not understand that his own, slothful, interpretations might be refuted, nor can he accept that the signs which he himself offers might meet with refusal. Here he resembles a rich man who is himself so attached to money that he cannot believe that any thing or person might be beyond his purchasing power. His fatherly affection, coupled with his words of authority, should, he believes, be enough to buy Mariane's love for Tartuffe.

This belief in the creditor's ability to decide what form repayment in any transaction shall take would appear to function not only as an attempt to assign a precise referent to every sign but also as an effort to assign a specific sign to every referent. Just as Mariane must manifest her gratitude according to her father's expectations, Tartuffe should respond to Orgon's kindness according to the host's plans. Near the end of the play, when the wife, Elmire, has exposed Tartuffe's deceptions, Orgon says little of his own folly but instead stresses the guest's duplicity in reacting in unforeseen ways to the favors lavished upon him: "Ce sont des nouveautés dont mes yeux sont témoins, / Et vous voyez le prix dont sont payés mes soins [These are novelties which my own eyes have witnessed, and you see the price at which my care has been paid]" (act 5, scene 3, 1644–45). Tartuffe's debts should produce signs of indebtedness and gratitude rather than treachery. The host has initiated a series of exchanges, and, in Orgon's eyes, Tartuffe has cheated in an incomprehensible manner. Rather than reward his benefactor with expressions of gratitude, Tartuffe will plunge into poverty the man who wished to give him his daughter and all his worldly goods.

As the use of the words *prix* and *payer* in the passages cited above remind us, Orgon, despite his efforts to bind unequivocal signs to referents, cannot escape the use of metaphor. He refuses to acknowledge, however, that persons, objects, or concepts designated by the same word might not be interchangeable. Orgon places money, daughter, and his expected reward, the riches of heaven, on the same level. In exchange for Orgon's good deeds, including the gift of Mariane and of the family's fortune, Tartuffe must guarantee salvation, this "richesse à nulle autre seconde [wealth second to none]" (act 2, scene 2, 530). Even when Orgon appears to use the verbal sign in a figurative fashion, he uses the sign to efface difference.

This tendency to take metaphors literally or at least to assume that they have a solid motivation may again recall Orgon's preference for the concrete. Yet, Orgon's attitude toward signs cannot be explained completely as belief in his senses or even as belief in the value of gold and silver. If Orgon's beliefs depended on the solid proof alone, he might discern the economic motives behind Tartuffe's friendship. Orgon may presume to tell the members of his household how signs should be interpreted, but he has the confidence to do so only because he has found a guarantor for his readings. The hypocrite retains his power in the household because Orgon, like the recipient of any coinage, supplements faith in the concrete with faith in authority.

As other subjects may accept the right of Louis XIV to tell them how they must interpret the coins which bear his effigy, Orgon has surrendered his own right to interpret signs to Tartuffe.[7] Thus, all those who do not attend church as frequently or as visibly as the *dévots* become "libertins" in Orgon's eyes. Thanks to Tartuffe's lessons, Orgon can, as he tells his brother-in-law, regard the world as manure and human affection as nothing (act 1, scene 5). With his guest's help, Orgon can even agree that a lie would, for technical reasons, be truth. If he relinquishes his exiled friend's compromising papers to Tartuffe, he does so because of the shelter of the casuistry which Tartuffe offers:

> J'allai droit à mon traître en faire confidence,
> Et son raisonnement me vint persuader
> De lui donner plutôt la cassette à garder,
> Afin que pour nier, en cas de quelque enquête,
> J'eusse d'un faux-fuyant la faveur toute prête,
> Par où ma conscience eût pleine sûreté
> A faire des serments contre la vérité.

> [I went straight to my traitor to confide this,
> and his reasoning came to persuade me
> to give the strongbox to him instead of keeping it,
> so that for a denial, in case of some investigation,
> I would have some subterfuge ready,
> by which my conscience would rest easy
> while taking oaths against the truth.] (act 5, scene 1, 1586–92)

If Tartuffe can convince Orgon that oaths against the truth are still true, this comes as no revelation to the reader or spectator who has, since the beginning of the play, watched Orgon reread every indication of Tartuffe's good health, enjoyment of his meals, and sound sleep as proof of all the pain which the devout man endures in the world. Just as the dupe later finds a meaning which benefits Tartuffe in Mariane's expression of gratitude, he manages to discover in Dorine's description of a glutton the "pauvre homme," the poor man, to whom he has abdicated the right to read (act 1, scene 4, 235, 241, 249, 256). Tartuffe determines all meanings and can conveniently dispose of any ambiguity which Orgon may encounter.

If ambiguity makes Orgon uncomfortable, I would suggest that it does so because of his social and economic background. Some critics have convincingly argued that Orgon has not yet become accustomed to the social status of his family. A man of bourgeois origins, Orgon probably enjoys noble status because of a royal office, and Orgon's son, Damis, is very likely the first member of the family to be noble by race. Gaines has suggested that uneasiness and guilt over the family's new position explains both Mme Pernelle's disapproval of her daughter-in-law's spending and Orgon's eagerness to serve a true noble, one whose rank comes from his blood and not from services recently rendered to the Crown (200–206). Tartuffe, in Orgon's eyes, can justify the family not only by interceding with heaven but also by using his prospective father-in-law's wealth to reestablish his own noble but vanished fortune.

Thus, in response to Dorine's insistence that a wealthy man should not choose a poor son-in-law, Orgon replies:

> Mais mon secours pourra lui donner les moyens
> De sortir d'embarras et rentrer dans ses biens:
> Ce sont fiefs qu'à bon titre au pays on renomme;
> Et tel que l'on le voit, il est bien gentilhomme.

> [But my help will be able to give him the means
> to get out of difficulty and to come back into his possessions:
> these are fiefs which with good reason are famous in that region;
> and however one sees him here, he is certainly a gentleman.]
>   (act 2, scene 2, 484–94)

Through Tartuffe, Orgon believes that he may overcome the ambiguity of the family's position in the world and display a virtue, liberality, attributed to the Second Estate. At the same time, Tartuffe can allow Orgon to conflate that virtue with Christian charity rather than with the excessive displays of riches which offend a man of bourgeois upbringing. As Orgon substitutes Tartuffe for his own son and heir, moreover, he believes that he can both repair the ill fortunes of a member of the nobility and make of his own descendants *nobles de race* whom other members of the Second Estate could not easily dismiss as upstarts. The marriage of Mariane and Tartuffe can obscure the double status of Orgon's heirs, who would have been nobles but merely recent nobles with bourgeois race and money in their background.

Orgon's guilt and discomfort with his place in society help to explain why this man who has the "bourgeois" tendency to value the real and the concrete fails to read certain economic signs which all those around him recognize. As little resemblance as there is between Orgon and a

Monsieur Jourdain, Tartuffe's host, like the "bourgeois gentilhomme," appears to have deliberately abandoned the financial savvy attributed to his class of origin (Molière 2:711–87). Other members of the household see Tartuffe as a penniless fellow who exploits his host's kindness. Orgon has chosen to see only charity and noble liberality, practiced by him and his guest alike. Instead of imitating a cautious merchant, who might weigh coins before accepting them, Orgon has accepted counterfeit.

This is not to say, however, that Orgon has totally ceased to think along the lines of a stereotypical bourgeois. As we have seen, he misreads obligations as debts and attempts to predict and to control the repayment of those debts.[8] His own equivocal stance in the world has led him to assign monetary readings to moral contexts and vice versa. Even as the dupe ignores the monetary import of his actions and those of others, he misunderstands the workings of the reciprocal obligations which govern the conduct of *honnêtes hommes* and courtiers.[9] Services rendered by one noble to another may function as a challenge to the second, who will act to show his own virtue through a second series of services. The individual with lesser social status may remain the *obligé* of a protector and thus feel loyalty toward that protector's interests. Obligations are not, however, financial debts. The person who repays obeys a social and moral code practiced by men of his rank rather than a legal one. Were the code in question to become legally enforceable, repayment would no longer be an occasion for the *obligé* to display his own noble virtues. Admittedly, the structures of obligation and financial debt parallel each other, and, if these similarities grow too obvious in a text, then the codes of the *honnête homme* may also be mocked as glorified bookkeeping. In *Tartuffe*, the text aims ridicule not at the similarity of obligation and debt but rather at the character who cannot or will not grasp the dissimilarities of financial and social codes and who has chosen an inappropriate authority to interpret both.

The individual who does understand the difference between debt and obligation is also the legal authority who can govern monetary and linguistic signs. When Tartuffe tries to ruin his benefactor by delivering certain compromising papers to the king, the monarch imprisons Tartuffe and pardons Orgon. Orgon may have kept the papers of a rebellious friend, but he himself was faithful during the Fronde. The monarch therefore remembers Orgon's past services. Louis presents the reward for these services not as obligatory repayment due at a given time, however, but rather as a voluntary gift. As the arresting officer explains, the king acts as he does

Pour montrer que son coeur sait, quand moins on y pense.
D'une bonne action verser la récompense,

Que jamais le mérite avec lui ne perd rien,
Et que mieux que du mal il se souvient du bien.

[In order to show that his heart knows how, when one least expects it,
to pour out the reward for a good action,
that merit never loses anything with him,
and that rather than evil he remembers goodness.]
    (act 5, scene 7, 1941–45)

Since the sovereign knows how to show gratitude, he appears as the opposite of the hypocrite. The monarch's understanding of the workings of gratitude and obligation also contrasts with Orgon's own misconceptions. The king's generosity and spontaneity in giving rewards provide the model which his fallible subject should have followed.

The king reinstitutes the interpretive difference which his deceived subject has tried to eliminate. As he declares Orgon's donation of goods to Tartuffe null and void, Louis distinguishes true respect for the laws of the land from legalistic enforcement of a contract obtained in a fraudulent manner. Louis can see in Orgon both the imprudent friend of a *Frondeur* and a loyal subject. Contradictions do not bother this monarch who gives rewards when they are least expected. The king can validate signs, but he does not aim at the suppression of ambiguity. He is a competent reader, and the competent reader must renounce any quest for the unequivocal sign.

Such renunciation seems to have always been difficult to accomplish. If Molière's text, as we know it today, places such emphasis on the necessity of reading well, this is in part a result of the original play's fate. According to La Grange, the actor in Molière's troupe who kept a record both of theater receipts and of various events in the history of the group, Louis himself feared a shortage of competent readers. Though the king enjoyed the play when it was created at court, he forbade Molière to perform it in public. The monarch, says La Grange, recognized that this was an attack not on religion but on hypocrisy. Nonetheless, the king argued, false and true devotion have the same appearance: to let the public at large view this play would be dangerous (La Grange 65, 77, 100).

Thus, the contrast between Orgon's inability to read and the king's analytic power echoes the difference which Louis supposedly claimed to see between himself and his subjects. Good sense, as Descartes had written some twenty-seven years before Molière created this play, might belong to everyone (568). The king nonetheless fears that bourgeois, even bourgeois like Orgon who have moved in noble circles because of their service to the Crown, remain less capable of discernment than the king and his courtiers. While the exact form of Molière's original text remains unknown, the king's decision to impose a ban confirms one of the major tenets of the play as we know it today. Many readers, Orgon among them, cannot acknowledge that one sign may cover more than one meaning. This inability to read is, moreover, closely connected to the individual's social position. Bourgeois, in general, are not expected to interpret society's signs as ably as do nobles.[10] People who know their own place in society and are satisfied with it cannot be as easily confused as a character like Orgon, caught in transition between two social groups.

Here we should note that the dupe, though he learns of Tartuffe's hypocrisy, never makes any progress in interpreting the signs around him or in learning how to respond to the exchanges offered him. He falls from one error into another, as his brother-in-law says, and, no longer believing in Tartuffe, claims that he will henceforth hate all "gens de bien," all pious people (act 5, scene 1, 1604). At the play's conclusion, when Louis has condemned Tartuffe and pardoned Orgon, Orgon starts to admonish the criminal: "Hé bien, te voilà, traître [Well, there you are, traitor]" (act 5, scene 5, 1949). The reasonable Cléonte must once again intervene and remind the dupe that signs and exchanges have multiple meanings. Louis may have found Orgon's offense pardonable, but this does not justify Orgon's rapid acceptance of his own righteousness. Orgon may impose binary oppositions on the world and see only extremes of good and evil, guilt and innocence. Others, including the king, see gradations, and Orgon would do well to remember that he is innocent only because of the king's wisdom and mercy. Rather than rail against the now-defeated Tartuffe, Orgon ought to respond to the king's generosity by falling at his sovereign's feet. That he does so only at Cléonte's prompting bodes ill for any possible future improvement in his interpretive powers.

In showing Orgon's incorrigibility, the play both affirms and threatens the differences upon which the seventeenth-century understanding of the world depends. On the one hand, the text maintains that there are essential differences between those destined to rule and those meant to serve. The play contrasts the insight of the sovereign and the gullibility of the subject. On the other hand, Orgon, deprived of Tartuffe, still needs an authority to interpret for him. With luck, this authority might be Cléonte or, indirectly, the king himself, but the dupe will in all probability continue to search for unequivocal readings of the world and to impose them on his family. If Orgon is indeed a royal officer, his misreadings could be harmful to any members of society who have business with him. Moreover, the reader/spectator might wonder whether other men of bourgeois origin who hold noble offices might experience similar difficulties in interpreting society. Orgon's family is but one of many in which the education and wealth both necessary to obtain offices have modified the social differences based on ancestry. This man of ambiguous status still has power and influence at the comedy's end. Orgon may be foolish, but he furnishes an example of money's ability to restructure a society in which an individual's place is supposedly determined at birth.

While the monarch and his court might have a vested interest in denying that money might obscure differences in ancestry, Orgon and readers like him menace not only the distinction between bourgeois and noble but also any concept of law and authority. This may seem paradoxical since, as we have seen, Orgon is eager to find an authoritative figure who can read for him. Nonetheless, the insistence with which he strives to attach a single referent to every sign can ultimately undermine any transcendent truth which church and state invoke. Relyea states that this play rests upon the assumption that truth exists and can be discovered (37), but the text also emphasizes the elusiveness of truth and the difficulties involved in making an individual exchange one truth for another. Rascals such as Tartuffe will continue to scramble society's codes and to pass themselves off as law-abiding citizens, as true *dévots*, and as real nobles. When their schemes are revealed, people who have observed their tricks may reject Cléonte's distinction between good and bad coinage and find all representatives of law, religion, and nobility suspect. Should Orgon and those like him continue to place their faith in signs rather than in the things and ideas which signs represent, distinctions between truth and falsehood will lose all meaning, as will respect for religion and the sovereign.

Like money itself, signs treated as money, as currency which can efface differences between dissimilar items, can reorder the seventeenth-century world. Molière's comedy cannot and does not disarm this threat. Instead, the text poses a challenge for its readers and spectators, be they commoners, nobles, or the king himself. Molière's audience should not imitate Orgon in seeking a single meaning for every sign and text.

Le Tartuffe uses the parallels between monetary and linguistic signs in order to show how the characters read their world and how they define their place within that world. The world is fraught with interpretive risk, and no foolproof guard against counterfeit exists. Both attachment to the concrete and excessive submission to authority lead first to error and then to the destruction of authority. Though Orgon remains recalcitrant, the readers and spectators of the play must learn to weigh all currency carefully and to recognize that the richest signs are never unequivocal.

NOTES

1. I am using here the Saussurean model of the arbitrary sign, composed of a signifier (for instance, a word) and a signified (the idea or image associated with that word) (146–57). For the purposes of this chapter, I am applying that model to money in the following manner. The coin acts as the signifier, the concept of its value then becomes the signified, and the goods and services which

that money might purchase serve as possible referents. These three parts, signifier, signified, and referent, allow for further divisions. The coin itself incorporates several signs, including inscriptions and the monarch's effigy. The *livre tournois*, the money of account of the *ancien régime*, can be regarded both as an alternate signifier of value, the bookkeeper's way of expressing the worth of all coins in circulation, and as the signified of those coins. On the monetary system of seventeenth-century France, see Dessert 28–39. For the monetary system of signs during the classical period, see Foucault 60–91, 214–25.

2. Molière first created *Tartuffe* at Versailles in 1664. The first two versions of the play were banned, and the version that we know today dates from 1669 (La Grange 65, 77, 100). Orgon, Tartuffe's host and dupe, is not the only character in the play who has difficulty in reading the world, but, as the head of the household, he is the individual whose misreadings can do the most damage.

3. For discussions of money as an effacer of difference, see, among others, Aristotle V.v.14–15 and Marx 64–65.

4. See Saussure 115. See also Foucault, who suggests that, in the classical *épistémè*, the analysis of differences and identities replaces the Renaissance method of apprehending the world through similarities and analogy (32–72).

5. On the distinctions between the *gentilhomme*, who inherits nobility through a long line of noble ancestors, and the nobles whose rank derives from royal office, and on the system of estates in seventeenth-century France, see Loyseau 494–95 and Mousnier 537–51. Discussion of *libéralité* as a noble virtue may be found in Apostolidés, especially 21–22, Bénichou 182, and Faret 22.

6. Cf. Gossman, who shows that the idolater, Orgon, uses his idol, Tartuffe, in order to increase his own power (101–44).

7. Despite the attraction of money's substance, treatises on money acknowledged that, in theory at least, money's value came from the king's authority. Thus, Scipion de Gramont, a royal officer writing some forty years before Molière, explained that coins in France "empruntent leur valeur et leur cours de la loy du Prince [gain their value and their currency from the law of the prince]" (17). A discussion of the king's ability to set and to measure value may be found in Goux 85. For some of the difficulties which the sovereign might encounter in setting that value, and for some of the ways in which he might use his power to redefine the value of coins for his own benefit, see Dessert 29–39.

The suggestion that Tartuffe, an unsuitable authority, takes the place of the king here is not novel. See Gossman 119.

8. For another perspective on the workings of obligation in *Tartuffe*, see Gross 16–34.

9. On the *honnête homme*, see Magendie and Stanton.

10. Here I would argue that other members of the household, except of course Dorine, are closer to nobility than Orgon. As Gaines has shown, Damis is probably the first member of Orgon's own family to be noble by race (200–206). The worldliness of Cléonte and Elmire, their clear ideas about how one does and does not behave in *honnête* society, suggests that they are at least used to frequenting nobles and may indeed come from a family of higher station than Orgon's own. As for Dorine, her acumen is no argument for the perspicacity of the bourgeoisie but is rather an example of the good sense which Molière often at-

tributes to the *peuple*, particularly to servants who know better than to question their role in society.

REFERENCES

Apostolidés, Jean-Marie. *Le Roi-machine: Spectacle et politique au temps de Louis XIV*. Paris: Editions de minuit, 1981.

Aristotle. *The Nicomachean Ethics*. Trans. H. Rackham. Cambridge: Harvard University Press; London: William Heinemann, 1982.

Bénichou, Pual. *Morales du Grand Siècle*. Paris: Gallimard, 1941.

Descartes, René. "Discours de méthode pour bien conduire sa raison et chercher la vérité dans les sciences." *Oeuvres philosophiques*. Ed. Ferdinand Alquié. 2 vols. Paris: Garnier, 1963, 1967, 1:567–650.

Dessert, Daniel. *Argent, pouvoir et société au Grand Siècle*. Paris: Fayard, 1984.

Faret, Nicolas. *L'Honnête homme, ou l'art de plaire à la cour*. Ed. M. Magendie. Paris, 1925. Reprinted Geneva: Skatkine, 1970.

Foucault, Michel. *Les Mots et les choses: Une archéologie des sicences humaines*. Paris: Gallimard, 1966.

Gossman, Lionel. *Men and Masks: a Study of Molière*. Baltimore: Johns Hopkins University Press, 1969.

Goux, Jean-Joseph. *Freud, Marx: Économie et symbolique*. Paris: Seuil, 1973.

Gramont, Scipion de. *Le Denier royal*. 1620.

Gross, Nathan. *From Gesture to Idea: Esthetics and Ethics in Molière's Comedy*. New York: Columbia University Press, 1982.

La Grange, Charles de. *Le Registre de La Grange, 1659–1685*. Ed. Bert Edward Young and Grace Philpott Young. Paris: Droz, 1947.

Loyseau, Charles. *Les oeuvres de Maistre Charles Loyseau, contenans Les Cing Livres d'Offices: des Offices, les Traitez des Seigneuries, des Ordres et simples Dignitiez du Deguerpissement & Delaissement par Hypotheque, de la Garantie des Rentes, et des Abus des Justices de Village*. Paris, 1966.

Magendie, Maurice. *La Politesse mondaine et les théories de l'honnêté, en France au XVIIᵉ siècle, de 1600 à 1660*. Paris, 1925. Reprinted Geneva: Skatkine, 1970.

Marx, Karl. *A Contribution to the Critique of Political Economy*. Ed. Maurice Dobb. New York: International Publishers, 1970.

Molière [Jean-Baptiste Poquelin]. *Le Bourgeois gentilhomme. Oeuvres complètes*. Ed. Georges Couton. Bibliothèque de la Pléiade. 2 vols. Paris: Gallimard, 1971. 2:711–87.

———. *Le Tartuffe. Oeuvres complètes*. Ed. George Couton. Bibliothèque de la Pléiade. 2 vols. Paris: Gallimard, 1971. 1:833–984.

Mousnier, Roland. *La Vénalité des offices sous Henri IV et Louis XIII*. Paris: PUF, 1971.

Relyea, Suzanne. *Signs, Systems, and Meanings: A Contemporary Semiotic Reading of Four Molière Plays*. Middletown, Conn.: Wesleyan University Press, 1976.

Saussure, Ferdinand de. *Cours de linguistique générale*. Ed. Rudolf Engler. 4 fasc. Wiesbaden: Otto Harrasowitz, 1967.

Stanton, Donna C. *The Aristocrat as Art: A Study of the* Honnête Homme *and the Dandy in Seventeenth- and Nineteenth-Century French Literature*. New York: Columbia University Press, 1980.

15

Economics as Lure in *Madame Bovary*

Patricia Reynaud

To read *Madame Bovary* as a novel dealing with political economics, to see how economic metaphors are disseminated in the narrative, seems more to pertain to the category of wager (*gageure*) than to rest on a certainty best symbolized by the gold exchange standard (*gage-or*) as the full convertibility of currency into gold. The play on words (better rendered in French) can appear rather far-fetched and even unreliable, but it will subsequently be justified within the perspective of this chapter, in which falsity is certainly the surest value upon which to rely. When Flaubert's novel was published, the system of the gold exchange standard, although still in existence, was undergoing the first signs of its decline. This system gradually became a wager, a shift that enables me to elaborate the uses of metaphors. If traditionally this figure of speech consists in giving to a thing a name that belongs to another, how is it still possible to adequately convert the meaning? In linguistics and in economics the sign is losing credibility and the security of money, or of the repository of signifieds backing it up, is gradually eroding. Metaphor as a transfer of meaning invests homologous relationships in the prosaic route of transfers of money scattered throughout the book and might lead to abusive uses and to the likelihood of fraud.

The metaphor, however, cannot be bypassed and is a necessary detour claimed as an act of renunciation to the literal in order to apprehend economics in Flaubert's text. Like metaphors, economics is prone to distance itself from the nominal value, which, after all, is a conventional value, to substitute for it with a market price. In this light, the homology between economics and metaphor becomes striking and is portrayed by the logic of the detour of meaning and/or funds. Metaphor is a borrowing of a figurative meaning which is in transit between contexts. Another type of borrowing at the level of the plot makes Emma fall in the economy of loss. Certain episodes of the book are relevant to this logic: an example is the letter from Rodolphe to Emma, breaking off their relationship, which yields a twofold interpretation. Through some words, some clichés, the process of writing acts as the revealing principle of an underlying economic system. For instance, the French term *usure* (usury and erosion) is a metaphor for the writing of the letter since Rodolphe is tired of his involvement, which he sees only as an erosion of feelings; but *usure* also connotes the effigy on a coin which has worn off with time. Illegitimate intercourse is like forged currency in circulation and usury is, in the book, the prohibitive interest rate that Lheureux (a merchant and a usurer) applies to the money he lends to Emma. *Usure* is a result of a too-frequent "use" of partners, feelings, and objects. This concept is in direct opposition to scarcity, according to which the value of a good is so high that it is beyond reach, outside of use. Proliferation of objects and signs from domains so opposed as the sentimental and the monetary conspires and leads to their irremediable devaluation.

Mystification is indeed a problem in this context: the monetary sign represented by the promissory note is autonomous and unchecked in its circulation. Instead of losing value with repeated uses, its value increases even more with each endorsement, each signature. It poses a challenge to the economic law of scarcity and constitutes the keystone upon which surplus value is erected.

One possible interpretation of the letter from Rodolphe to Emma is the portrayal of her lover as a forger, one who writes inflamed but false feelings using *lieux communs* and clichés. This letter is but the epiphenomenon of a generalized piece of trickery, whereby great principles never pass the stage of good intentions. Economics is to be found everywhere in the letter: in various metaphors, in either the comparing or the compared term which relates to precise economic categories such as debt, borrowing, and investing. Economics is also explicitly present in other episodes such as the ball of La Vaubeyssard, which equates (and trivializes) the aristocratic world with the power of money in an all-too-obvious manner. A dazzled Emma perceives only the deceptive appearance of wealth as she reduces the signs of wealth to their exchange value. Thus she fits into the definition of fetishism as conceived by Marx. The general equivalent of commodities in its money form was first constituted to be a reflection of any possible commodity and therefore to facilitate transactions. But it soon assumes a dominant position as it becomes the reflection of that for which it was originally created, that for which it was playing the role of an equivalent. This general equivalent finally imposes its domination by the enforcement of the law and by the forgetting of its genesis as a supplementary and cultural creation. This alienation proper to the capitalist system is better known as "the ideology of the owner" or an absolute contamination by wealth which attributes a price to everything, human beings included. Even if Emma is contaminated to the point of yielding to the principle of exchange, her relatively free space should not be denied. Because of her ties to the imaginary world, she somehow manages to exceed the principle of exchange. Not having to earn the money she lavishly spends on her lover, she can even afford to spend more than her husband's earnings. That is, for a time, before accounts are settled and she has to pay back society for her debts as much as for her provocative behavior. Her squandering, however, cannot be confused or reconciled with the notion of the total gift seen as the direct negation of a world of bourgeois calculations.

The tangible secret of her spending lies in the signature of promissory notes. The amount of these notes soon becomes uncontrollable and their circulation follows the particular logic of circularity. The monetary standard, or what we have called the general equivalent, originates in a legal decision but eventually acquires a transcendental position resulting in the imposition of its norm on all other commodities, excluding itself from them. It activates the principle of reiteration: the standard is guaranteed by a reserve of gold but what guarantees the gold itself? The spiraling movement proves that gold does not guarantee anything anymore and that the mechanisms of repetition are self-generated without anyone's being accountable. The gold reserve, once safe and reliable is, in the text, shattered in its founding principle by lies and fiction. The mechanisms of the promissory note are just a way to anticipate the necessary evolution toward a script currency whose reserve is no longer actual: such are the instruments of credit when payments are made by simple compensation and when banknotes are unconvertible. But Emma, trapped by the implacable mechanism of borrowing, hangs her only hope of escape on the ethereal mystification of religion. This escape meets economic utilitarianism in a dual fashion: first, she conveniently forgets a pressing need to repay her debts, and second, she only accepts the precious religious objects (she wants to buy a prie-dieu encrusted with emeralds in order to pray properly!). For all her flaws, she refuses to the end to be constituted according to the thematics of detour, a fundamental category in economics which replaces immediate consumption with consumption that is deferred and based on anticipated calculations.

Emma's system can be apprehended as a reflexive deflation, a paralysis in the flow of narration. The heaviness of her dominant mood, the spleen, is then rendered in ways escaping ordinary temporality. But, when economics or calculation is described, directly or metaphorically, the rhythm of the novel accelerates as if inflation were creeping into the plot and prevents further descriptive pauses. At these frantic moments, writing becomes a factual narration with no intervention or value judgment from the narrator, with no mention of intentionality. This symbolically means that surplus value can be calculated without its formation being comprehensible. While being created, surplus value follows a mysterious process of development. According to a similar logic, the careful management of the couple's budget (before Emma starts spending on lovers) and Emma's practical sense, reflecting her bourgeois constitution (which she can never totally overcome, even in her fantastic dream world), are a set of attitudes formally expressed in the lack of interpretative statements, as if the author's strategy were to save his words now, in order to better waste them on gratuitous descriptions, metaphors, or images defying a common logic, the reductive logic based on calculations.

Some microepisodes consist of indirect indictments of Flaubert's society on a global level. Such is the episode of the blind man, who, at the end, is imprisoned. The episode bears witness to the change of perspective of public authorities with respect to the definition of poverty. According to the new mentality (and morality), every individual must be useful, must somehow serve the productive machinery which itself serves the higher purpose of profitability. In another instance, Emma remains utilitarian even when she throws her money to the poor. Her bourgeois character, being used to reduce costs, resurfaces in her most generous gestures. Her gift is thus a disguised loan in which the giver is not the loser in the transaction. The scheme of unproductive spending is reduced to the principle of the balancing of an account, of compensation between profits and loss. For these very reasons, the relationship between debtor and creditor prevails in a book in which everything and everybody have become exchange values. By operating another detour, this time through Hegelian philosophy, we come back to the character Lheureux, the usurer who speculates on the work of others and makes profitable investments while Emma, seen from an economic perspective, does not accomplish much. All her endeavors are doomed to fail. The reality of a housewife's work was at best imaginary and, at worst, the lot of lower social strata such as Emma's daughter's wet nurse. Thanks to her supposed idleness, however, Emma subverts the classical category of utility. Her (few) grandiose gestures are evidence of her way of overcoming rational economics, a category also called restrictive economics by George Bataille. Her countersystem is diffused and experienced by the reader through sensations of liquidity, lost energies, degradation, and death. Emma re-creates unproductive values, the most subversive being her downfall, which she accepts as the only option offered to her by society. The Hegelian dialectic also applies to Emma's masculine counterpart, Lheureux, who loses in autonomy (with respect to the system) what he gains through speculation as he becomes debtor of a society which uses him to reproduce itself.

Flaubert's novel is a complex book, impossible to read without attributing an array of contradictory meanings to the deeds, thoughts, and words of the characters. As soon as simplification by approximation is applied, falsification can easily be a consequence. Measure, regularity, and norms only provide an ideal case of representation not accountable in terms of residues, discrepancies, and overflow. This appreciation is also another way of rendering the main impression made by this literary work: the real is a considerable impoverishment of the imaginary world. The principle of liquidity, blood as well as meaning, pertains to the era of a defiant economy, an economy that challenges utility, an economy gradually becoming pleasurable. But what are we to do with a meaning which is no longer reducible to its usefulness and whose value henceforth is derived from the price paid for renouncing the affective needs it has previously crushed? The dichotomy between the two economies, between the twofold meaning of liquidity, the restrictive economy as mastery over meaning and general economics as "sovereignty" (in Bataille's words) linked to loss, is struggling throughout Flaubert's novel.

Flaubert seemingly deals with a realistic topic, that of portraying the morals of a French woman living in the provinces during the nineteenth century. In fact, and this fact is corroborated by his correspondence, he denounces the servility of meaning to become the subject of an all-powerful master: style, which he sees as a noncompensated loss, a style through which knowledge and truth disintegrate when faced with the creative impulse in the signifiers, metaphors, and images. Such an attitude leaves the reader with the impossibility of attributing an authoritative meaning to a text lacking any conclusive value or statement. Flaubert's vaunted doctrine of impartiality and formal innovations are partly responsible for the reader's invigorating sense of alienation. His point, claimed in one of his letters, is "to make a mystery of the moral and beneficient meaning of the book" (*Letters* 229). This provocative idea is not as original as it seems. It is an idea flowing in the *air du temps* as it tries to extricate any signs of a detested social anchoring from literary texts. Following the same vein, in the poetic genre, the influence of the movement called "Le Parnasse" touches larger audiences as it defines the beautiful as the negation of the useful, consequently becoming a marketable endeavor but, ironically, one which contests the no less successful theories on the market economy and free enterprise.

This unheard-of superiority of nonmeaning over meaning leads Flaubert to be fascinated by the problem of stupidity made manifest by the massive use of accepted conventions, consumed in abundance by all of the characters in the novels. Using clichés sparingly would contradict Flaubert's perspective, as he bets on stupidity to become a conceptual category which has invaded all relations in his society. Stupidity is also a structural category for his novel, as it touches everyone, regardless of his or her intelligence. Stupidity is a social illness which contaminates first and foremost the bourgeois without respecting privileges due to social hierarchy. Thus the particular (and most insidious) stupidity of the pharmacist Homais is concretized by his adopting a rhetorical discourse inflated with anticlerical statements, in fact a mere reprise of the official discourse of science, one which pays off at the time. Homais is always prone to adopting the fashionable traits reinforcing his image of a modern man emancipated from the obscurantism of the Catholic priests. His critical attitude, however, never questions in depth the sociopolitical and economic order since this order enables him to climb the social ladder (in the end, he is decorated by the state authorities for his alleged contributions to the progress of science). Of a different kind is Emma's stupidity. Hers consists of accepting the forged currency of her society as well as forging it herself in her imagination: "She sees the sentimental world as a market where it is only necessary to pay so that desired realities materialize" (Riggs 258).

The most devastating stupidity is the one wanting to conclude or to close the text. The author categorically refuses to yield to the hackneyed mechanisms of closure, a refusal expressed through the use of formal techniques such as indirect free style, or by assigning an obsessive role to the object, by using provocative narrative tenses which often freeze the plot and dilate durations in an unprecedented manner, and by giving more importance to the musicality of signifiers than to the set meaning of signifieds. For Flaubert knows, by contemplating Emma in her contradictions, that words, when reduced to signifieds, are also traps retaining only an exchange value. As for their use value, it is a myth. Flaubert's resistance also demonstrates the inscription of his book into modernity, a consequence which leads me into the intricacies of a Derridean analysis as it ill treats logocentrism in the dyad identity-truth.

In his book *Philosophical Perspectives on Metaphor* Marc Johnson examines the semantics of metaphor. His point of departure is the Aristotelian definition according to which metaphor is considered "a deviance from literal usage, since it involves the transfer of a name to some object to which that name does not properly belong" (6). Thus, for Greek philosophers, the separation between literal and figurative meaning had serious consequences since metaphorical use is necessarily inscribed in a subsidiary use of a word challenging its initial definition. This history of metaphors has not been fixed and reduced to this classical interpretation. Recent works by Jacques Derrida, for instance, have aimed to reinsert in its prerogatives that which was previously excluded, the other of a universal definition. These works have enabled new elaboration with respect to the alleged illegitimacy of a transfer of meaning, with a view to reestablishing the analogy in its justified right to existence. As Aristotle would have it, metaphor is a deceptive device, which destroys the identity of the proper meaning since this meaning should not be scattered in derivative tracks. It also privileges feeling over reason, only because metaphors function as a reserve of meaning, a threatening residue capable of subverting an absolute meaning closed onto itself. Modernity has warned us against the arbitrariness of this closure which has to exclude the metaphoric game as well as the notion of exchange to preserve its coherence. The fraud resulting from a literal use supposedly uncompromised can be, in our semantic system, appropriately transferred to the economic detour of production, as well as the circulation of the monetary sign. If a fraud does exist as soon as a metaphor is used to convey a meaning, an easy inference could claim the existence of a premetaphorical thinking as a repository of an integral truth according to the logic that "metaphor is a deviant use of words in other than their proper senses, which accounts for its tendency to confuse and to deceive" (Johnson 13). Such is the argument claimed by empirical philosophers who argued that figurative meaning hinders the adequate expression of the integrity of our thinking. In *Madame Bovary*, I can exemplify this thematics of deceit in various ways and see how it functions in one episode of the book. This episode is narrated at the moment when Rodolphe writes to Emma, letting her know of his decision to put an end to their love affair, thus ruining her dreams of an escape with him. Ironically (irony is the main mode of this passage) Rodolphe adopts for himself the statement on metaphor we have just quoted as the narrator conveys to the readers the total indifference of his character hidden under romantic love clichés.

Approaching the metaphor, in a text which reads as a lie, is a tautology, since the trope, by definition, implies the replacement of a word by another. Furthermore, mystification as a higher form of deception represents the economic metaphor par excellence in Flaubert's book (an array of mystifying forces from the sentimental to the religious, from the value to the semiotic system as a whole). The choice of this episode is thus legitimized as the representative of the metaphor or arch-metaphor, subsumed in the economy of mystification to be inferred from the mystification of economics.

Metaphors also "save" in a literal reading which is sacrificed to a figurative meaning. The homology between this second level of reading and the fiduciary character of currency in which a fictitious value replaces the nominal value is now corroborated. Success depends on making an appropriate use of the metaphor, on not abusing the transfer of meaning that the trope implies, and on not being abused by the underlying economic system as is Emma. "A good metaphor places things in a new light, so that we can see them in a way we have never seen them before" (Johnson 7). The economic metaphor does shed a new light on the opacity of the Flaubertian novel.

Johnson argues that the decline of the metaphor in medieval thought

was a consequence of its depreciation since "treated traditionally under
rhetoric, it becomes a stylistic device divorced from serious philosophical
argument" (9). But how could an economic logic be ignored, a logic still
to be interpreted by resorting to the metaphorical thinking of detour and
deviation? In this context, nominal would be to literal what real value is
to figurative value. The real values still need further investigation in *Madame Bovary*. The point, however, is not to impose on Flaubert intentions alien to his artistic endeavors: Flaubert has not spoken explicitly
and literally about economics. Yet, economics is implied all through his
book. Thanks to his numerous references such mechanisms as the promissory note, debts, and bankruptcy, the portrayal of a coherent system in
the context of a liberal bourgeois society emerges. The interpretive task
has to be pursued according to the principle that the reader provides the
thesis of the novel and that this task is no longer a privilege reserved for
the writer. The references to economics can be found on different levels:
in the psychology of the characters (the relationships between Emma and
Lheureux, the usurer), in the role of the objects and their proliferation
(inflation), and even in the style, which is not exempt from value judg-
ments despite the claimed impartiality of the narrative mode. For instance, the fragmentation of certain passages at times prevents the reader
from giving a coherent meaning to some episodes, thus posing the problem of meaning, of property and ownership as well as their credibility.

The classical conception which tries to reduce the metaphor to an el-
liptical simile is also relevant to our analysis. Metaphors of the diegesis
rest upon analogies in Flaubert's style. Here is one selected among many.
The context is the following: Charles Bovary's mother comes to pay a
visit to the young couple, and she makes known her bitterness now that
her son neglects the maternal affection for his devoted love of his new
wife, Emma: "and she observed the happiness of her son with a sad
silence, like some ruined man who watches through the window-panes
people sitting at table in his own old house" (Flaubert 55). A metaphor
cannot be reduced to an analogy, but, for my purpose, the elimination
of similes in which economics can be read, would have resulted in the
denial of valuable information which helps sustain the main argument.
This metaphor involves somebody who has gone bankrupt and for whom
a windowpane acts as a screen to prevent the unmediated perception of
phenomena observed inside his former house. It informs about the analogy between the decay of filial love and the loss of a fortune and is linked
to the motive of opacity as the main economic motive of the book. Opacity, as the indirect cause of Emma's bankruptcy, symbolizes the impossibility of making sense of economic calculations as well as, on a larger
scale, the mystified relationships of woman to man, objects, and institutions. The quotation is otherwise relevant. In the course of the philo-

sophical tradition, opacity has been associated with a degradation of a prime vision, a solid ground for meaning as if the figurative ground on which metaphors are built is slippery.

Jacques Derrida sets out to deconstruct the contradictory presuppositions of a metaphysics embedded in the Western mythology of the logos and the proper. Since, without resorting to metaphors, the task of reasserting an original and nonmetaphoric meaning is an impossible one, the faulty reasoning has proven its inadequacy and its constructedness is confirmed. There is no original meaning anchored in a presence even through infinite regression. The Derridean logic (or the lack of it) about the impossibility of the proper to be rendered in a total transparency not yet attacked by a metaphor is useful for this chapter in revealing that, if opacity is considered the property of the metaphor, it can also appropriately be considered the property of economics. A conventional image used to describe metaphor is that it is part and parcel of the definition of the trope "as if, so to speak, a word would be in a borrowed house" (Derrida 302). This deceptive definition, combined with the previous one on the obscure character of the trope, thematically corroborates Flaubert's quotation and reasserts my concern to read it following a logic determined by economics. Derrida, in *Margins of Philosophy*, quotes Du Marsais, a French philosopher who, in the seventeenth century, tried to reinstate the argumentation of the classical philosophers. For Du Marsais, the double context of obscurity and dwelling is that which defines the metaphor ontologically, precisely because, as Derrida points out, the economic value of the house, or the proper, is systematically referred to as soon as the definition of the metaphor is at stake:

It is a metaphor of the metaphor, expropriation, to be outside of one's own home, but still to be in a dwelling place, outside of one's home but in another metaphoric home where one can find oneself, be oneself, be together outside of oneself in oneself. Such is the philosophical metaphor as a detour in view of reappropriation. (302)

I would like to borrow and play with the presupposition attacked by Derrida according to which "philosophy as a theory of metaphor was at first a metaphor of theory" (303). Literature in the nineteenth century, when read as a means to inform one about Flaubert's unconscious, appears as an economy of metaphors because it is first and foremost an economic metaphor. And since opacity is encouraged by modernity in Flaubert and post-modernity in Derrida, I will suppose that and justify how any permutation of my terms remains adequate. In this way, it is also plausible to read economics as the theory of the metaphor, in that economics deals with exchange mechanisms and, as in the metaphoric transfer of meaning, any exchange can finally result in a dupery. It is also permissible to see an inscription of the metaphor in economics which, like the trope, cannot escape its constitutive premises more than the metaphor escapes its own. And at last, why not consider economics as a metaphor of literature, both fields participating in the process of regulation of exchanges?

Returning to Derrida's metaphor (on dispossession subsequent to the loss of an origin defined in its fullness) leads to further consequences. "To be outside of one's home but still in a dwelling place" could also mean, following a metaphorical logic of substitution, to be in an inn. One of *Madame Bovary*'s critics considers that Emma's somnambulistic journey goes through several inns. He defines it as somnambulistic because "she never meets the real, which is also the one defined by class conflicts" and not only the other of her dream world:

Fake subsidiaries of her original home, landmarks on a closed-in tour: Lion d'Or–Croix Rouge–Hotel de Boulogne–Croix Rouge–Lion d'Or–home. Each of these places looks like the first one of the Quartier Saint Gervais at which her father stopped with her on the way to the convent and where she had already discovered on painted plates the rudimentary spells keeping her forever prisoner of the dominant ideology. (Picard 94)

With the journey to these inns evolving in a circular way, metaphor as a turn of language is finally evoked, as the last metaphor defining the metaphor. The previous Derridean statement is once more asserted in that it is impossible to return to the original home, or proper meaning, without resorting to a metaphor, a home temporarily borrowed. This is a difficult statement to prove faulty in our Flaubertian quotation, since the original home henceforth belongs to its new owners and since the transfer of money and title have abolished the initial guarantee of property.

This diegetic metaphor, as we have discussed, deals with an opacity of vision. Max Black studies the image of the screen to describe how metaphors work:

Suppose I look at the night sky through a piece of heavily smoked glass on which certain lines have been left clear. Then I shall see only the stars that can be made to lie on the lines previously prepared upon the screen, and the stars I do see will be seen as organized by the screen's structures. We can think of a metaphor as such a screen and the system of "associated commonplaces" of the focal work as the network of lines upon the screen. We can say that the principal subject is "seen through" the metaphorical expression—or, if we prefer, that the principle subject is "projected upon" the field of the subsidiary subject. (Johnson 75)

The theory of the metaphor and economic analysis meet in the similarity of their preoccupation with such themes as the proper/property, appropriation or its contrary, exchange, usury and detour. But the notion of metaphor goes beyond the simple analogy of words or syntagmas:

We use one entire system of commonplaces to filter or organize our conception of some other system. The interaction is a screening of one system of commonplaces by another to generate a new conceptual organization of, a new perspective on, some subject. (Johnson 28)

In Flaubert's case, the one system of commonplaces is the ruined person and the other is the end of the privileged mother/son relationship after the son's marriage. The filter, as the attitude in front of a bankruptcy and the incomprehension of its inner mechanisms, pertains to economics. I regard it as the theoretical way of understanding a possible reading of the novel, one which reveals a new interpretation of a canonical work of literature.[1] Any metaphor is puzzling in dispersing an alleged primary meaning read through a second one, thus inscribing itself as a loan between two series, "a transaction between contexts" according to I. A. Richards (Johnson 40). Just as a black room is necessary to render the image of a normal vision, ideology offers the readers the image of inverted relationships which, thanks to the metaphorical eye, will be able to reappear noninverted.

As a conclusive remark, I offer a quotation of M. Black: "If some metaphors are what might be called cognitive instruments indispensable for perceiving connections that, once perceived, are then truly present, the case for the thesis would be made out" (Johnson 41). This statement corroborates my own work on the space of intersection of literature and economics when applied to *Madame Bovary*. The reading strategy offered here would not have been possible without the possibility offered by metaphors of bringing into fruitful relationships new conceptual rapports. If originality is indeed the result (with respect to traditional readings of the well-known novel), it is no longer based on the metaphysics of the proper and property. This reading needed the use of metaphors as a loan in order to exist and can no longer claim to be a creation *ex nihilo*, another common ideology caught in the problematics of logocentric interpretation.

NOTE

1. Certain difficulties arise when a critique of canonical works is at stake. The sacred edifice of Culture has taught us that its authorities monopolize the discourse of truth. Any new interpretation is an adventure and any adventure entails a risk. But, after all, the risk is a basic concept of liberal economics.

REFERENCES

Bataille, Georges. *La Part maudite*. Paris: Les Editions de Minuit, 1967.

Derrida, Jacques. *Marges de la philosophie*. Paris: Les Editions de Minuit, 1972.

Flaubert, Gustave. *Madame Bovary*. Trans. W. Blaydes. New York: P. F. Collier and Son, 1902.

————. *The Letters of Gustave Flaubert*. Vol. 2 Trans. Francis Steegmuler. Cambridge: Harvard University Press, 1982.

Johnson, Marc. *Philosophical Perspectives on Metaphor*. Minneapolis: University of Minnesota Press, 1981.

Picard, Michel. "La prodigalité d'Emma Bovary." *Littérature* 10 (mai 1973): 94.

Riggs, Larry. "La Banqueroute des idéaux reçus dans *Madame Bovary*." *Aimer en France: 1760–1860*. Clermont-Ferrand: Association des Publications de la Faculté des Lettres et Sciences Humaines, 1988.

16

Mammon's Finger in the Novels of Balzac, Zola, and Gide

John A. Frey

No servant can be the slave of two masters; for either he will hate the first and love the second, or he will be devoted to the first and think nothing of the second. You cannot serve God and Money.

Matthew: 6,24

Money is a metaphor, a medium of exchange for goods and services; it is also a symbol of power and control. Images on currency denote intentional metaphorical value. Coins are imprinted with representations of presidents, queens, and kings. Religious and political slogans are presented, such as "In God we Trust" or "Liberty, Equality, and Fraternity." Economics and aesthetics join on script and postage stamps to pay homage to the arts and sciences, to our heroes and heroines. Money language offers positive similes: "he is as good as gold," and negative ones: "as phony as a three-dollar bill"; "not worth a red cent."

In this chapter money is regarded as intrinsic to the narrative structure and to the metaphorical fields accompanying it. The main argument is that focus on money can be seen as a unifying device for the pondering of moral dilemmas of modern societies under the impact of the development of capitalism and the rise of the middle class as a power agent with its own ethical agenda.

Molière's *Miser* (1668) marks the first appearance in France of the modern money problem. Although derived from Plautus, this play does go beyond stock dramatic figuration, suggesting dark personality problems more complex than the simple hoarding of money. On its heels, Lesage's

Turcaret (1709) develops what is incipient in Molière, that is, the development of the modern money-oriented personality. Turcaret starts out as a lowly lackey, but financial speculation turns him into a powerful financier. At the play's end he is financially ruined, and another lackey replaces him at the top of the financial world.

Lesage's world of servants becoming masters is overshadowed and transformed by the consequences of the French Revolution, and these changes will be first noted fictionally in Balzac's depiction of French society in the first half of the nineteenth century. Zola's depiction of the Second Empire shows the acceleration of forces unleashed by the events of 1789–1815, and by the developing Industrial Revolution. Gide can rightfully be viewed by his dates (1869–1951) as a man of both centuries. He continues the pondering, through fiction, of the meanings of money as found in Balzac and Zola, but in his work there are some fundamental shifts or modifications of the money metaphor.

Balzac's *Human Comedy* depicts the triumph of the bourgeois spirit following the French Revolution. The novel presents a world of money-lenders, bankers, speculators, creditors, and gamblers. It also portrays an underworld of criminals wearing disguises so as to infiltrate, sabotage, and capture the world of money and its facades. Talented crooks, like Balzac's Vautrin, anticipate the world of Gide's adolescent counterfeiters and the swindlers of *Lafcadio's Adventures*.

Money in Balzac's world is a metaphorical code for moral turpitude. Moral flaw is ultimately traced back to obsession with power, be it sexual, political, or religious. Zola's focus is just more intense than that of Balzac. In the *Rougon-Macquart*, money indeed makes the world go round; the stock market is the motor piece of the series, but it implies other moral equivalencies.

Obsessive behavior in the novels of Balzac entails the expenditure of great sums of money, leading to the destruction of stable households (entities). Balzac, expressing a conservative outlook, believes that honesty and the practice of virtue can right financial wrongs. Thus, lascivious males are frequently if only temporarily rescued by redemptive females (angels). In *Search for the Absolute* (*La Recherche de l'absolu*), the mad alchemist loses the family fortune in his efforts to change raw ores into gold. Virtuous women work with success to reestablish financial stability, only to see it lost again, like the daily ups and downs of the stock exchange. Sexual obsession also leads to moral and financial ruin. *Cousin Betty* (*La Cousine Bette*) reiterates the sexual perversions of the Baron Hulot. His compulsive sexual behavior persists to the end of the novel, destroying family honor and fortune. Money in the world of Balzac has stolen society's soul; it is the springboard for moral decay.

Figuratively speaking, Balzac and Zola share a metaphorical field in which money as power is seen in terms of bellicose conquest and predatory behavior, wars, battles, attacking, destroying, consuming. Young romantic idealists learn quickly that society is not a realm of virtue but the site for monetary acquisition. Eugène de Rastignac, a young idealistic provincial, comes to Paris to study (*Old Goriot* [*Le Père Goriot*]). As a witness to the excessive filial devotion of Balzac's Goriot, who increasingly depletes his fortune to give money to his undeserving daughters, he attends the poor man's funeral (where only the daughters' empty carriages attend, for they are too preoccupied with their own affairs, getting their hair fixed, preparing for a ball), and from the heights of Père-Lachaise cemetery realizes the meaning of Paris: one must become an *arriviste* and obtain power through money and sex. Balzac's Restoration Paris is a dog-eat-dog world, and animal comparisons aptly pinpoint the ardent desire for money. To explain the avarice of Monsieur Grandet (*Eugénie Grandet*), the narrator uses a comparison with the predatory habits of cobras and tigers:

Financially speaking, Mr. Grandet resembled the tiger and the boa: he knew how to stretch out, squat, consider for a long time his prey, and then to leap onto it; then he would open the mouth of his purse, swallowing up a load of coins and then going peacefully to sleep, like the serpent which digests its prey, without feeling, cold, methodical. (Balzac, III, 486; English translations of Balzac and Zola are by Frey)

Consistent metaphorical structures back up the money narrations in Balzac. The color yellow is dominant in *Eugénie Grandet*, relating to the color of gold and Monsieur Grandet's monetary obsessions. The miser's eyes are described as yellow; on his deathbed, as the priest presents a crucifix for his final kiss, it is only the yellow color of Christ's body which he sees.

Zola builds on the money novels of Balzac, amplifying for the Second Empire what Balzac had done for the world of the Restoration. Balzac's world represents the birth of bourgeois power, of nascent mercantilism, the start of the Industrial Revolution and its potential for enrichment. Zola's world of the *Rougon-Macquart* represents the frenzy of acquisition and consumerism. It also underlines the economic extremes of the very rich and the very poor (Furst).

That money relates to power and class ascendancy is poignantly revealed in the plight of Mother Perou of *Pot-Bouille*. This poor old lady is employed by Gourd, the concierge of an apartment building, to sweep the courtyard and do other domestic duties. Her earnings are four cents per hour. Gourd himself had been a servant, but having risen to the rank of concierge, he will take his revenge on what he used to be: "He spoke . . . of old woman Perou with a spirit of brutal domination, the enraged need for revenge of former domestics who in their turn are being waited upon" (Zola, III, 99).

The revenge pattern of former servants persecuting servants echoes class warfare as perceived in Balzac's *The Peasants*. Zola is summarizing what was intuited by the mature Balzac, namely that modern capitalism induces cupidity and the desire for upward mobility (Vernon 147).

Zola's novels explain economic suppression and demonstrate economic power and the lust for it. Such is the world of *La Curée* and *Money* (*L'Argent*), wherein real estate and stock market speculation are the enriching elements of the nouveaux riches of the Second Empire. Zola calls it the "rage to spend" (III, 187), and his novels abound with examples of lurid consumerism, spending for its own sake, vulgarly, without discretion or discrimination. Uncle Bachelard, a minor character in *Pot-Bouille*, likes to eat out in expensive restaurants, ordering meals not from a sense of taste, but from the idea of spending: "He would order whatever was the most expensive, gastronomic curiosities, even the uneatable" (Zola, III, 187).

Au Bonheur des dames, a novel exploring the development of the new idea of the department store, analyzes modern techniques of merchandising. Interpreted in terms of our own society, it could be called the novel of the credit card syndrome. Given the extreme poverty of late nineteenth-century France, the supercilious spending of the rich is morally untenable. The conclusion of *La Curée* describes the death of the heroine, Renée, who leaves behind a bill with her hairdresser, a debt of 257,000 francs (Zola, I, 599).

Money is symbolic of the entire *Rougon-Macquart* series. It reintroduces Aristide Saccard of *La Curée*, husband of Renée, back in Paris trying to rebuild his fortune. Previously Saccard had made a fortune through real estate speculation during the rebuilding of the right bank of Paris by Haussmann. Saccard now plunges into financial speculation. His scheme is simple enough: he asks for investments from pious Catholics for his *banque universelle*, which plans to create a new Christian kingdom of Jerusalem, with the idea of moving the Pope there from Rome. In his financial dealings, Saccard is in financial warfare with the Jewish banking firm of Gundermann, and these two forces of capitalism, associated with two religious cultures, are played out against a third force, that of Sigismond, the scholarly revolutionary and friend of Karl Marx. The elements of socialism and communism, unspoken in Balzac, erupt now in the world of Zola.

As with Balzac, the narrative structure of finance is reinforced with metonymic and metaphorical fields which give the narration its symbolic meaning. *Money*'s narrative hammers away at the idea of an increasing tempo of increase in capital value, the division and subdivision of stocks, increases in growth and national productivity. These inflationary modes are translated into an imagery which suggests relationships with idolatry and conquest, culminating in a major metaphorical field of money.

Balzac and Zola, unlike Gide, represent an argument against capitalism and materialism, based on fundamentally old-fashioned conservative arguments—Balzac, regretting the loss of prerevolutionary France, Zola, seeking an honest bourgeois way of dealing with life, based on a work ethic. Gide will turn the money argument into one of escape from bourgeois restraints.

Zola believed that the materialism of the Second Empire was destroying the very fabric of French society. He saw a new liturgy coming into being in the cult of money. *Nana* tells of the adventures of a sex goddess created by money. Berthe Josserand of *Pot-Bouille* has been raised in a society which recognizes only money as God: "all this religion of money whose cult she had learned in her family" (Zola, III, 243). In *Germinal* the workers do not know for whom they work, but they sense it is some hidden god somewhere in Paris. It is plainly stated in *Money*: "Money, king money, god money" (Zola, V, 220). Money is sacred and will take on the garments of religion, which give it respectability. In *Money*, Saccard supervises the decoration of his new bank. It must have a severe look, should smell like a sacristy, and customers will get the impression that they are entering a devout establishment. Employees are taught to speak in measured tones, and "money is received and given with an entirely clerical discretion" (Zola, V, 139).

Money as warfare, as battle, was noted in Balzac, in Rastignac's challenge to the business world of Paris. This imagery is intensified in Zola with the financial challenges accepted by Saccard. Saccard's Middle East scheme for swindling gullible Catholics of their money involves a curious constellation of images combining echoes back to the Crusades with more recent images of the conquests of Bonaparte. What had not been accomplished by the Crusades, and what Napoleon had failed to do, would now be realized by Saccard's financial enterprise: "What Napoleon could not do with his sword, this conquest of the Orient, a financial company would accomplish it" (Zola, V, 253).

Saccard's financial empire, however, collapses, and instead of conquest we have rout and defeat. The narrator changes Saccard into a Bonaparte, and the floor of the stock market into the battlefield of Waterloo:

Instead of the expected help, was this a new enemy coming from the neighboring woods? As at Waterloo, Grouchy was not showing up, and it was betrayal which completed the rout. . . . Well, during the last half hour it was debacle, the rout growing and carrying along the crowd. . . . There were no more purchases, the field was strewn with cadavers. . . . But in the hall of the stock market panic had above all been blowing around Saccard, and it was there that the war had done its damage. (Zola, V, 328–30)

The most important metaphorical field in all of Zola's novels is that of variants on money as gold, coin, golden rain, seas of gold. They are found across the series, but specifically in *La Curée* and in *Money*. In the first, Saccard sits at a restaurant from the heights of Montmartre, and he sees the financial possibilities of Paris, a fabulous city transformed into a vision from a *Thousand and One Nights*, a city of gold. Money indeed becomes the central image of Zola's novels:

"The rain of gold striking against the walls would come down more heavily every day." (Zola, I, 387)

" . . . this mad dance of millions." (Zola, V, 55)

" . . . the hail of gold pieces, the dance of millions." (Zola, V, 116)

" . . . the rain of gold which was to rain on him and around him." (Zola, V, 127)

As in the boa and tiger image of Balzac, there is the fusion of the real world of finance and its metaphorical equivalencies. Money in these nine-teenth-century novels is a figure representing moral decay, empower-ment, and disenfranchisement. Gide will also explore the meaning of money, but will relate it less in terms of the rich and the poor, and more in terms of moral depravity. He attacks money as a symbol of the moral hypocrisy of the French middle class. This occurs as a product of his Calvinistic upbringing, and his confrontation with his homosexuality. Money will be Gide's metaphor for exploring inauthenticity and sincerity, enslavement and liberation. A complicated web of personality issues re-lated to society comes into focus in two of his major prose works, *Laf-cadio's Adventures* (*Les Caves du Vatican*, 1913), and *The Counterfeiters* (*Les Faux-Monnayeurs*, 1926).

Money is the backdrop for *Lafcadio's Adventures* and acts as symbolic motif for multiple character permutations in *The Counterfeiters*. The com-plex story of Lafcadio, a modern picaresque hero, is played out against the absurd plot of a so-called kidnapping of Pope Leo XIII by the free-masons, and the installation of a fake masonic pope on the papal throne. This is a hoax to get rich pious Catholics to contribute money for the pope's release, a scheme devised by the underworld antihero, Proto. Tex-tually, the plot seems to be a humorous and sardonic continuation of Zola's *Money*. The word *counterfeiters* in the title alludes not only to a novel of the same name being written by one of the main narrators, the novelist Edouard, but also to a ring of small-time crooks at a Protestant boarding school whose ring leader, Strouvilhou, is an underworld anar-chist. *Counterfeit* is code in this novel for a variety of artificialities and reversals of moral orders.

In both of these works there exists a tension between what is and what seems to be, between sincerity and hypocrisy, between social conventions and hidden mores, between the world of bourgeois conventions, and a hidden world, a demimonde. Disguise is an important element in both Balzac and Zola. The criminal Vautrin takes on many masks as he tries to hoodwink bourgeois society, and in Zola villains and crooks rise to the heights of power in society. Gide's world seems to be populated by persons who are not what they seem to be; they are fake, they are counterfeit. Gide wants to know how to get beyond that artificiality. Lafcadio has as a basic character trait the dissimulation of his true feelings and nature. This is a lesson he learned from an old school chum, Proto. Lafcadio had once scolded Proto about his ability to imitate anything and everything, and was told in reply that the "important thing in this world was never to look like what one was" (Gide, *Lafcadio*, 90).

Proto is a master of disguise as he sets about his embezzlement schemes. Disguised as a canon of Virmonthal, he gets a huge sum of money from a pious countess. Dressed as a French abbé, he enlists Amedée Fleurissoire into the crusade for the deliverance of the pope. In a final disguise which fools and entraps Lafcadio, he presents himself as a lawyer from the Bordeaux law faculty.

Both Gide texts present a world where moral values are tottering. There is widespread cheating, lying, stealing, snooping, reading other people's journals and letters. In both works illegitimacy becomes a major concern and interrelates with financial survival and inheritance. Lafcadio is illegitimate, as is Bernard Profitendieu. *The Counterfeiters* deals with one of society's deepest social disguises and the metaphors used for it, namely the question of homosexuality. Robert de Passavant is a notorious decadent and contrasts with Edouard the novelist. Both are homosexual and have affairs with young men (Bernard and Olivier). But all is concealed—the code word or metaphor for lover or kept boy is "secretary."

There is in addition the facade of bourgeois morality. In *Lafcadio's Adventures* this inauthentic world is represented by Julius de Baraglioul, whose burning ambition is entrance into the French Academy. *The Counterfeiters* allows Gide to scrutinize the French Protestant middle class from which he is seeking liberation. One example among many is that of Oscar Molinier, a proper father, concerned with the conduct of young people, including his sons, who seem to be engaging the services of prostitutes and also passing counterfeit coins. Trouble is in the air, and Molinier attributes this to the bad influence of Bernard, viewed as a corrupting influence because of his status as bastard.

I had rather Olivier saw as little as possible of that young fellow. I have heard the most deplorable things about him—not that I'm much astonished at that. We must admit that there are no grounds for expecting any good from a boy who has been born in such unfortunate conditions. I don't mean to say that a natural child mayn't have great qualities—and even virtues; but the fruit of lawlessness and insubordination must necessarily be tainted with the germs of anarchy. (Gide, *Counterfeiters*, 215)

This judgmental attitude of Oscar Molinier is close to the moral hypocrisy found in Zola's novels. Here we have a man worrying about the education of children when he himself has a mistress which could also lead to the birth of a "bastard." Zola and Gide are both concerned with the double standards of society. Money becomes a discourse betraying other social categories: marriages and extramarital affairs, heterosexual love and homosexual liaisons, honest faces and masks, nakedness and disguise, real money and counterfeit.

Lafcadio is a young man who knows many languages and many currencies. Recounting his life story to Julius, the money images pop out of the page. It was his "uncle" Heldenbruck who contributed to his financial education:

He was, it seems, a distinguished financier. As well as his own language he taught me arithmetic. . . . He made me what he used laughingly to call his "cashier"—that is, he gave into my keeping a whole fortune of petty cash and wherever we went together, it was I who had to do the paying. Whatever he bought . . . he insisted on my adding up the bill in as short a time as it took me to pull the notes or coins out of my pocket. Sometimes he used to puzzle me with foreign money, so that there were questions of exchange; then of discount, of interest, of brokerage and finally even of speculation. (Gide, *Counterfeiters*, 86)

With such training in money and language, Lafcadio becomes the perfect multinational (another disguise), which for a brief moment leads him down the road to serious crime (the gratuitous murder of Amedée by pushing him off the train), much as the secret society manipulations lead to the suicide of young Boris in *The Counterfeiters*.

Both works, however, indicate a way out of a life of scheming and counterfeiting. Lafcadio is capable of virtue and he practices it by saving children from a burning building. He is also generous. As the work concludes, Lafcadio, who had always taught himself to hate possessions, is a whole person, liberated. We do not know his final decision; we cannot know whether or not he will turn himself over to the police. As for Bernard, having left home because of his discovery of his illegitimacy, he too is capable of generous actions (his feelings and love for the pregnant Laura). In a master stroke, the narrator has Bernard meet an angel from heaven at the Sorbonne; he wrestles with the angel and then returns home to be with the man who is not his real father. The novel announces the beginning of an authentic human relationship.

Gide has given new dimensions to the money question. He has turned the question of bourgeois morality, expressed through a money value system, into a discussion of the meaning of freedom, a freedom he had hoped to find in communism. Gide's quest for a communal society is partly born of his reading of the Acts of the Apostles, and from his recognition that a truly liberated person cannot· serve both God and mammon.

In the works herein discussed, money has been viewed as meaning power (Vernon 99) but in the words of Marx, alienated power:

In the *Grundrisse*, Marx shows how money can appear in the form of collateral. Men place their faith in this collateral because it is an objectified mutual relation between their productive activity. Every other collateral may serve the holder directly in the function of objectified exchange value. Money, however, serves him merely as "the dead pledge or mortgage" of society, but it serves as such only because of its social (symbolic) property; and it can have a social property only because individuals have alienated their own social relationship from themselves so that it takes the form of a thing. (Shell, 126. Shell cites the Marx test)

This alienation is certainly the meaning of money as accurately perceived by Gide in these two works, and it is an amplification of Zola's rage against the bourgeois world of the Second Empire, as well as Balzac's Marxist inclinations, albeit before the fact.

REFERENCES

Balzac, Honoré de. *La Comédie humaine*. Paris: Bibliothèque de la Pléiade, 1967, III.

Furst, Lillian R. *L'Assommoir: A Working Woman's Life*. Boston: Twayne Publishers, 1990.

Gide, André. *The Counterfeiters, Les Faux-Monnayeurs*, translated from the French by Dorothy Bussy. New York: Alfred A. Knopf, 1947.

———. *Lafcadio's Adventures, Les Caves du Vatican*, translated from the French by Dorothy Bussy. Garden City, N.Y.: Doubleday and Company, 1953.

Shell, Marc. *Money, Language, and Thought*. Berkeley, Los Angeles, London: University of California Press, 1982.

Vernon, John. *Money and Fiction: Literary Realism in the Nineteenth and Early Twentieth Centuries*. Ithaca and London: Cornell University Press, 1984.

Zola, Emile. *Les Rougon-Macquart*. Paris: Bibliothèque de la Pléiade, 1960, I, III, V.

Part V

Money and English Literature

17

"Cut My Heart in Sums": Shakespeare's Economics and *Timon of Athens*

Sandra K. Fischer

G. Wilson Knight asserts that "in studying, normally, everything but economics, great poetry necessarily studies, though indirectly, economics too" (224). In *Econolingua*, I have chronicled how the works of Shakespeare reveal a habit of mind that links love and money in an intricate metaphorical system. For the bard, parallel spheres exist in relation to natural processes and artificial financial connections.[1] The two worlds share a common lexicon, each with its own type of bonds, debts, dues, accounts, estimates, increase, profit, thrift, value, and use. The plays often investigate the relation between the two realms, as we see most blatantly in *The Merchant of Venice*. Because of their linguistic overlap, the systems often become confused, and thus a notion of correctly interpreting the right use of money becomes central in the theme and structure of the plays.

No single image in Shakespeare portrays the link between natural and economic processes as potently as the connection of usury and prostitution. Usury, according to E. C. Pettet, appears in Shakespeare as an inclusive metaphor for the operations of a society based on the money ethic. In the natural realm of human relations, usury becomes equivalent to prostitution, "because they are the degeneration of a human relationship into a purely mercenary one" (335). For Shakespeare the processes of nature are to be desired over social processes contrived by people. This natural/artificial dichotomy reiterates notions of intrinsic and exchange value and implicates the concept of double seeing, or a discrepancy between appearance and reality.[2] Nature teaches a kind of economics that instructs us in our reciprocal obligations, the right use of nature's gifts. Our abilities and attributes are not true donations but rather loans; the receiver is obliged to put the sum of the loan "to use" so that he can repay nature with interest upon the day of reckoning (judgment). Most often that interest is viewed as the outcome of breeding or propagation: nature's "use" produces more heirs. Breeding is an investment in the future, for a child is entered on the asset side of the ledger. Nature is thus bountiful to those who understand her system of economics, those who, themselves "free," repay her in kind.

The connection between nature's system of "natural" economics and man's contrived system of high finance is prolific in Shakespeare. However, the similarity of expression for markedly different functions—the one a "natural" relationship whose activities are of the greatest good in creating and cementing society, and the other an "artificial" relationship that breeds an unnatural offspring of financial profit and that tends to isolate and alienate individuals—ultimately contributes to problems in discerning between the two. Timon of Athens, for instance, believes that he lives in the sphere of natural connection and finds his appropriately gauged behavior thwarted by a society operating on the "unnatural" system of financial ethics. The ability to recognize true but hidden value is a virtue allied with the side of nature and "natural" economics. Irresponsible financial behavior more often than not expresses itself in an inwardly empty show of finery. The greatest wealth attainable shows in a congruency between inner worth and material riches and extends itself socially in bounty, hospitality, and generosity.

Directly pointing to this double sense inherent in economics, Pompey the clown in *Measure for Measure* comments on the social encroachment of merchandising ethics into the natural processes of love: "'Twas never merry world since of two usuries the merriest was put down, and the worser allow'd by order of law" (3.2.5–7). This distinction of the "two usuries" is at the core of Shakespeare's economic theory. The worse is, of course, moneylending at 10 percent interest; the merrier is "the generating of offspring construed as a payment made to nature in recompense for the use of the body" (Pearlman 217).

Alongside *The Merchant of Venice, Timon of Athens* (1607) is Shakespeare's most "economic" play, and it reveals a structural confusion resulting from the treatment of its economic theme as it moves toward a reckoning with a new financial system of morality obviously here to stay.[3] Although Shakespeare and his editors did not assign a generic title to this play—alone among the tragedies, it is merely *The Life of Timon of Athens*—we can see how it partakes of the characteristics of overlapping genres. Act 1 ostensibly presents to us the world of comedy. Timon reigns over a benevolent household with himself installed as king of giving. He pays the debt of Ventidius, a sizable sum, and then supports him from his own income. Only lines later he donates to Lucilius a sum that allows him to marry for love, basing his gift on the bond of service that Lucilius has faithfully incurred: "For 'tis a bond in men" (1.1.144). For Timon human bounty reiterates and reenacts nature's free bounty. Thinking himself wealthy in his friends, in the community of concord harmonious as nature's hierarchy, he gives in order to celebrate and acknowledge his social bonds: "We are born to do benefits; and what better or properer can we call our own than the riches of our friends? O, what a precious comfort 'tis to have so many like brothers commanding one another's fortunes!" (1.2.101–5).

Within this harmonious and "natural" first act, however, hints appear of threats to Timon's order, of motives not quite properly understood, regardless of their outward manifestations. As in *The Merchant of Venice* we must view the characters and their actions with the eyes of double vision, for they inhabit a world in economic transition and are temporarily suspended in a limbo of values. The Jeweler is first to warn us by emphasizing relative rather than absolute standards of value. Showing Timon his stone, he says,

> My lord, 'tis rated
> As those which sell would give; but you well know,
> Things of like value differing in the owners
> Are prized by their masters.   (1.1.168–71)

The role of human value in exchange transactions becomes even clearer when the old Athenian, father of Lucilius' fiancée, in effect auctions off his daughter to the highest bidder without regard for her affections. Apemantus and Flavius both seem to understand the danger of Timon's anachronistic economic action, especially in the Athenian society of opportunists. Their warnings, which Timon refuses to accept, indicate a structural change from comedy to something more resembling tragedy, focusing on a character who suffers because of his blindness.

The values of the new economic order indicate that while worth is measured almost totally in monetary terms, anything may become currency, a medium of exchange.[4] Timon discovers both of these unhappy truths when he becomes impecunious and is repaid by his friends in a variety of commodities like rejection, false pride, and empty words. Shakespeare capitalizes on the imagistic connection of words and coins, as he did in the portrayal of Shylock, to demonstrate both the workings of the commodity ethic and the lack of sound inner merit that the rich so often hide. Early in the play, when Timon squanders his estate in recklessly extravagant gifts and promises of more gifts, his steward is prompted to exclaim, "what he speaks is all in debt: he owes / For ev'ry word" (1.2.198–99), and later, when Timon finally listens to Flavius, he admonishes his master with:

> O my good lord, the world is but a word;
> Were it all yours to give it in a breath,
> How quickly were it gone!   (2.2.152–54)

The final blow is represented by the vapid speech of Lucius (3.2.44–58) as his portion of repayment for the "small kindnesses from him, as money, plate, jewels, and such like trifles." These images support Shakespeare's conception of value in a mercantilist society as infinitely various and variable.

Although we are prone to view Timon sympathetically as a man wholeheartedly subscribing to old values in the context of a changed society that mocks these ethics, the character also has shortcomings that temper this sympathy. We may pity the man "shattered and disillusioned to the point of madness by his discovery that the traditional beliefs he has lived by are no longer the beliefs of the world around him" (Pettet 329), but we also realize his own economic faults. In a sense he is an inverse Shylock, for he gives and gives but never learns to accept. Early on, when false friends offer him gifts, he takes them only in order to present even better gifts in return. Even by the end of the play he vehemently refuses help and good counsel from his best devotees, Apemantus and Flavius. According to Kenneth Burke, Timon gives so excessively in a sort of desperate attempt to make his bounty replace the human bonds that he lacks or feels inadequate to form. While these gifts do represent bonds, sadly enough they do not constitute bonds (122).

Part of Timon's inability to form satisfying human bonds stems from a Lear-like fault. In the guise of bounty, Timon actually establishes himself as an economic judge who rewards good socioeconomic behavior and who tests the economic fidelity of his friends (2.2). While Lear eventually learns both to give and to receive, Timon makes no such progress. His giving is faulty in motive and his inability to receive a crucial failure, "an attempt on the part of man to ape divine bounty, ever spontaneously giving without receiving anything in return, . . . presumptuous and . . . inevitably . . . frustrated" (Maxwell 201). To the end of the play he ignores the necessity of reciprocity. His economic abuses, although erring on the side of prodigality rather than frugality, are judged almost as harshly. His excessive bounty, according to one of the senators, is itself a type of usury or counterfeiting that partakes of the "unnatural" side of economic fertility:

> If I want gold, steal but a beggar's dog
> And give it Timon, why, the dog coins gold.
> If I would sell my horse and buy twenty more
> Better than he, why, give my horse to Timon,

> Ask nothing, give it him, it foals me straight
> And able horses.   (2.1.5–10)

Dogs and horses are not so very different from the ewes and rams of Shylock's parable of usury, and evidently just as productive.

By introducing usury into this play along with the tangible bonds that invariably accompany moneylending transactions, Shakespeare shows us an equivocation on bonds at least as disturbing as in *The Merchant of Venice*. Burke finds *Timon* as well to be a play "almost wholly concerned with relations among men (as though all the world were a kind of secular monastery devoted perversely to a universal god of gold)" (118). As the money ethic gains precedence, the nature of human bonds changes. The senator who comments on Timon's unnatural propagation of wealth also eventually finds his financial bond more pressing than the bond of friendship and sues an impecunious Timon for repayment. In his decision of utility the material wins out over the intangible. Similarly, in act 1 all of the false lords counterfeit the actions that generally indicate traditional bonds, but they do it only to profit from Timon's gifts and feasts. Alcibiades offers a refreshing counterpoint in that he knows and upholds the bonds of war, fidelity, and honor and lives by their ethics; yet when he argues the case of his friend and fellow soldier before the Senate, he knows enough of their priorities to couch his argument in terms of economic bonds (3.5.76–84). According to O. J. Campbell, "The senators who rule the city value riches more than virtue" (194), and their morality has extended into the majority of the citizenry as well. This is the problem of Timon when, pressed by creditors and aware of the betrayal of his friends, he cries out "Cut my heart in sums" (3.4.92) as payment for the bills. Mingling love and money, this image crystallizes Timon's dilemma: he tried to give his heart, but false friends find such a gift ultimately worthless in a money economy.

As the play moves toward tragedy with Timon's realization of his prior blindness and betrayal and with his isolation, it falls short of a satisfying structure because of the economic lessons that remain unlearned. Timon never achieves the proper balance: as Apemantus observes, "The middle of humanity thou never knewest, but the extremity of both ends" (4.3.300–301). Timon still persists in giving without receiving. Having placed too much faith in human bonds, he now denies and curses all bonds, even economic ones. A man can rely only upon their being broken (4.1.3–21). Similarly, he is slow to recognize his bond to Flavius, who has been faithful all along, and when he does accept his service, Timon yet again rewards and repays this human debt with gold, as does Lear his "bonded" servant, Kent.

By the end of the play, Timon still fails to understand the true nature and right use of money. He has learned accurately of his society's dedi-

cation to the money ethic and of its faith in the ability of gold to trans-
mute human action; some values, however, cannot be touched by gold.
Timon neglects to acknowledge the role of intrinsic values, even with
Alcibiades as his teacher. When Timon flees Athens and society for the
solace of natural economy as a hermit living in a cave, nature tries one
last time to turn him around. Ironically, Timon digs for roots to eat and
finds only gold; the women who visit and offer him succor are prostitutes.
Here Shakespeare stunningly encapsulates the theory of the two usuries.
In a passage that was influential in helping Karl Marx to theorize about
the galvanizing effects of gold, Timon rails against a society in which the
money morality tends to negate all traditional bonds:

> O thou sweet king-killer, and dear divorce
> 'Twixt natural [son] and [sire]! thou bright defiler
> Of Hymen's purest bed! thou valiant Mars!
> Thou ever young, fresh, lov'd, and delicate wooer,
> Whose blush doth thaw the consecrated snow
> That lies on Dian's lap! thou visible god,
> That sold'rest close impossibilities,
> And mak'st them kiss! that speak'st with every tongue
> To every purpose! O thou touch of hearts,
> Think they slave man rebels, and by thy virtue
> Set them into confounding odds, that beasts
> May have the world in empire!   (4.3.381–92)

But there is still a remnant of humanity that finds value in serving its
siblings. Timon can only rail against a society that has disappointed him;
Alcibiades, in contrast, takes arms against a sea of troubles and emerges
victorious. While the money ethic and its companions of usury and financial bonds threaten society, all money is not therefore bad. Alcibiades
in fact uses the gold that Timon gives him to put down the economic
corruption of the Senate. Timon cannot see the positive power of gold
because he confuses the two usuries. As Ellis-Fermor notes, when Timon
lashes out at nature, he misreads the function of natural use, which can
be productive (265). Nature is not a thief; it merely operates by a system
of reciprocal obligation that Timon does not understand. "Natural" usury
and use are desirable. Accepting as well as returning are essential in the
hierarchies of both nature and society. Friends, then, are to be "used"
in the sense of reciprocal human obligations rather than "put to use"
with only the hope of pecuniary gain. Having been slow to recognize the
latter, Timon persists in refusing the former.

Timon's persistent wrongheadedness attains its final expression in the
first epitaph he proposes, "nothing brings me all things" (5.1.188).[5]
Nothing brings him only a self-imposed solitude and an irrational, all-
consuming hate. Bounty, used correctly and with discretion, is able to

achieve the true sense of community for which he strives. Comparing this last act with act 5 in *The Merchant of Venice* instructs us in Shakespeare's theory of proper economics. While wealth may lend itself to abuses, withdrawal is not the right answer. Even Shylock is in a sense incorporated into the society. Like Shylock, who hangs between censure and sympathy, Timon is an unsatisfying hero. In both structure and character the playwright can only expose the abuses of this new money economy without finding a workable solution. Some traditional values, like those of Alcibiades and the servants of Timon, show themselves strong enough to fend off the corruption of economic ethics, but these values are no longer widespread. Shakespeare acknowledges the presence of a money economy but cannot yet answer the question of how to cope with its attendant morality. The issue itself breaches the gap in time and setting from ancient Greece to Renaissance England: "If usury then was responsible for this social disintegration and the misery it entailed, one can easily see why . . . Timon [was] so sympathetic to an Elizabethan audience, which saw itself, like [him], in the clutches of griping creditors" (Draper 26–27).

One hope seems to reside in those who can recognize the necessity of human interrelation and interdependence, those who believe in enduring values and have the ability to discern them truly. Flavius, as steward and faithful servant, epitomizes the hope of man in *Timon of Athens*. From the beginning he understands prudent economic management, loves Timon because of his inner values rather than his external shows of wealth, and stands by his master in the direst circumstances. Like Bassanio, he is eventually rewarded materially for his knowledge of and participation in "natural" economics.

Critics may have trouble with the structure and characters in this play if they give short shrift to its economic emphasis. Its minimal character development sets the play firmly in the tradition of the moral interlude, which concerned itself with a similar nexus between the worldly and the spiritual (Collins 97). The confused generic structure of the play also reflects its economic theme. While the subject of money in relation to love and friendship usually lies within the province of comedy, Shakespeare found the threats of traditional values growing too menacing to resolve as easily as in *The Comedy of Errors*. The intervening fifteen years witnessed an expanded acceptance of mercantilism and the money ethic. Even though Timon's world initially is the world of comedy, economic threats to this social stability drive the play toward tragedy. The work eventually falls short of true tragedy, however, for Timon never reaches a proper balance in reconciling the two realms of bonds. While *The Merchant of Venice*, written eleven years earlier, at least made a pro forma attempt at the standard comedic ending, by 1607 even this was no longer possible. Structurally *Timon of Athens* demonstrates the effect of the new mercantilism on society and decries its moral uncertainties in unresolved tragedy.

NOTES

1. This distinction may derive from Aristotle's original separation of household economy (as allocation for the primary needs of life) from chrematistics (acquisition for its own sake). See *Politics*, Bk. I, Ch. 9.

2. The interest in how to distinguish between intrinsic and exchange value was, with usury, one of the paramount concerns of late medieval and Renaissance "economists." See Bowley 64–90.

3. The Renaissance in England was a time of confused economic transition. While mercantilism and its ethics, defined then as "commerce," "merchandising," and "dedication to money as the sole embodiment of wealth" (*Oxford English Dictionary*), constituted more often than not one's daily activities, the traditional morality governing socioeconomic transactions was anachronistic and inadequate. These moral precepts were typically derived from medieval church doctrine and the Schoolmen, passed on to the Renaissance in morality plays and moral interludes. The economically reactionary *Liberalitie and Prodigalitie*, for example, was performed before the queen in 1603. The Renaissance witnessed a proliferation of sophisticated economic machinery, like bills of exchange, insurance, investment in mercantile and exploratory ventures, and representative currency. These developments, coupled with a distrust of the currency stimulated in part by the coinage debasements of the mid-sixteenth century in England, resulted in an economic ethical confusion caused by a divergence between economic theory and practice. Much of Renaissance drama wrestles with questions of a changing system of economic morality and human value. A *bond* became confusingly equivocal in actual as well as lexical terms. See Fischer, *Econolingua* 23–27.

4. For a similar suggestion, linking words and coins, see Sigurd Burckhardt 23, 232; Marc Shell, *Economy* 3, "Verbal Usury" 66, 71; and Fischer, " 'He means' " 150–53.

5. According to Aristotle, money was barren and could not propagate; this concept was commonly expressed in the truism "Nothing comes of nothing." Timon plays on the proverb by inverting it.

REFERENCES

Aristotle. *Politics and Economics*. Trans. Edward Walford. London: Henry C. Bohn, 1853.

Bowley, Marian. *Studies in the History of Economic Theory before 1870*. London: Macmillan, 1973.

Burckhardt, Sigurd. "*The Merchant of Venice*: The Gentle Bond." *English Literary History* 29 (1962): 239–62.

Burke, Kenneth. *Language as Symbolic Action*. Berkeley: University of California Press, 1966.

Campbell, O. J. *Shakespeare's Satire*. London: Oxford University Press, 1943.

Collins, A. S. "*Timon of Athens*: A Reconsideration." *Review of English Studies* 22 (1946): 105.

Draper, John W. "The Theme of 'Timon of Athens.' " *Modern Language Review* 29 (1934): 26–27.

Ellis-Fermor, U. M. *The Jacobean Drama*. London: Methuen, 1936.

Fischer, Sandra K. *Econolingua: A Glossary of Coins and Economic Language in Renaissance Drama*. Newark, Del.: University of Delaware Press, 1985.

————. " 'He Means to Pay': Value and Metaphor in the Lancastrian Tetralogy." *Shakespeare Quarterly* 40 (1989): 149–64.

Knight, G. Wilson. *Christ and Nietzsche*. 1948; reprinted n.p.: Folcroft Press, 1970.

Marx, Karl. *Selected Writings*. Oxford: Oxford University Press, 1977.

Maxwell, J. C. " 'Timon of Athens.' " *Scrutiny* 15 (1947–48): 201.

Pearlman, E. "Shakespeare, Freud, and the Two Usuries, or, Money's a Meddler." *English Language Review* 2 (1972): 217.

Pettet, E. C. "*Timon of Athens*: The Disruption of Feudal Morality." *Review of English Studies* 23 (1947): 330–35.

Shakespeare, William. *Complete Works*. Boston: Houghton Mifflin, 1965.

Shell, Marc. *The Economy of Literature*. Berkeley: University of California Press, 1978.

————. "The Wether and the Ewe: Verbal Usury in *The Merchant of Venice*." *Kenyon Review* 1, 4 (1979): 66, 71.

18

The Fusion of "Social Eminence with Divine Eminence": George Herbert and the King's Stamp

Jeffrey Powers-Beck

In 1953 Kenneth Burke put a prescient question to critics of devotional poetry. "Where matters of 'reverence' are concerned," he asked, "should we not consider such possibilities of fusing social eminence with divine eminence as would be indicated by the similarity between 'My Lord' and 'milord'?" (222). Recently, in articles and in his book *Prayer and Power*, Michael Schoenfeldt has eagerly answered Burke's challenge and found the fusion of "social eminence with divine eminence" in George Herbert's devotional practices (22). This fusion mingles diction and telescopes images from courtly and churchly realms. One such dual image, circulated by Dekker and Donne, as well as by Herbert, is that of the King's stamp. In Dekker's *Northward Ho*, his witty Doll quips: "Siluer is the Kings stampe, man Gods stampe, and a woman is mans stampe" (419). In preaching on Christ's command to give God and Caesar their due, Lancelot Andrewes also fused together the royal and the divine images on the coin: "Here is a systasie, a consistence, they will stand together well—both they and their duties—as close as one verse, one breath, one period can join them" (130). Such fusions of theology and politics (and sexuality, in Dekker's case) invite cultural criticism. So also do the fused images of Herbert's "Avarice," a sonnet that brings together the kingdoms of Christ and currency in a story of a noble's squandered authority. The sonnet dramatizes coining as a parody of redemption, while it ponders the origins of human, especially monetary, value.

Although Irving Blum has treated "Avarice" as part of the poet's teeming and paradoxical business imagery, it has long been one of the most slighted lyrics in *The Temple* (153–54). John Ottenhof calls it "conventionally impersonal" and classes it as one of "Herbert's least interesting sonnets" (3). Herbert's major critics (i.e., Martz, Summers, Lewalski, Strier, et al.) either do not discuss it or they politely disparage it. Helen Vendler finds the poem dry and incomplete, ending in a premature note of moral censure: "There is no breath of temptation in the poem, nothing to show that Herbert himself ever thought money powerful or attractive" (181). Unlike the passionate and graceful poem Vendler imagines, "Avarice" is speculative in the mythohistorical manner of Herbert's "Church Militant," and it ends with a blunt couplet. Even admitting these bases for Vendler's criticism, however, I hope to show the real power of money in the poem, which is not in the metal, so to speak, but in the stamp.

Depicting avarice as a temptational aura that surrounds a glistening hoard, as in the discovery scene of *The Jew of Malta* or the Mammon episode of *The Faerie Queene*, may be psychologically engrossing, but it is not the only way to imagine monetary power. Herbert chooses to convey that power in the paradoxical image of an ennobling and disgracing, incarnating and desecrating, stamp. The "stamp and seal" that mingles divine power and kingly authority in the poem leaves a deep impression. To resume the poem briefly, "Avarice" tells the story of a heavenly king's image, once stamped upon the soul, then transferred to molten metal. This transfer of human dignity to coins degrades humans to the status of dross and procures for personified money a mock kingdom. With the redemption of money comes the fall of humankind. I shall treat the poem in detail, after examining its sources in royalist myths and inquiries about the origins of value in money.

The censure of gold mining in "Avarice" derives in part from classical and biblical sources—from the gospels, from St. Paul, from Lucretius, and from Pliny, who in Book XXXIII of his *Natural History* might have suggested the sonnet's closing image of greedy gold diggers falling into their own mines. Herbert adds to such classical sources, however, an intriguing idea found in patristic writings, Donne's poetry, and Renaissance tracts— the idea that the king's stamp confers value upon some otherwise valueless metal. This paradox of this stamp, which produces and disperses kingly power, makes "Avarice" a dour critique of secular history. While the poem supposes an exalted view of the king's authority to create and confer value, it presents human history as an erosion of value and a diminishment of royal presence. This diminishment of presence threatens both king and priest alike, undermining their sovereign order with a new commercial and political order. Among Herbert's poems, only the ecclesiastical history of "The Church Militant" and the political history of the "Triumphus Mortis" rival the sonnet in bleakness.

The notion that the king's stamp imparts value to a worthless or nominally valuable lump of metal is a common Renaissance hyperbole. Winfried Schleiner and John Carey have treated the images of God's stamp on human souls as allusions to patristic ideas, current in the Renaissance, about the soul and the sacraments. On the other hand, the historian Max Beer attributes this commonplace of the king's stamp to the "exalted position of kingship" in the late Renaissance, and the demands implicit in the transition from a feudal to a mercantile economy (63). To some degree, those demands were to increase the movement of capital by giving national currency greater prestige, making wealth more fluid, and money, as distinct from bullion, more instrumental (Foucault 174). "The King," says Beer, "set his effigy on it [i.e., money]. He gave it valuation, which was thought to be 'its spirit that giveth life' " (63). The Crown's insistence upon the right to give coins "valuation" (i.e., denomination of value) and, by a hyperbolic leap, "value," was in the end patrimonial, a means of regulating trade resisted by a rising class of merchants.

The Frenchman Scipion de Gramont phrased the idea most succinctly: "Money does not draw its value from the material of which it is composed, but rather from its form, which is the image or mark of the Prince" (quoted in Foucault 175–76). Similarly, John Donne asserts this power of the king's stamp baldly in his "Elegy X": "As kings do coins, to which their stamps impart / The value" (106; 11. 4–5), and in his description of Elizabeth Drury's value-creating acts of pardon in the "Second Anniversary": "She coined, in this, that her impressions gave / To all our actions all the worth they have" (297; 11. 369–70).

This motif of Donne's poetry owes not only to a Thomistic philosophy of the soul, as Carey maintains, or to patristic metaphors for salvation history, as Schleiner interprets, but also to the mythology of Stuart absolutism. King James himself regarded the minting of coins as "one of the marks of the Prince his dignity and Soveraignty" (226). In fact, approaching Herbert's metaphors closely, the king claimed that he could determine the value of money much as he determined the value of men. In his "cristal mirror" speech to Parliament in 1610, James asserted the king's godlike power of creating and conferring value:

God hath power to create, or destroy, make, or unmake . . . : To raise low things, and to make high things low at his pleasure, and to God are both soule and body due. And the like power have Kings. . . . They have power to exalt low things, and abase high things . . . and to cry up, or downe any of their subjects, as they do their money. (307–8)

Here, theology fuses with politics, and patronage with economics. Courtiers and members of Parliament could not have ignored James' implicit threat in comparing patronage to the valuation of coins. In making both men and coins, the king claimed an absolute right.

With increases in trade and in royal requests for supply from Parliament, the Stuarts found absolutist monetary theories harder to maintain. Even the assay master of King James' mint, Gerard de Malynes, admitted that international bullion trade "over-ruleth" the king's valuation of coins (81). Any metaphysical claim the king might make for the creation of value would be suspected by merchants. In his essay "Donne and Coins" Carey considers "intriguingly questionable" the poet's repeated references to the king's stamp as conferring value (158). All too obviously, the frequent clipping of coins in England before the advent of milled edges testified to the real value of the bullion (Carey 167). No merchant of the time could neglect the varying bullion contents in the same coins. Many were tempted to trade with the lighter pieces and to save the heavier ones for melting into plate. And as the economist Marian Bowley observes, the commonsense notion that "utility on the one hand, scarcity on the other" determined value was widespread in the seventeenth century and earlier (65).

Still, the continued acceptance of clipped coins in commerce and the greater utility of coins than bullion argued that the king's stamp transferred to minted bullion at least some extrinsic value (Appleby 228–31). The origins of the value of money—whether a coin derives its value intrinsically, or from popularly valuable metals, from its instrumentality in exchange, or from some combination of factors—were disputed in a number of Renaissance works. For example, in *A Discourse of the Commonweal of the Realm of England*, written in 1549 and printed in 1581, a doctor named Pandotheus, a nameless knight, and sundry others discuss coinage and Britain's economic problems. Opposing the learned doctor, the knight affirms, by his skepticism toward bullion, the value-conferring power of the king:

Forsooth, such a dullard am I indeed that cannot perceive what hindrance it should be to the realm to have this metal more than that for our coin, seeing the coin is but a token to go from man to man. And since it is stricken with the King's seal to be current, what makes it the matter what metal it be of, yea, though it were but leather or paper? (Dewar 69–70)

Though the knight makes no metaphysical claims about the king's stamp, his tokenist view of money recognizes the king's power of minting and securing, and thereby envaluing, the state currency.

Later, in the early 1620s, during a "great and generall Dampe and Deadnesse in all the Trades of the Kingdome," the monetary debate went on in earnest (Misselden 29). In his tract *Free Trade* (1622), the merchant Edward Misselden blamed England's economic problems on unprofitable trade and bad coins, contradicting the view of Gerard de Malynes. As assay master of the mint, de Malynes took a different view of the economic crisis and of money itself. In *The Maintenance of Free Trade* (1622), de Malynes states that the weight and fineness of bullion constitute the intrinsic and essential value of coins. That value is determined in two disturbingly contrary ways: "the one by the Publicke Authority of Kings and Princes, the other by the Merchants in the course of exchange, and this is Praedominant and over-ruleth the Kings Valuation" (de Malynes 81). In effect, de Malynes sensed the greater power of the market in determining value, but, unlike Misselden, he still emphasized the king's role in deciding monetary policy. In a limited way, de Malynes still claimed that it was king's "Valuation . . . which giveth life" to trade. Although de Malynes did not assume the king's ability to create value *ex nihilo*, he still, through the myth of the live-giving stamp, attributed a divine regulatory power to the king.

This attitude—that the monarch knew best the value of money—was also shared by Queen Elizabeth's secretary of state Sir Thomas Smith. In *De Republica Anglorum*, Smith makes the double-edged observation that princes enjoy an absolute right in denominating coins, but they also suffer from attempts to manipulate the national currency. "The mony," says Smith,

is always stamped with the princes image and title. The forme, fashion, maner, weight, finenesse, and basenesse thereof, is at the discretion of the prince. For whom should the people trust more in that matter than their prince, seeing the coine is only to certifie the goodness of the metall and the weight, which is affirmed by the princes image and marke? But if the prince will deceaue them and give them copper for siluer or golde . . . , he is deceaved himselfe, as well as he doth go about to deceaue his subjectes. (45)

While Smith esteemed the prince's image as an ensuring mark of sovereign authority, he realized pragmatically that princes took considerable risks in abusing their national currency systems. If the king debased the coinage in order to fill his treasury, he faced both political and commercial revenge. The market would take its revenge by inflation, and, even barring rebellion, the impoverished citizens would be little able to pay future subsidies to the king. This two-sided realization about the power of the king's stamp, in fact, very much resembles the doubleness of Herbert's "Avarice," which extols a divine stamp, but deplores a base coinage.

Through this rehearsal of sources and history, I might seem to have strayed a long way from Herbert's *The Temple*. Yet, the poem "Avarice" insistently combines material and theological concerns. The speaker's question in the second line of the poem, "Whence com'st thou, that thou art so fresh and fine?" puns on the numismatic meanings of "fresh and fine," that is, freshly minted and pure of alloy. He asks not only where money has come from—that is, the mine and the mint—but also why it is accorded such value. While Herbert probably knew nothing of the tract wars over monetary policies, he certainly knew the commonplace of the king's stamp and associated it with the *Imago Dei*, the image of God in human beings. In "The Church-porch," he warns the young gallant: "Wine above all things doth Gods and stamp deface" (1. 48); and he advises his readers to give alms: "Man is Gods image; but a poore man is / Christs stamp to boot: both images regard. / God reckons for him, counts the favour his" (11. 379–81). In other words, God considers alms as gifts to himself, counting the "favour" or face of the poor to be his own, while counting the "favour" of the king's face on the coin to the credit of the almsgiver.

In "Avarice," Herbert treats the question of money's source of value by combining a mock redemption with a fall from grace:

> Money, thou bane of blisse, & sourse of wo,
> > Whence com'st thou, that thou art so fresh and fine?
> > I know thy parentage is base and low:
> Man found thee poore and dirtie in a mine.
>
> Surely thou didst so little contribute
> > To this great kingdome, which thou now hast got,
> > That he was fain, when thou wert destitute,
> To digge thee out of thy dark cave and grot:
>
> Then forcing thee, by fire he made thee bright:
> > Nay, thou hast got the face of man; for we
> > Have with our stamp and seal transferr'd our right:
> Thou art the man, and man but drosse to thee.
>
> > Man calleth thee his wealth, who made thee rich;
> > And while he digs out thee, falls in the ditch. (93)

The opening paradoxes of "Avarice" set the dryly mocking tone of the poem and the central method of inversion: wealth is dross, getting is losing, and redeeming is enslaving. The repeated addresses to personified money as "thou" and "thee" and the impugning of money's birth expose the pretensions of fluid wealth toward kingly authority.

In regard to the origins of money's value, the speaker rejects the intrinsic value of rare metals with aristocratic disdain. The stuff of wealth is "base and low," crude and ill-born, found "poore and dirtie" in a mine. In requesting parliamentary supply to King James in 1610, Robert Cecil, the lord treasurer and earl of Salisbury, personified money similarly as "a base creature whearof never any wise man spake without contempt" (Gardiner 2). The implication was that no obedient subject would withhold such dross from his Majesty. This "base creature" of money appears "fresh and fine" in Herbert's poem only because of the value accorded it by nobility. The speaker or "we" of the poem, like the James of the "cristal mirror" speech, can create and value money at will. As Herbert describes it, the mining, forging, refining, and, most crucially, the stamping of metals give them their value as coins. All the noble qualities of coins—fineness, freshness, brightness, and their stamped faces—derive either from human industry ("Then forcing thee, by fire he made thee bright") or from a transfer of authority.

Clearly, the fateful act that fully effects the transfer of authority is the stamp: "Nay, thou hast got the face of man; for we / Have with our stamp and seal transferr'd our right" (11. 10–11). Here, Herbert combines the imagery of minted coins and signet rings to describe the loss of power. The idea of nobility itself being marked by a stamp or *charactere indelible* is hardly novel: Shakespeare's nobles speak scornfully of those who seek to "be honorable / Without the stamp of merit" (*MV* 11. 9.38–39), and they warn those young men against presumption whose "fire-new stamp of honor is scarce current" (*R3* I. 3. 255). In "Avarice," the loss of that stamp forfeits not only an individual's title to nobility, but also the human title of kingship over the earth. The "we" and "our" of lines 10 and 11 refer to a right that is both communal and kingly. By the stamp, money takes over "this great kingdom," to which it brings little tribute or kingly wealth itself ("thou didst so little *contribute*," 1.5).

Perhaps most troubling to the speaker is the human parody of redemption that coining enacts. As Schleiner has illustrated amply, a long line of writers use the image of the stamp or seal to represent the crucial events of Christian salvation history. Schleiner summarizes the central tropes:

First, in his creation in God's image, man received a seal that was impressed upon him by the divine Logos. . . . Second, through the Fall the divine image in man was defaced, and it became necessary therefore to restamp the image. The possibility of restamping was opened by the Incarnation of the archetypal Logos. Thus . . . man may receive the renewal of the image. (109)

In the bleak world of "Avarice," however, the final possibility of the restamping of the Logos does not appear. In fact, the loss of the divine stamp comes through the imposition of the human stamp on gold.

Specifically, the metal buried in a "deep cave and grot" recalls Christ's burial in a cave before the Resurrection and the filth of sin cleansed in baptism. Yet, in this poem there is only ironic resurrection and redemption. The transfer of the human face to the coin parodies God's creation of Adam in his image and Christ's incarnation in human flesh. In line 12, the speaker hails the money-king bitterly: "Thou art the man, the man but drosse to thee." So, he sardonically admits that money is the man— that is, money enjoys a noble stature—and he echoes Pilate's *Ecce Homo* ("Behold the Man") to Christ in John 19:5. By redeeming gold and silver, humankind loses its kingdom, becoming dross itself and sacrificing its higher aspirations.

If the sonnet progresses bitterly, nothing in the couplet attenuates the bleakness. The poet reinforces the message by repeating the inversions of getting and losing. The monosyllables and the emphasis on "thee" make the lines strident and lecturing; and the rhythmic stumbling of the final syllables mimics a fall. The couplet recalls Christ's parable of the blind falling into the ditch in Matthew 15:14 and may also allude to Pliny's condemnation of gold mining: "We trace out all the fibres of the earth, and live above the hollows we have made in her, marvelling that occasionally she gapes open" (3). Thus, the poem ends with a deep pessimism about the rise of material culture from the earliest times. The fall of the poem comes not merely from mining metals but from endowing them with human dignity, transposing the image of God in man to a coin for narcissistic gratification.

While the poet's perspective on avarice is implicitly Christian, it is also implicitly aristocratic. The poem presumes distinctions between God and man, noble and commoner, which money disrupts in its circulation through the social order. Furthermore, the increase in affluence seems not only to secularize society but also to diminish the king's prerogatives. In *The Economy of Literature*, Marc Shell makes the fascinating argument that the mass minting of coins "destroyed the aura of individual objects and encouraged a sense of the universal equality of things" (86). This concept, based on a reading of Walter Benjamin's critique of mimesis, views the rise of coinage and commerce as replacing cult value with exhibition value: "Instead of being based on ritual, [art began] to be based on another practice—politics" (quoted in Shell 87). Hence, it may be that Herbert's art, which is imbued with ritual and assumes the numinous presence of both God and king, finds the secularizing influence of money so disturbing. Without the myth of the king's stamp, the face on the coin mocks and undermines the cultic authority of king, poet-divine, and divine king.

Shell's analysis also helps explain the endurance of the myth of the king's stamp—why King James, Donne, and Herbert would assume the king's conferring of value upon bullion, and why de Malynes would honor the king's power to "give life" to trade through denominations and exchange rates. The myth of the king's stamp enabled his Majesty to maintain some cultic presence while exercising political control over the national wealth. When the king's effigy stands on the coin as God's image in the nation, guaranteeing and regulating commerce, aristocratic prerogatives may endure. When coins are valued primarily for their bullion, as determined by the clipping and culling merchants, or when coins are seen as passive indicators of the merchant's commodities, the "stamp of nobility" loses both cultic and political value. Ironically, the double-sided stamp of Herbert's poem reinforces the power of the king's image, while it argues against the power given to fluid wealth. The metal is dross, but the stamp is truly noble, theologically and politically powerful.

Perhaps with no little coincidence, when Herbert's spiritual confrere Nicholas Ferrar remembered his friend's saintly life and death, he also referred to the myth of the king's stamp. In commemorating the rebuilding of Leighton Ecclesia and recalling Herbert's judgment, "It is a good work . . . if it be sprinkled wth the bloud of Christ," Ferrar compared natural goodness unsprinkled by Christ's blood to a piece of brass unstamped by the king. In this rather legalistic metaphor, Ferrar's speaker, the "Learner," says of the true Christian:

And that, wch would comport it [Christ's blood] in its own Nature, if it want the Effectual application thereof, is but like brasse wthout the Princes stamp. which howeuer it be of the same mettall, weight & Forme, y^t the Coine it self is, yet is it no waies currant, nor available for the purchase of any good & needful Commodities. (Ray 7)

Here, the speaker uses "comport" in the obsolete sense of "bear, endure, or allow." The willing nature requires a transforming act. This transforming "Effectual application" of Christ's blood involves both personal devotion and priestly mediation. Serving as God's (and the king's) agent, the priest applies the seal of Christ's blood upon his parishioners in the sacrament of baptism. That royal seal of baptism renders the Christian's soul to both God and the king.

In conclusion, let me reiterate that the deep impression of "our stamp and seal" upon Herbert links his religious life to his politics, and divine eminence to social eminence. To make this claim is not to doubt the sincerity of the poet's despising of greed or of his charity for the poor (as illustrated in Walton's life and in the *Country Parson*), but to construe their foundation in his vision of an aristocratic social order. While the absolutist state sometimes came into overt conflict with emergent commercialism, it also, as Perry Anderson points out, "accomplished certain partial functions in the primitive accumulation" of capital. The relationship between the dominant and emergent orders was never purely adversarial, since there was "always a potential field of compatibility at this stage between the nature and programme of the Absolutist State and the operations of mercantile and manufacturing capital" (41). Characteristically, Herbert sometimes feared the political power of mercantile wealth, as in "Avarice," and at other times extolled trade "from sunne to sunne" as a proof of God's providence ("Providence," 1. 108). To analyze these manifold political implications of Herbert's devotional poetry need not detract from that poetry, as Schoenfeldt has demonstrated very ably (261). Such study should enrich the poetry by widening our purview of religious history to see the full sway of swords and scepters, and pounds and pence.

REFERENCES

Anderson, Perry. *Lineages of the Absolute State*. London: Verso, 1979.

Andrewes, Lancelot. *Ninety-Six Sermons*. Vol. 5. Oxford: John Henry Parker, 1843.

Appleby, Joyce Oldham. *Economic Thought and Ideology in Seventeenth-Century England*. Princeton: Princeton University Press, 1978.

Beer, Max. *Early British Economics from the XIIIth to the Middle of the XVIIIth Century*. London: George Allen & Unwin, 1938.

Blum, Irving D. "The Paradox of Money Imagery in English Renaissance Poetry." *Studies in the Renaissance* 8 (1961): 144–54.

Bowley, Marion. *Studies in the History of Economic Theory before 1870*. London: Macmillan, 1973.

Burke, Kenneth. "On Covery, Re- and Dis-." *Accent* 13 (1953): 218–26. Rev. of Rosemund Tuve's *A Reading of George Herbert*.

Carey, John. "Donne and Coins." *In English Renaissance Studies Presented to Dame Helen Gardner*. Oxford: Oxford University Press, 1980. 151–63.

Dekker, Thomas. *The Dramatic Works*. Ed. by Fredson Bowers. Vol. 2. Cambridge: Cambridge University Press, 1965.

Dewar, Mary, ed. *A Discourse of the Commonweal of This Realm of England*. Charlottesville: University Press of Virginia, 1969.

Donne, John. *The Complete English Poems*. Ed. by A. J. Smith. London: Penguin, 1986.

Foucault, Michel. *The Order of Things*. Trans. of *Les Mots et les Choses*. New York: Random House, 1970.

Gardiner, S. R., ed. *Parliamentary Debates in 1610*. Camden Society Publications 81. London: Nichols and Sons, 1862.

Herbert, George. *The English Poems*. Ed. C. A. Patrides. London: J. M. Dent & Sons, 1974.

James I. *The Political Works of James I*. Cambridge: Harvard University Press, 1918.

Malynes, Gerard de. *The Maintenance of Free Trade*. London: 1622.

Misselden, Edward. *Free Trade*. London: 1622. New York: Augustus Kelley, 1971.

Ottenhof, John H. "Herbert's Sonnets." *George Herbert Journal* 2.2 (1979): 1–14.

Pliny. *Natural History, Libri XXXIII–XXXV*. Trans. H. Rackham. Vol. 9. 10 vols. Loeb Library. London: William Heinemann, 1952.

Ray, Robert H. *The Herbert Allusion Book*. *Studies in Philology* 83 (Fall 1986; Special Edition).

Schleiner, Winfried. *The Imagery of John Donne's Sermons*. Providence R.I.: Brown University Press, 1970.

Schoenfeldt, Michael. *Prayer and Power: George Herbert and Renaissance Courtship*. Chicago: University of Chicago Press, 1991.

Shakespeare, William. *The Riverside Shakespeare*. Ed. G. Blakemore Evans. Boston: Houghton Mifflin, 1972.

Shell, Marc. *The Economy of Literature*. Baltimore: Johns Hopkins University Press, 1978.

Smith, Sir Thomas. *De Republica Anglorum*. London: Henrie Midleton, 1583.

Vendler, Helen. *The Poetry of George Herbert*. Cambridge: Harvard University Press, 1975.

19

Robinson Crusoe and South Sea Trade, 1710–1720

LEE MORRISSEY

Most Defoe scholarship has neglected, on the one hand, the particular economic arguments Defoe made throughout his career, and on the other hand, any connections between these arguments in the pamphlets and those dramatized in the novels. Critics and editors have taken *Robinson Crusoe* out of its very specific historical, political, and economic context, frequently reshaping the "meaning" of the story in supposedly universal terms. However, despite what some recent critics might contend, Defoe himself admitted that "writing on Trade was the whore I really doated upon" (quoted in Novak, *Economics* vii).

It is no mere coincidence that Defoe should write a novel with a protagonist who proves that a generous existence can be carved from the land off the coast of northern South America. At that time, Chile, Argentina, and Peru were collectively referred to as "the South Seas," and, between 1711 and 1720, they were the focus of an influential plan to expand British commerce. For, in 1711, Defoe's employer, Robert Harley, unveiled the South Sea Company, a plan, which, nine years later, would be known as the South Sea Bubble.

Between 1710 and 1720, various "projectors," Defoe being one of them, argued over the issue of a trade to the South Seas. In a way, because the South Seas were a *tabula rasa* upon which British pamphleteers could, on behalf of City insiders, write their colonial aspirations, these pamphlets are a map of British international desire in the early eighteenth century. Since the South Sea Company never fulfilled the promise made by its original proponents, these political pamphlets remain a kind of a fiction, a simulacrum—"the map that precedes the territory . . . the map that engenders the territory" (Baudrillard *Simulations* 2).

Most writing directly concerned with the South Sea happened in two distinct flurries: 1711–14, and 1719–22. During the first period, pamphlet titles such as *A Letter on Settling a Trade* (1711) and *Considerable Advantage of a South Sea Trade* (1713) indicate the City's optimism for a South Sea trade. In the later years, pamphlet titles such as *An Argument to Show the Disadvantage . . . from Obliging the South Sea Company* (1720), indicate the pamphleteers' sense that the South Sea Company was squandering the trade. In fact, one pamphlet even commented on the difference between that decade's two kinds of South Sea Companies: *A True State of the South Sea Scheme as It Was First Formed . . . with the Several Alterations Made in It* (1722).

In many ways, *Robinson Crusoe* is a liminal, or threshold work: between the Company's formation in 1711 and its failure in 1720, between Defoe's specific arguments for a South Sea trade and his general arguments for any foreign trade, and between a pamphlet's relatively small London audience and a novel's increasingly enfranchised national audience. I would argue that, by dramatizing the economic possibilities of a South Seas trade, *Robinson Crusoe* falls between the novel and the pamphlet form. That is, in the same way that the South Sea pamphlets partake of the "fictional," so too we might say that Defoe's *Robinson Crusoe* partakes of the "factual," in this case, the potential South Seas trade.

In an argument concerning the relationship between the South Sea Bubble and Defoe's *Journal of the Plague Year* (1722), Pat Rogers states, "I do not claim that Defoe was 'really' writing about the South Sea episode when he composed the *Journal*. My contention is that some of the deeper imaginative currents of the book must have been set in motion by his recent experience in witnessing—and chronicling for the press— the traumas of the Bubble year" (164–65).

In this chapter, I suggest that *Robinson Crusoe*'s "deeper imaginative currents" represent, in part, Defoe's response to "his recent experience in witnessing" the unraveling of the South Sea trade, an unraveling which may have led to the South Sea Bubble. *Robinson Crusoe*, published three years before *A Journal of the Plague Year*, was also published about a year before the South Sea Bubble. In other words, *Robinson Crusoe*, unlike the *Journal*, might imaginatively predict—or "project"—a possible solution to the oncoming financial collapse.

Of course, *Robinson Crusoe* comes late in the decade. Before getting to how its argument fits there, let's see how the South Sea Company developed and progressed. Initially, Robert Harley, a Tory, intended it as a way to retire early eighteenth-century British war debt which, after 1707, placed at least 30 percent of the state's income into debt service. In the spring of 1711, Harley proposed a South Seas Company in which "£9 million worth of unfunded government securities . . . be exchanged . . . for shares at par in a joint stock company to be set up . . . to carry on the sole trade and traffick . . . into . . . and from the Kingdoms, Lands etc. of [South] America" (Carswell 54). Harley does not say—for it was implicitly understood—that besides selling British commodities for South American gold, the South Sea Company would also organize a South American trade in slaves, a trade which required the Spanish Asiento.

The Company responded quickly to capitalize on their new-found cartel, and apparently the South Sea Company began as an astounding success (in its own terms). According to the *The Design and Advantage of a Trade to the South Seas*, "in the few days the books were open, which did not exceed 3 weeks, near four millions were subscribed" (36). Bolingbroke wrote that "Mr. Harley's project for providing a fund of interest for the national debts, is agreed to with great applause" (Biddle 190). Lady Dupplin wrote home to her aunt that it was "a glorious thing" (Carswell 53). Defoe, writing in *The Review* in October 1711, points out that "the plain English of this is, that had your South Sea Trade been entered upon seven years ago, it had rendered you 'ere now compleat victors over the French" (no. 86, 347).

In July 1713, the South Sea Company subcontracted with the Royal African Company to ship "healthful, sound negroes of all sizes, in such conditions as to be able to go over the ship's side" (Carswell 65). By the end of the year, three ships had sailed with 1,230 slaves. In 1714, they sent seven more ships with 2,680 people, thirteen in 1716, twenty in 1717 and twelve in 1718, leaving a total of 13,000 Africans, a number which averages 4,333 a year, or just a few hundred short of the Asiento's annual allowance of 4,800.

During 1714, however, Spanish colonial administrators in South America refused to recognize Madrid's understanding of the Asiento. The difficulties that the South Sea Company encountered highlighted a basic problem: Spanish settlement and administration. The very definition of *South Seas* implies the circumstances under which it was first seen by a European: "Since [Balboa, in 1513] viewed it looking southwards from the isthmus, he named it the South Seas" (Williamson 145). Defoe's own definition, first given in *The Review* in 1711, practically bristles with resentment toward that etymology: "this is the coast which we very improperly call the South Seas" (170).

No argument concerning South Sea trade could get around the fact of Spanish presence there. In this way, the efforts of the South Sea Company are like those of Robinson Crusoe, who at one point decided to escape his island by hewing a canoe from a fallen tree. Cutting down an appropriate tree took twenty days, removing branches and twigs took fourteen days, shaping the tree into a hull took one month, while clearing out its inside took another three months. When he finished all this work, Crusoe had, stranded one hundred yards uphill from water, a canoe big enough for twenty-six men. In order to get this massive boat to the water, Crusoe began to dig a canal. Eventually he abandoned the attempt when he realized that digging a canal to the requisite depth of twenty feet would take him twelve years. Reflecting on his failed project, Crusoe wrote, "my thoughts were so intent upon my voyage over the sea in it, that I never once consider'd how I should get it off the land" (*Robinson Crusoe* 93).

The South Sea Company, with its thoughts more on getting across the sea than on getting off the ground, never fully implemented a satisfactory administration committed to working with, or, as the case may be, against the Spanish. As a consequence, there is a great difference between the South Sea trade as it was proposed from 1711 to 1714, and the operations of the South Sea Company before its fall in 1720. Or, as Trevelyan says, "the South Sea company was not in 1711 the wild cat scheme it had become by 1720" (123).

In 1714, the same year that colonial administrators contested the Asiento, the South Sea Company's status was further complicated, this time by governmental corruption and scandal. Rumors suggested that the queen would be keeping 25 percent of the South Sea Company profits, and that Bolingbroke had already been skimming 7.5 percent for his "financial advisor." "When all this was discussed at a General Court of proprietors on 24 February 1714 nearly a third of the 1,200 present were against accepting the Asiento at all . . . and the Government had to withdraw [its claims to the profits]. . . . The atmosphere was thoroughly poisoned." Before an investigation could be pursued, "the Queen intervened . . . [and] renounced her share of the Asiento contract, turning it over to the South Sea Company; early in July . . . she prorogued Parliament" (Carswell 67).

In the end, however, the home offices thought that South American administrative obstructions precluded the South Sea Company's pursuing a profitable trade there. And so the Spanish question slowly forced the South Sea trade into the South Sea Bubble. After 1714, conventional wisdom had it that there could be no South Sea trade without a South Sea struggle. Britain did not tackle that perceived challenge, and the South Sea Company foundered, so to speak.

Like Robinson Crusoe, the South Sea Company became stranded somewhere between Britain and South America. Difficulties so reshaped the Company's objectives that the South Sea Company and the South Sea trade became separate entities. Despite real hardships inflicted by the short-lived trade, the trade and the Company are remembered as but two different kinds of paper ghosts, the former emphasizing commerce, the latter emphasizing finance. Like Crusoe, when he reflects upon his stranded canoe, the South Sea Company now "saw too late, the folly of beginning a work before we count the cost, and before we judge rightly of our own strength to go through with it" (*Robinson Crusoe* 94).

As it turned out, however, a book detailing M. Frézier's explorations

(1712–14) of South America's western coast, published in 1717 as *A Voyage to the South-Sea*, suggested that Spanish hegemony in South America was exaggerated—precisely the kind of information that a South Sea company, supposedly committed to a South Sea trade, would want their supporters to know. The English preface admits that "our people are very much unacquainted with those seas" (unnumbered preface).

For example, Frézier reports that at Lima "the walls of the city . . . [have] no one place broad enough to mount a cannon, which makes [him] believe, that they were built only to oppose any attempts of the *Indians*" (217, original emphasis). When he reviews the condition of Penco, Chile, he says that "at this time, there are no remains of any fort . . . [and] the cannon are in no better condition . . . [being] cast at Lima in 1618 and 1621" (54). The weaponry is nearly one hundred years old and cast to South American standards, not European ones. In the end, Frézier asserts that "this want of fortifications is not made good by men and able officers" (54).

To acquaint some portion of the British population with the South Seas, the South Sea Company translated this book into English and published it in England. Because the catalog issued for the sale of Defoe's library—*The Libraries of Daniel Defoe and Phillips Farewell*—is still extant, we know that Defoe owned a copy of Frézier's *A Voyage to the South-Sea*. Thus, we can conjecture that Defoe was familiar with 1717's revisionist understanding of Spanish colonial rule.

By 1717, after being turned away by Spaniards abroad and accepting graft money at home, those in the South Sea Company still interested in a South Sea trade needed to reclaim public confidence. By 1717, Daniel Defoe, having devoted his last issues of the *Review* in 1711, along with several pamphlets in 1712 and 1713 to a South Seas trade, had a commitment to reviving a potential vehicle for expanded British trade. As Pat Rogers says, "everyone agrees that Defoe had a life long concern with the threat of financial disaster" (159).

In 1719, only two years after the South Sea Company reprinted Frézier's *A Voyage to the South Seas*, Defoe published *Robinson Crusoe*. In fact, on 7 February 1719, Defoe's *The Weekly Journal* advised readers to "expect . . . a most flaming Proposal from the South Sea Company . . . [for] the establishing a Factory and Settlement [in the South Seas]" (quoted in Novak *Realism* 26). A few weeks later, in April 1719, Defoe published *Robinson Crusoe*. Perhaps that novel is the "flaming Proposal." In this way, *Robinson Crusoe* could represent a (desperate? last?) pamphlet on behalf of a South Sea trade, written in the light of Frézier's information, and meant to stave off the demise of the South Sea Company.

Crusoe dramatizes the possibility of a South Sea trade regardless of the fate of the South Sea Company: a model small businessman investing his time in a South Sea trade, or, as Christopher Hill puts it, "an exemplar of the Protestant and bourgeois virtues" (7). For this reason, it is important that Defoe direct his arguments for a South Sea trade to a different audience. As Defoe says, the "preaching of sermons is speaking to a few of mankind, printing of books is talking to the whole world" (Defoe quoted in Hill 6).

Defoe's original, pamphleteering audience consisted principally of London insiders highly unlikely to become involved in the actual trade. In a way, these insiders resemble Robinson Crusoe's father, whose reminders about "the middle station of life" would have prohibited Crusoe's entrepreneurial initiative. That is, the pamphleteering audience—City insiders—are, like the father against whom Crusoe rebels, "in easy circumstances sliding gently through the world" (*Robinson Crusoe* 6).

Although City insiders were probably unwilling to subject themselves to the vicissitudes of international trade, Defoe could expect a different attitude from those who might gain from the hard work a South Sea trade would require. Defoe mentions his fears of a French, Catholic "universal monarchy," and wonders "where [he] shall you find a man knowing in what we call Universal commerce?" (*General History* 13).

Robinson Crusoe *is* that man "knowing in Universal commerce." Thus, in *Robinson Crusoe* Defoe advances an argument similar to that found in the South Seas trade pamphlets. The "novel" form, which includes narrative and allusive elements of spiritual autobiography, could reach a different audience than the pamphlets, "familiarizing" them. That is, as Halley puts it in *A Voyage to the South Seas*, "your design must answer your expectation." In this, Defoe and Halley agree; fictional forms are so frequently conventional that a fictional argument intended for a large audience fulfills "expectations."

In terms of page length, plotting, and popularity, *Robinson Crusoe* and South Sea trade pamphlets are very different forms. As most people have read one version of these very similar arguments—*Crusoe*'s—and have not read the other one—the pamphleteer's—critics ought to concern themselves with the similarities between the two forms. Having suggested the contextual and historical similarities of *Crusoe*'s and the trade pamphlets' arguments, I submit that the important issue is not that Defoe could "transform" the South Seas pamphlets' issues into such a resounding commercial success, but rather, how and why.

REFERENCES

Anonymous. *An Argument to Shew the Disadvantage That Would Accrue to the Publick from Obliging the South Sea Company to Fix What Capital Stock They Will Give for the Annuities*. London, 1720.

————. *Considerable Advantage of a South Sea Trade to Our English Nation*. London, 1713.

————. *A Letter to a Member of Parliament on the Settling a Trade to the South Seas of America*. London, 1711.

————. *A True State of the South Sea Scheme As It Was First Formed, Etc. with the Several Alterations Made in It, before the Act of Parliament Passed. And an Examination of the Conduct of the Directors in the Execution of That Act; with an Enquiry into Some of the Causes of the Losses Which Have Ensued. As Also an Abstract of Several Clauses of the Acts of Parliament, Made against Those Directors, and the Grounds of Them; with Some Remarks on the Whole*. London, 1722.

Baudrillard, Jean. *Simulations*. New York: Semiotext(e), 1983.

Biddle, Sheila. *Bolingbroke and Harley*. New York: Knopf, 1974.

Carswell, John. *The South Sea Bubble*. Stanford, Calif.: Stanford University Press, 1960.

Defoe, Daniel. *A General History of Trade*. London, 1713.

————. *The Life and Strange Surprising Adventures of Robinson Crusoe of York, Mariner*. Ed. G. N. Pocock. London: Everyman, 1945.

————. *A Review of the State of the British Nation*. London, 1711.

————. *A True Account of the Design and Advantage of a Trade to the South Seas*. London, 1711.

Frézier, A. F. *A Voyage to the South-Sea, and along the Coasts of Chile and Peru, in the Years 1712, 1713, and 1714. Particularly Describing the Genius and Constitution of the Inhabitants, As Well Indians As Spaniards: Their Customs and Manners, Their Natural History, Mines, Commodities, Traffick with Europe, Etc.* London, 1717.

Hill, Christopher. "Robinson Crusoe." *History Workshop: A Journal of Socialist Historians*. 18 (1980) 6–24.

Novak, Maximillian. *Economics and the Fiction of Daniel Defoe*. Berkeley: University of California Press, 1962.

————. *Realism, Myth, and History in Defoe's Fiction*. Lincoln: University of Nebraska Press, 1983.

Rogers, Pat. *Eighteenth-Century Encounters: Studies in Literature and Society in the Age of Walpole*. Totowa, N.J.: Barnes & Noble, 1985.

Trevelyan, G. M. *England under Queen Anne: The Peace and the Protestant Succession*. London: Longmans, Green, 1934.

Williamson, James A. *The Ocean in English History*. Oxford: Oxford University Press, 1941.

Metrical Experimentation in Swift's *Wood's Halfpence Poems*

John Louis DiGaetani

Financial problems clouded much of Jonathan Swift's childhood. Since his father died when he was only two years old, his mother had to depend on the kindness and generosity of her relatives to support and educate her precocious son. As a result, Swift often was forced into the position of the poor relation, asking uncles and aunts for money for school and clothing (Forster 18–22, Van Doren 4). Such a pattern of want and humiliation generated in Swift a special sensitivity to money matters, the possibilities of exploitation through money matters, and the close connections between money and power.

Thus, when Sir William Wood, an English ironmonger, received a writ from the British government and its monarch, George I, allowing Wood to produce and spread into circulation some coin currency for the Irish population, those facts struck Jonathan Swift as suspect and ultimately reprehensible. Wood received his patent on 12 July 1722 and there was a general protest in Ireland (Murry 356). Swift felt that this was once again an example of the English exploiting the Irish—in this case by foisting a worthless currency on the victimized Irish. Biographers of Swift, however, disagree about whether Wood's halfpence currency would indeed have harmed Ireland, but in any case, the fight against this currency provided an early opportunity for an organized Irish effort to thwart an English monetary decree that failed to consult the Irish or the Irish Parliament about the matter. Irish feelings were never consulted in regard to Wood's currency—the decision was made unilaterally in London—and Swift felt that the effect on Ireland of this currency did not concern the English, though it would enrich Mr. Wood (Murry 356–59).

The occasion of Jonathan Swift's battle with William Wood over his worthless coinage resulted in the four justifiably famous *Drapier's Letters*, in which Swift uses the anonymous persona of a Dublin drapier, and these letters caused a successful boycott of the money in Ireland. This boycott also produced eleven poems by Swift, called as a group the *Wood's Halfpence Poems* and written in 1724 and 1725. The poems are propagandistic; they were intended to supplement the *Drapier's Letters* in urging the Irish people to resist the introduction of Wood's money. As a group, these poems are also very comic, abounding especially in puns on *wood*, though Swift didn't use puns often in his writings during this period. Too, the poems include praise for the archbishop of Dublin, several satires on Judge Whitshed (who was involved in the case), a mock epic of sorts, plus several epigrams. We are dealing, then, with a very mixed group of poems, and the variations appear not only in theme and form but also in meter. The subject matter for all these poems concerns people or incidents connected with the Wood's halfpence conflict, and Swift used both prose and poetry to fight the introduction of Wood's currency.

Swift's favorite meter was always the iambic tetrameter, and he uses it in this group, but he also experiments with a variety of meters and line lengths. Iambs, trochees, and anapests are tried here as well as pentameter, hexameter, tetrameter, and the fourteener. A close look at the metrics and line lengths of each of the *Wood's Halfpence Poems* discloses exactly where Swift was experimenting, how he manages each of the meters and line lengths, and for what effects. Such a study will hopefully provide an insight into Swift's complex use of metrics in these poems.

The first poem in the Wood group, "A Serious Poem upon William Wood," exemplifies an interesting variation of Swift's octosyllabic couplet:

> When Foes are o'ercome, we preserve them from Slaughter,
> To be Hewers of Wood and Drawers of Water,
> Now, although to Draw Water is not very good,
> Yet we all should Rejoyce to be Hewers of Wood.
> I own it hath often provok's me to Mutter,
> That, A Rogue so Obscure should make such a Clutter. (270)

Swift is using four beats in most of these lines, but he avoided the iamb in favor of the anapestic foot. The basic anapestic tetrameter couplet form of this poem is varied with an extra final syllable in lines 1, 2, 5, and 6, creating a feminine rhyme. Too, not all the opening feet in each of the lines are anapestic. "When Foes" and "I own" start their respective lines iambically and thereby provide some variety. The metrical variations are contained in individual lines for the same necessary purpose of avoiding monotony. "That A Rogue so Obscure should make such a Clutter" is varied both by the irregular iamb in the third foot and the extra syllable at the end for the feminine rhyme. Such irregularity is necessary to manipulate the couplets effectively and avoid a doggerel sound. The fact that each of the lines is end-stopped emphasizes the rhymes, yet a sing-song effect is avoided through the metrical variations. In this poem, then, Swift has used rhythm very skillfully to get the maximum impact from his meter and line. He has also avoided the iambic tetrameter, his usual meter, for something different. The effect is smooth and conversational, rare for couplets, and witty because of the often silly rhymes. For example, the pun on *wood* appears in the rhyme and is emphasized by being monosyllabic and end-stopped. Metrics clearly aid both meaning and wit in this poem.

The short "Epigram on Wood's Brass Money" contains some successful uses of metrics as well. Here Swift uses as his subject matter the appearance of Lord John Carteret in Dublin, sent by the English prime minister, Sir Robert Walpole, to investigate the Wood's halfpence uproar.

> Cart'ret was welcom'd to the Shore
> First with the brazen Canons Roar,
> To meet him next, the Soldier comes,
> With brazen Trumps and brazen Drums,
> Approaching near the Town, he hears,
> The brazen Bells salute his Ears:
> But when Wood's Brass began to sound,
> Guns, Trumpets, Drums, and Bells were drownd'd. (274)

The scansion here remains the usual iambic tetrameter, a form Swift had become very skillful with at this point in his literary career. Yet he wisely varies the meter with trochaic feet in the first two lines: "Cart'ret was welcom'd" and "First with the brazen." The last line also remains metrically significant because of its use of the hypercatalexis, which ends the poem with an extra stressed syllable. This serves to conclude the poem with a metrical flourish, with even "Guns" and "Trumpets." The hypercatalectic finale is something Swift had rarely used in his earlier poems. This clever, witty, short poem is so unlike the poetics of the period that prescribed the poem's proper dedication to the Muse; one can easily imagine what Sir Robert Walpole would have thought of poetry written to encourage a boycott of British money. Walpole, the prime minister, and his special envoy to Ireland, Carteret, clearly knew they were dealing with a clever literary and political opponent in Swift.

But even Walpole would certainly have approved of the panegyric, "To His Grace the Arch-Bishop of Dublin." This poem consistently uses the iambic tetrameter, the octosyllabic couplet. In this regard, it is very conventional since it uses Swift's favorite metrical form and since the rhymes are all perfect. The first and eighth lines in this poem make an interesting contrast: "Great, Good, and Just was once apply'd" and "Because thou'rt Great, and Good, and Just." Neither line is very exciting, but the first one is more interesting because of its meter. The initial spondee in this line opens the poem forcefully, while the use of the "and's" in the eighth line smoothens the meter to form perfect iambs but is so obviously filler that the line simply plods dully along. Aside from the comparative lack of rhythmical inventiveness, this poem is also not very exciting because of the absence of Swiftian wit. Swift just does not seem very good at the panegyric, even when he sincerely wants to praise someone; this poem rings hollow because Swift failed to find a very exciting way to praise a man he obviously admired, a problem we also find in some of the Stella poems that also lack Swift's usually witty repartee.

The next poem in the series, "An Excellent New Song upon His Grace Our Good Lord Arch-Bishop of Dublin," succeeds more as a panegyric primarily because it has some metrical ingenuity. Swift uses a completely different metrical pattern for this poem, the iambic heptameter, which lengthens the line considerably and minimizes the sound of the rhyming couplets:

> I Sing not of the Draper's Praise, not yet of William Wood
> But I sing of a Famous Lord, who seeks his Country's Good,
> Lord William's Grace of Dublin Town, 'tis he that first appears,
> Whose Wisdom and whose Piety, do far exceed his Years,
> In ev'ry Council and Debate he stands for what is Right;
> And still the Truth he will Maintain, what'er he loses by't. (276)

This poem represents one of the very few times Swift used the rhymed fourteener, which certainly demands many syllables to fill out. Swift's use of it here must have been experimental since he doesn't use it elsewhere in this group. He apparently had some difficulty in filling out the long line, for there are filler-words here. The redundancy of "Dublin Town," "Whose Wisdom and whose," and "will maintain" suggests that Swift was uncomfortable with the line and had difficulty sustaining it. Too, the meter remains amazingly regular and lacks Swift's usual variations. But the long line does deemphasize the rhymes simply by putting them further apart, and this does much to keep the poem moving rapidly and rather conversationally.

Swift's use of caesuras is also significant in this poem. In five of the six lines quoted above there is a caesura in the middle of the line. What Swift has done in effect is reduce the heptameter length to the tetrameter he was more accustomed to and found more manageable. Of course he doesn't do this in all the lines, but the majority of them do contain medial caesuras. Alexander Pope, in a letter to Walsh dated 22 October 1706, gives his opinion on the use of the caesuras: "Ever nice Ear, Must (I believe) have observ'd, that in any smooth English Verse of ten syllables, there is naturally a Pause at the fourth, fifth, and sixth syllable. It is upon these the Ear rests, and upon the judicious Change and management of which depends the Variety of Versification. . . . Now, I fancy, that to preserve an exact Harmony and Variety, the Pauses of the fourth or sixth shou'd not be continu'd above three lines together, without the Interposition of another; else it will be apt to weary the Ear with one continu'd Tone, at least it does mine" (23). Pope is suggesting that the poet alter the placement of the caesura to avoid monotonous rhythmical repetitions. In Swift's poem, however, each one of the caesuras in the passage quoted above appears invariably after the first four feet, creating a constant pattern of tetrameter, then trimeter. Swift places the caesuras after the first eight syllables almost always to facilitate the tetrameter form, but at the expense of diversified rhythmical patterns.

In "Prometheus," Swift returns to his usual medium, satiric iambic tetrameters, and the result is more effective than the two preceding panegyrics to the archbishop of Dublin. Swift even uses some mock epic elements toward the end of this poem:

> Ye pow'rs of Grub-Street make me able,
> Discreetly to apply this Fable.
> Say, who is to be understood,
> By that old Thief Prometheus? Wood
> For Jove, it is not hard to guess him,
> I meant His Majesty, God bless him.
> This Thief and Black-Smith was so bold,
> He strove to steal that Chain of Gold,
> Which links the Subject to the King:
> And change it for a Brazen String. (279)

A primary source of the humor in this invocation to the Grub Street Muse is the obviously forced rhymes; "able/fable" and "stood/wood" are especially emphasized because of the shortness of the line, and the very regularity of the iambs adds to the comically doggerel effect. The comparative lack of caesuras also helps the poem to proceed more quickly, more conversationally, and as a result more comically.

"Whitshed's Motto to His Coach" combines in an interesting way both octosyllabic couplets and caesuras, rarely paired in Swift's verse. The second stanza typifies the metrics in the poem:

> Libertas bears a large Import;
> First, how to swagger in a Court:
> And, secondly, to shew my Fury
> Against an uncomplying Jury:

> Add, Thirdly: 'tis a new invention
> To favor Wood and keep my Pension:
> And, Fourthly; 'tis to play an odd Trick,
> Get the Great Seal, and turn out Brod'rick. (280)

Most of the lines are end-stopped and also contain caesuras, with the resultant effect of interrupted movement through a series of short phrases. The last four lines quoted above provide good examples of the poem's progression through short spurts of phrasing. The tone that results is neither conversational nor comic but biting and testily satiric. Swift was apparently quite angry with Judge Whitshed, and the poem's metrics reflect this attitude and help to dramatize it. This judge found the publisher of the *Drapier's Letters* guilty of libel; when a jury disagreed with the judge's decision, he dismissed them. Swift naturally tried to defend his publisher.

The three short "Verses on the Upright Judge, Who Condemned the Drapier's Printer" continues Swift's attack on Judge Whitshed, though the poems themselves are not very notable metrically. They use the iambic tetrameter form that Swift was so fond of, and the meter remains entirely regular. The only exception to this appears in the last poem of the series, "The Judge Speaks":

> I'm not the Grandson of that Ass Quin;
> nor can you prove it, Mr. Pasquin.
> My Grand-dame had Gallants by Twenties,
> And bore my Mother by a Prentice.
> Then, when my Grandsire knew; they tell us he,
> To Christ-Church cut his Throat for Jealousy.
> And, since the Alderman was mad you say,
> Then, I must be so too, ex traduce. (281)

The first four lines contain nine syllables, ending with an unstressed feminine rhythm. The last four lines, however, include an extra syllable and end with a stressed masculine rhyme, which serves to add an extra iambic foot to these last lines. Why Swift changed line lengths midway through the poem I do not know. In any case, it certainly is a clever way to call Judge Whitshed a bastard.

The only instance of the heroic couplet in this group of poems occurs in "Horace Book I, Ode XIV, Paraphrased and Inscribed to Ireland." The lines remain quite facile and effortless and the syntax is generally natural:

> Unhappy Ship, thou art return'd in Vain:
> New Waves shall drive thee to the Deep again.
> Look to thy Self, and be no more the Sport

of giddy Winds, but make some friendly Port.
Lost are thy Oars that us'd thy Course to guide,
Like faithful Counsellors on either Side. (282)

Three of the lines above included caesuras, but the caesuras don't become so monotonously fixed in the same position all the time as they did in "An Excellent New Song." All the rhymes are masculine and all the lines are end-stopped, but there is enough movement within the lines themselves to ensure smooth progressions. Swift happily avoids here the extremes of singsong and staccato abruptness since they would not be appropriate for the poem's intended meaning. The metrics help to create a tone that is both earnest and sincerely concerned yet controlled.

On the other hand, "Wood, an Insect" was written in the humorous, punning vein that characterizes so many of these poems. In cataloging the different kinds of wood insects, the most odious of which is of course the William Wood insect, Swift uses metrics very functionally to enhance the comic tenor and meaning of the poem:

The Louse of the Wood for a Med'cine is us'd,
Or swallow'd alive, or skillfully bruis'd.
And, let but our Mother Hibernia contrive
To swallow Will. Wood either bruis'd or alive,
She need be no more with the Jaundice possess't;
Or sick of Obstructions, and Pains in her Chest.
The Third is an Insect we call a Wood-Worm,
That lies in old Wood like a Hare in her Form. (284)

The basic meter, anapestic tetrameter, is varied with both iambs and trochees to resemble more closely natural speech with all its various rhythms. Each of the lines begins with an iamb rather than the anapest one would expect. Too, some of the lines end with iambs (1, 3) but the rest end anapestically. All the lines, however, do end on stressed syllables and are end-stopped; the preponderance of masculine rhymes emphasizes the rhymes, yet there are enough caesuras variously placed to keep the poem's rhythm nicely varied. Swift's comic verse forms generally succeed in this group of poems and are especially vivid in this one. Interesting too are the variations of the four-beat line Swift handles so adroitly. Swift obviously remains most comfortable with lines of four stresses whether in eight syllables or two, iambs or anapests.

Significantly enough, the last two poems of the series, "On Wood the Iron-monger" and "A Simile on Our Want of Silver," return to the iambic tetrameter couplet that had been Swift's chosen meter before the *Wood's Halfpence Poems* and continued to be so after them. The first poem is

broadly comic and compares Wood to a "mad Copper-Smith" who made
so much noise that Jove himself knocked him down:

> Then what a high Delight were all in,
> To see the wicked Varlet sprawling;
> They search't his Pockets on the Place,
> And found his Copper all was base;
> They laught at such an Irish blunder,
> To take the Noise of Brass for Thunder! (286)

The narrative moves easily yet in a quietly humorous tone, and the metrics and rhymes are obviously basic causes for the effect. The second
poem, "A Simile," more directly calls for a boycott of the worthless
money and here too the octosyllabic couplet appears:

> But, to this Parchment let the Draper
> Oppose his Counter-Charm of Paper,
> and ring Wood's Copper in our Ears
> So loud, till all the Nation hears. (287)

The run-on lines plus the smooth syntax aid the metrics to create an easy,
sloganizing line. After the whole series, Swift returns once again to the
line and meter he had become famous for, yet the experimentation with
the different meters represented in these poems surely helped Swift to
understand his art more thoroughly and control language more
effectively.

The eleven *Wood's Halfpence Poems*, then, provided Swift with an opportunity to do much experimentation with metrics. The poems were all
written within a year and, aside from their value in helping the cause of
the Irish boycott, Swift developed and matured as a poet through them.
He managed the anapestic tetrameter, heroic couplet, iambic heptameter,
iambic tetrameter, and combinations of these feet for varying audial qualities and different tonal effects with varying degrees of success. By the
end of the series Swift was once again using his old favorite, the iambic
tetrameter couplet, but he had learned from these metrical experimen-
tations. He had learned to use language more flexibly and gained an
increased control of meter, and his later poems show this in their greater
metrical variation and flexibility.

In addition, the *Wood's Halfpence Poems* fulfilled their immediate purpose. Wood's patent was surrendered on 19 August 1725; the Wood's
halfpence coins were not introduced into Ireland (Murry 356). In part
because of Swift's *Drapier's Letters* and *Wood's Halfpence Poems*, England was forced to retreat on this issue. Whether the coins would have
really hurt Ireland or not, though still debatable, obscures a more im-

portant accomplishment of these poems. Swift and his satire—whether in prose or poetry—provided Ireland with one of its first successful resistances to English control and hegemony over Ireland.

It is interesting that money and monetary interests inspired Swift to write the poems. Money, an important personal issue for him, became symbolic of England's determination to exploit Ireland for her own ends. That Swift's anger at English injustice should be balanced with metrical experimentation indicates that Swift remained for most of his career both propagandist and writer. Perhaps his main allegiance was ultimately to neither Irish drapers nor English money, but to language.

REFERENCES

Barnett, Louise K. *Swift's Poetic Worlds*. Newark: University of Delaware Press, 1981.

Cook, Richard I. *Jonathan Swift as a Tory Pamphleteer*. Seattle: University of Washington Press, 1967.

Ehrenpreis, Irvin. *Swift: The Man, His Works, and the Age*. Cambridge: Harvard University Press, 1962.

Forster, John. *The Life of Jonathan Swift*. London: John Murray Press, 1875.

Murry, John Middleton. *Jonathan Swift: A Critical Biography*. New York: Noonday Press, 1955.

Pope, Alexander. *The Correspondence of Alexander Pope*. Edited by George Sherburn. Oxford: Clarendon Press, 1956.

Quintana, Ricardo. *Swift: An Introduction*. Westport, Conn.: Greenwood Press, 1979 (originally 1955).

Reilly, Patrick. *Jonathan Swift: The Brave Desponder*. Carbondale: Southern Illinois University Press, 1982.

Swift, Jonathan. *Poetical Works*. Edited by Herbert Davis. London: Oxford University Press, 1967. All the poems quoted are from this edition.

Van Doren, Carl. *Swift*. Port Washington, N.Y.: Kennikat Press, 1964 (originally 1930).

Feminine Transactions: Money and Nineteenth-Century British Women Writers

Vanessa D. Dickerson

I had made but about 540 £ at the close of my last affair, and I had wasted some of that. However, I had about 460 £ left, a great many very rich cloaths, a gold watch, and some jewels, tho' of no extraordinary value, and about 30 £ or 40 £ in linnen not dispo'd of.
—*Moll Flanders* (1722)

Few female characters in British fiction have tallied their possessions or counted their pence and pounds with as great a relish as Daniel Defoe's Moll Flanders. This is not to say that money does not figure in works of succeeding writers, or, more specifically in the writings of nineteenth-century British women. Living in a century so preoccupied with "getting and spending" that hell itself, according to Thomas Carlyle, was "equivalent to not making money" (149), Victorian women, who had such limited means of getting and making it, were keenly aware of money.[1] From Jane Marcet's Socratic dialogues on the science of economics to Harriet Martineau's illustrations of political economy to Virginia Woolf's declaration that the woman writer needs money as well as a room of her own, not just the economic but the social and political significance of the sterling pound has proven a subject both open and attractive to women writers. The fiction of such writers as Austen, Brontë, Eliot, and Oliphant shows, however, that even where women appear entrenched in financial affairs and most involved in the business of money, they are rarely accorded direct control of the sovereigns or publicly recognized for their fiscal knowledge. To put it another way, women's relations to money tend to make them the stewards of petty cash, whereas men are the controllers of hard cash.

In *Literary Women* (1977), Ellen Moers says that "money and its making were characteristically female rather than male subjects in English
fiction." She points to Jane Austen first and foremost, noting that all
Austen's "opening paragraphs, and the best of her first sentences have
money in them" (101). While it is true that money means a great deal to
Austen and her characters, her young women hardly handle real capital
in any official capacity. Women's financial endeavors are always domes-
ticated. Thus in *Persuasion* (1818) when it becomes evident that Sir Walter Eliot "was growing distressed for money," Lady Russell rallies and
instigates a "scheme of retrenchment" whereby she "drew up plans of
economy . . . made exact calculations, and . . . did what nobody else
thought of doing: she consulted [another woman,] Anne" (14, 17). As M.
Jeanne Peterson has observed in her case study of "one circle of upper-
middle-class women," "women were not isolated from money and the
facts of financial life" (125). Lady Russell's and Anne's plans to help rec-
tify the family's grave financial problems highlight this observation. Yet
in Austen's novel, the female-engineered rescue is carefully presented.
That is, it is kept within the bounds of decorum. The women devise ways
of curbing spending and think of economizing activities that fall within
or comfortably near their socially prescribed roles of managers and keep-
ers of the household. "While Lady Eliot lived, there had been method,
moderation, and economy which had just kept him [Sir Walter] within
his income." Anne's "more rigid requisitions" and Lady Russell's gentle
reformations do not center in the buying, selling, and trading of the Exchequer, but in the frills and luxuries, as well as the creature comforts,
underwritten with household funds. "What every comfort of life knocked
off!" cries Sir Walter, presented with the women's financial proposal.
"Journeys, London, servants, horses, table—contractions and restrictions
everywhere." Finally the women's sally into financial management is "of
little consequence" because Sir Walter objects outright to the idea of
living "no longer with the decencies even of a private gentleman" and
so rejects their economical proposals (18). Overriding the women's fiscal
control over the domestic sphere, Sir Walter demonstrates Friedrich Engels' historical contention that man really takes "command in the home
also" (189). If Lady Russell and Anne are not to have the ultimate say
about domestic spending, then these women are clearly not to have a
hand in the nitty-gritty world of money and high finance. They are to
"suffer and be still."[2]

In Austen's fiction, not only do women not handle the money, they do
not make it. Instead they tend to acquire it through marriage, which, as
Moers herself admits, "makes money a serious business in Austen fiction"
(102). While "marriage and a husband," as Peterson contends, "far from
putting women outside the realm of decision making" may "often [have]
widened their realm of financial power" by way of marriage settlements,

the fact remains that without the "private legal creations of marriage settlements . . . and trust" (123, 131), the husband was automatically and
legally recognized as the owner of money, property, and children. In
truth, then, for women the acquisition of money through marriage was
at best secondhand. As the American Charlotte Perkins Gilman, who
wrote about "sexo-economic relations" near the end of the nineteenth
century put it, "The economic status of the human race in any nation, at
any time, is governed mainly by the activities of the male: the female
obtains her share in the racial advance only through him" (572). Under
such circumstances, any woman who sought thus to secure a living was
engaged in a risky financial venture. Harriet Martineau would write
around 1834 in a sociohistorical review of the marriage compact, "But
new difficulties about securing a maintenance have arisen. Marriage is
less general and the husbands of the greater number of women are not
secure [as in feudal times] of a maintenance from the lords of the soil,
any more than women are [made financially secure by] . . . being married" (62). In *Moll Flanders* Defoe had created a lowly female character
who maneuvered a succession of marriages to amass a modest fortune;
by the turn of the century, Jane Austen depicted genteel female characters
ostensibly in search of a cultivated and wise male companion, not a
purse. It is fair to say that Austen recognized the financial impact of marriage, but was careful not to reduce that sacrament solely to a principle
of feminine economics.

Dorothy Lampen Thompson's study of women's contributions to the
development of economics sheds light on Austen's handling of money as
an important but delicate matter. Thompson observes that

early nineteenth-century England was not a propitious time or place for a woman
to become an economist. Economics was still neither a scholarly nor a popular
study. It had, in fact, only recently gained respectability. In the opinion of the
seventeenth century and much of the eighteenth century, the study of trade was
beneath the dignity of learning, and the view that "the gentleman does not sully
his hands in trade" was one that was slow to be overcome. . . . The prevailing
view was that "no gentleman, and especially no self-respecting scholar, would
study the profession if he were forced to." (9)

Tradition required that gentlemen maintain a respectable distance between themselves and their money, that it be inherited instead of made.
Of course it followed that for a woman, a lady in particular, to concern
herself too markedly with the acquisition of money, whether she earned
it or sought it through marriage or inheritance, was, if not unthinkable,
then as outrageous as Defoe's Moll's and much later Thackeray's Becky
Sharpe's financial machinations.[3]

By the mid-nineteenth century, with the growth of manufacturing and the middle class, the Victorians who enjoyed among other things great material and economic progress, did not necessarily feel, like their more fastidious predecessors, that money and the trade that brought it sullied the hands.[4] Still, in the fiction of Austen's British female successors, the treatment of money remains as circumspect as Austen's. In *Jane Eyre* (1847), for example, Jane earns thirty pounds per annum as a governess until she inherits a fortune, then marries the master; Catherine Earnshaw marries the wealthy landowner, Linton, to secure comfort and respectability in *Wuthering Heights* (1847). George Eliot's Gwendolyn Harleth weds the languid and sinister Grandcourt to rescue her financially distressed family in *Daniel Deronda* (1876). In such stories, there is little evidence of female protagonists who go to the bank, finger their coins, or balance the accounts, as the women maintain a commercial "anonymity," to borrow Carolyn Heilbrun's words, "long believed . . . the proper condition of woman" (12). Like the sisters Brown in the Amazonian stronghold of Elizabeth Gaskell's *Cranford*, where "we none of us spoke of money, because that subject savoured of commerce and trade" (41), good strong women represented in these fictions are seldom found in any blatant contact or sustained relation with money that would betray good but vulgar business sense or an undecorous preoccupation with lucre.

By the end of the nineteenth century, Dinah Mulock, later Dinah Craik, would argue that good business sense was exactly what women needed to cultivate. In a volume of essays, *About Money and Other Things* (1886), Mulock declared,

I know that I shall excite the wrath or contempt of the advocates of the higher education of women, when I say that it is not necessary for every woman to be an accomplished musician, an art-student, a thoroughly educated Girton girl; but it is necessary that she should be a woman of business. From the day when her baby fingers begin to handle pence and shillings, and her infant mind is roused to laudable ambition by the possession of the enormous income of threepence a week, she ought to be taught the true value and wise expenditure of money; to keep accounts and balance them to repay the minutest debt, or, still better, to avoid incurring it; to observe the just proportions of having and spending, and, above all, the golden rule for every one of us, whether our income be sixpence a week or twenty thousand a year—*waste nothing*. (6–7)

Bold as Mulock's observations sound, they finally call for energies that are meant to be channeled back into the domestic sphere. Mulock admonishes women to "observe the just proportions of spending" so that they can be better "helpmeets to the men they marry." For after all, Mulock continues, "very few men know how properly to use money:"

They can earn it, lavish it, hoard it, waste it; but to deal with it wisely, as a means to an end, and also as a sacred trust, to be made the best of for others as well as themselves, is an education difficult of acquirement by the masculine mind; so difficult that one is led to doubt whether they were meant to acquire it at all, and whether in the just distribution of duties between the sexes it was not intended that the man should earn, the woman keep—he accumulate, and she expend; especially as most women have by nature a quality in which men are often fatally deficient—"the infinite capacity for taking trouble." (4–5)

Even as Mulock questions the male's aptitude for financial management, she describes conditions whereby woman's relation to money is etherealized and so deflated in any real professional or worldly sense. For if woman does handle money, she does so in her angelic role as the keeper of a "sacred trust," as one who traditionally sacrifices and troubles to do her best for others.

In the phrase "just distribution of [economic] duties between the sexes" Mulock does not describe what her American counterpart Charlotte Perkins Gilman calls a partnership. "The comfort a man takes with his wife," writes Gilman, "is not in the nature of a business partnership, nor are her frugality and industry. A housekeeper, in her place, might be as frugal, as industrious, but would not therefore be a partner" (573). While Mulock re-presents the hierarchy that financially subordinates women instead of making them partners, Jane Welsh Carlyle, in a composition which is said to have greatly amused Thomas Carlyle, gives good evidence of woman's economic position in the "just distribution of duties." In "Budget of a Femme Incomprise" (12 February 1855), Jane lightly but sarcastically addresses her husband as "the Noble Lord" as she explains why she must "*speak* again on the money question!" She reminds him that "through six-and-twenty years I have kept house for you at more or less cost according to given circumstances, but always on less than it costs the generality of people living in the same style." As a woman and wife she is put in the uneasy and marginal, if not demeaning, position of having not only to "pester your [Carlyle's] life out about money" but also to account to her modern "lord of the soil" throughout the twenty-six years of marriage for expenditures, "though," as she caustically remarks, "I am not strong in arithmetic." Jane Carlyle sees and states clearly the role of husband and wife in what she terms the "money row": "No, my Lord, it has never been my habit to interfere with your ways of making money, or the rate which you make it at; and if I never did in early years, most unlikely I should do it *now*. My bill of ways and means has nothing to do with making money, only with disposing of the money made" (235–42).

Though not what Gilman calls the "producers of wealth" or for that matter the disposers of substantial sums, middle- and upper-class women like Jane Carlyle contributed "in the final processes of preparation and distribution" (573).[5] Nevertheless, their contributions were not perceived to be as important as those of men. As Gilman wrote, the Mulock too understood, "The labor of women in the house, certainly enables men to produce more wealth than they otherwise could; and in this way women are economic factors in society." However, as Gilman goes on to say, "like the labor of women, the labor of horses [also] enables men to produce more wealth than they otherwise could. The horse is an economic factor in society. But the horse is not economically independent, nor is the woman" (573). In the money row, Jane Carlyle must have certainly felt that she was pulling the plow.

The nineteenth-century British writer Eliza Lynn Linton did not equate the position of middle-class woman with that of a beast of burden; however, she did recognize the servility of a woman in Jane Carlyle's position. She saw that a wife was no more than the servant of her husband:

an honoured servant if you will, but a servant all the same. . . .
No one but women themselves know how bitter this dependency is to them. Many a wife even after long years of marriage, and when kindly treated by her husband, the mother of his children and used to the manipulation of the housekeeping allowance, many even of this blessed class, feel bitterly that nothing is theirs, that it is not *their own*. It is their husband's. . . .
This is the real meaning of modern revolt—women want to be independent, and to be on terms of monetary equality with men. (227–28)

As domestic guardian of the welfare of others, woman, no better off than a horse or a servant, finds herself a "femme incomprise" whose financial powers are severely qualified.

For a good portion of the nineteenth century most women who dealt with money tended to deal not with pounds but with shillings and pence because, in fiction as in real life, women's acquisition and management of their rights to the real sources of power and governance—land, houses, and, the focus of this chapter, money—were restricted by laws of coverture. Even if a middle- or upper-class woman had property or a fortune, there was a dissociation of her womanliness from cold hard cash. In Charlotte Brontë's *Shirley* (1849), in which Shirley Keeldar has so much money, property, and character that she earns the title of Captain Keeldar, Robert Moore and Shirley's uncle Simpson take charge of the counting houses and manage both the property and financial affairs of the heiress. Shirley proves more an angel of mercy than a captain of industry as she herself finds in her money a sacred trust. Having "money in hand," Shirley feels compelled to "do some good with it": "It is not an immense sum, but I feel responsible for its [her fortune's] disposal; and really this responsibility weighs on my mind more heavily than I could have expected. They say that there are some families almost starving to death in Briarfield: some of my own cottagers are in wretched circumstances: I must and will help them." Money carries with it the responsibility of caring and helping, yet even for Shirley that money is something with which a lady does not directly deal. Caroline, Shirley's sisterly friend, suggests that Shirley let the old maid Miss Ainsley "distribute the cash" since Shirley "will not manage properly" (267–68).[6] Indeed, the old maid Miss Ainsley, Caroline, who fears she is on the way to becoming an old maid, and Robert Moore's spinster cousin Hortense come closer than Captain Keeldar to handling accounts, even if their approach to financial knowledge and experience tends to be by way of the socially sanctioned larders and the sewing boxes got up for charity.

One memorable female character who comes closer than Shirley Keeldar to being a real captain of commerce is George Eliot's Jane Glegg. The proper getting, saving, and disposal of money and material wealth is the business of the oldest Dodson sister Mrs. Glegg in *Mill on the Floss* (1860). The bulwark of the Dodson tradition is so committed to having and saving that she stashes her new dresses and hairpieces away, bringing them out for wear when they are quite moldy and outdated. Adept at putting away and pinching goods and money to amass wealth, Jane Glegg is legally and financially cognizant of how money may lend one authority, get one respect, and create family dependents. Armed with this knowledge, she lords it over weaker-willed and -minded sister Bessy Tulliver, directing that sister how to economize in her own household:

"It's a pity for you, Bessy, as you haven't got more strength o' mind. It'll be well if your children don't suffer for it. And I hope you've not gone and got a great dinner for us—going to great expenses for your sisters as 'ud sooner eat a crust o' dry bread nor help to ruin you with extravagance— . . . And here you've got two children to provide for, and your husband's spent your fortin i' going to law, and's like to spend his own too. A boiled joint, as you could make broth of for the kitchen," Mrs. Glegg added, in a tone of emphatic protest, "and a plain pudding with a spoonful o' sugar and no spice, 'ud be far more becoming." (110)

Unlike Mrs. Tulliver, Mrs. Glegg, who has the "strength o' mind" to abhor "extravagance," here shows in that tradition of sacred trust, a fitting and proper concern with money for the children's sake. Interestingly enough, she is critical not only of Mrs. Tulliver, who is so silly as to prepare a financially ruinous "great dinner for us," but also of Mr. Tulliver, who has "spent your fortin 'i going to law." Aware that the man of the house is not taking care of his family as he should, Mrs. Glegg points out her ability to lend financial assistance, if not to fill Tulliver's shoes, as the fiscally responsible individual. As Jane Glegg complains, she reveals her sense of her monetary knowledge and potential: "Well, Bessy, *I* can't

leave your children enough out o' my savings, to keep 'em from ruin.
And you mustn't look to having any o' Mr. Glegg's money for it's well if
I don't go first—he comes of a long willed family—and if he was to die
and leave me well for my life, he'd tie all the money up to go back to
his own kin" (111). Elsewhere, she comments on a Mrs. Sutton who had
died having "left no leggicies, to speak on—left it all in a lump sum to
her husband's nevvy":

There wasn't much good i' being so rich, then . . . if she'd got none but husband's
kin to leave it too. It's poor work when that's all you've got to pinch yourself
for—not as I'm one o' those as 'ud like to die without leaving more money out
at interest than other folks had reckoned. But it's a poor tale when it must go
out o' your own family. (114)

Given the limits placed upon women, Mrs. Glegg shrewdly and honestly
calculates upon one of the ways in which women could finally own and
manage money: the death of a husband meant, of course, widowhood,
but it hopefully also meant a will leaving money and material possessions
in the hands of the wife.[7] A dowry was a "fortin" that passed from the
father to the husband; a will could mean a whole new financial scenario
for a woman—a loophole to financial independence and freedom. Mrs.
Glegg is well aware of the financial possibilities this legal instrument may
offer or withhold when she chides her sister Sophy for bemoaning the
death of Mrs. Sutton: "You couldn't fret no more than this, if we'd heared
as our cousin Abbot had died sudden without making his will" (114).
Finally she gives a great deal of consideration to Mr. Glegg's "handsome
provision for her in case of his death." Because "Mr. Glegg, like all men
of his stamp, we extremely reticent about his will," Mrs. Glegg worries
"in her gloomier moments" that "he might cherish the mean project of
heightening her grief at his death by leaving her poorly off" (193). But
in her happier moments she dreams of surviving Mr. Glegg to

talk eulogistically of him, as a man who might have his weaknesses, but who had
done the right thing by her notwithstanding his numerous poor relations—to
have sums of interest coming in more frequently and secret it in various corners
baffling to the most ingenious thieves . . . —finally to be looked up to by her own
family and the neighborhood, so as no woman can ever hope to be who has not
the praeterite and present dignity comprised in being a "widow well left." (193–
94)

To be a "widow well left" is to be left a woman in control of her own
resources, to be left a woman with financial autonomy, to be left a woman
with the right to go to the bank.
     Even without benefit of a will, however, Mrs. Glegg comes to command
a part, albeit a small one, in business transactions usually left to men.

Indeed, Mrs. Glegg loans money out at 5 percent, secreting her profits in her home, if not taking them to the bank. She even engages in financial speculation with Bob Jakin the packman. However, all of Mrs. Glegg's financial transactions finally go forth more or less under the watchful eye of her noble "lord of the soil," Mr. Glegg, who has condescended to grant his wife some control over her own money. During a conjugal dispute, Mr. Glegg himself points up how unusual it is that a woman have such discretion: " 'Did ever anybody hear the like i' this parish?' said Mr. Glegg, getting hot. 'A woman with everything provided for her, and allowed to keep her own money the same as if it was settled on her, and with a gig new-stuffed and lined at no end o' expense and provided for when I die beyond anything she could expect' " (192).

While Mr. Glegg, who had found in "the eldest Miss Dodson . . . a handsome embodiment of female prudence and thrift" (187), gives his wife control of her money, he remains her adviser, the final financial authority to whom she ultimately listens. Thus, he advises the angry Mrs. Glegg not to "call in her money, when it's safe enough if you let it alone, all because of a bit of a tiff' (191). The emotional female here gets the calming and reasoned professional advice of the experienced man of business and behaves sensibly: "Mrs. Glegg felt there was really something in this [advice]" (190). It is Mr. Glegg who invites and condones Mrs. Glegg's investment in the business venture of Bob Jakin and the Glegg's nephew, Tom Tulliver. " 'What do you say, Mrs. G.?' said Mr. Glegg. 'I've a notion, when I've made a bit more inquiry, as I shall perhaps start Tom here with a bit of nest egg— . . . an' if you've got some little sums lyin' idle twisted up in a stockin' toe' " (416). Though Mrs. Glegg still conducts her business transactions under the paternal umbrella, she is guarded about her money and jealous of her right to make her own decisions about money, though finally Mr. Glegg steers her in a safe direction. Thus when Glegg suggests that his wife add twenty pounds of her own to the money he thinks of handing over to Tom, she replies, "You're not counting on me, Mr. Glegg, I hope, . . . You could do fine things wi' my money, I don't doubt." When an exasperated and tiffed Mr. Glegg invites her to keep her money and stay out of the whole affair, Jane reveals how she at some conscious and unconscious level resents Mr. Glegg's attempts to tell her what to do with her money: "I never said I wouldn't put money into it [the financial venture]—I don't say as it shall be twenty pounds, though you're so ready to say it for me" (417). Later when Mr. Glegg, Tom, and Bob, thinking they have concluded their discussion, prepare to go their several ways, Jane Glegg again feels the need to assert her financial weight:

"Stop a bit, Mr. Glegg," said the lady, as her husband took his hat, "you never *will* give me the chance o' speaking. You'll go away now, and finish everything about this business, and come back and tell me it's too late for me to speak. As if I wasn't my nevvy's own aunt, and th' head o' the family on his mother's side! and laid by guineas, all full weight for him—as he'll know who to respect when I'm laid in my coffin." (422)

Again Jane Glegg resists what she perceives as her husband's efforts to nudge her into the margins of the financial transaction. She would remind Glegg and particularly her nephew, who has money to gain by her death, that she is a substantive contender for his consideration and respect. Her money exacts inclusion: "I desire as nothing shall be done without my knowing. I don't say as I shan't venture twenty pounds, if you [Mr. Glegg] make out as everything's right and safe. And if I do, Tom,' concluded Mr. Glegg, turning impressively to her nephew, 'I hope you'll always bear it in mind and be grateful for such an aunt' " (422). As one who has some control over her own money, Jane Glegg no doubt feels that she should be able to speak for herself and not be patronized. Her husband as well as Tom and Bob, who are present during this exchange, see what women, economically dependent on men for so long, have known—that persons who have control over their money and therefore have economic independence must sometimes be humored. Having sized up Mrs. Glegg's financial disposition, a winking Bob Jakin outwits her, selling her damaged Laceham goods and thereby seeming to put Jane in her place. But while Jane Glegg's stinginess and flawed business acumen are underscored in the transaction with Bob Jakin, she is no worse off as a woman capable of increasing her capital. For finally, like Mr. Glegg, Tom, and Bob, she too turns a profit.

While Jane Glegg wields some power over her own financial affairs, the rich spinster Catherine Vernon in Margaret Oliphant's *Hester* (1883) manages a commercial concern. Her financial rescue of the failing bank of the Vernons is no small feat in a society where it is remarked that "ladies in this country have nothing to do with business," that "when ladies meddle with business everything goes wrong," and that when women get "mixed up with business they are entirely out of their place. It changes the natural relations—it creates a false position" (46, 54). Margaret Oliphant counters these preconceptions by putting the bank "in the hands of Miss Vernon, who, it turned out, had more than her grandfather's steady power of holding on, and was, indeed, the heir of her great-grandfather's genius for business. The bank throve in her hands as it had done in his days, and everything it touched prospered" (20).

In the hands of men like John Vernon, who embezzles money from the bank, and later of Edward Vernon, who secretly uses the bank's money to engage in speculation for his own personal gain, the Vernon bank is jeopardized. On the one hand, the idea of bank failure, upon which Margaret Oliphant builds the story of Catherine and Hester, was not unique.

As John Reed writes in *Victorian Conventions* (1975), "Considering the prevailing economic conditions and attitudes in nineteenth-century England, it is not unusual that financial failure was a major theme in Victorian literature" (176). On the other hand, that the threat of bank failure should become the occasion for a woman to become a financial power broker was not a common theme or story. For while women may have often been presented in fiction as the pawns of what Reed calls "commercial marriages" (108) which could secure money needed to, among other things, save a bank, women were not usually portrayed as individuals in any way capable of directly and nigh singlehandedly reversing a financial calamity of this magnitude and sort.

But in Catherine Vernon, Margaret Oliphant depicts a woman who, to the astonishment and admiration of the head clerk, had a head for business (17) and a fondness, though certainly not Moll's zest, for acquiring and keeping money. At one point, looking back over the days when she was at the helm of the bank, Catherine Vernon comments,

"For my part, speculation in this wild way is my horror. If you could see the proposals that used to be put before me! Not an undertaking that was not the safest and the surest in the world! The boys are well indoctrinated in my opinions on that subject. They know better, I hope, than to snatch at a high percentage; and love the substance, the good honest capital, which I love. I think," she continued, "there is a little of miser in me or perhaps you will say all women. I love to see my money—to count it over like them—By the way it was the king that did that [counted his money] while the queen was eating her bread and honey. That goes against my theory." (172)

As Catherine here recognizes, her position as the one who counts the coins reverses the order of the nursery rhyme that has the king or man provide and control, while the queen or woman merely consumes.[8] It is just such a scenario that Catherine's young kinswoman Hester hopes to avoid by having a career. Edward Vernon takes note of Hester's desire to be more than the queen eating honey and bread, commenting

"but you are a girl, what can you do [but marry Harry]? They would not let you work, and if you could work nothing but daily bread would come of it. And, my dear Hester, you want a great deal more than daily bread. You want triumph, power; you want to be as you are by nature, somebody." (154)

In short, though a jealous Hester resists the notion, she identifies with Catherine, who, as head of the Vernon bank, not only has the power and is recognized as "somebody," but also is a kingly giver of bread:

People spoke of her, as they sometimes do of a very popular man, by her Christian name. Catherine Vernon did this and that, they said. Catherine Vernon was the first thought when anything was wanted either by the poor who needed help, or the philanthropist who wanted to give it. The Vernon Almshouses, which had been established a hundred years before, but had fallen into great decay till she took them in hand, were always known as Catherine Vernon's Almshouses. Her name was put to everything. Catherine Street, Catherine Square, Catherine places without number. . . . She was, at least, a saint more easily within reach and more likely to lend a favorable ear. (20–21)

Significantly, Catherine's patriarchal role as head of the bank does not render her any less saintly or angelic. "The work of a successful man of business increased, yet softened by all the countless nothings that make business for a woman, had filled her days. She was an old maid to be sure, but an old maid who never was alone" (23). In that tradition of the spinsterish Miss Ainsleys and good housewives, Catherine keeps the sacred trust, reigning "with great benevolence . . . liberality . . . and firmness too" (20) and so realizing on a more sweeping scale the domestic idea.

And yet Margaret Oliphant suggests that the financial but especially the commercial empowerment of a Catherine Vernon is problematic. For one thing, the relations who are "indebted to her [Catherine] for their living, as well as their lodging" (27) are resentful of their rich and powerful kinswoman. For another, Catherine eventually discovers that Edward Vernon, the young relative whom she favors as the son she never had, despises what he perceives to be his servitude to her. When young Edward tries to explain why he does not want to discuss bank business with Hester, he also accounts indirectly for his aversion to his Aunt Catherine, as he calls her:

"Hester," he said, "that is not what a man wants in a woman, not to go and explain it all to her with pen and ink, and tables and figures, to make her understand as he would have to do with a man. What he wants, dear, is very different—just to lean upon you—to know that you sympathise, and think of me, and feel for me, and believe in me and that you will share whatever comes." (400)

What Hester unwittingly hears here is Edward's rejection of Catherine, to whom he has on occasion taken "my balance-sheet and my vouchers" (401). What she also hears here is the expression of a society for which, as Linda Hunt declares in *A Woman's Portion* (1988), "the [angelic] female character had become an alternative to the marketplace values that threatened to obliterate the aesthetic, moral, and emotional dimensions of life" (5).

Interestingly enough, while Hester finds Edward's call for "doggish fidelity" and "unreasoning belief," his "calm assertion that such blind adherence was all that was to be looked for from a woman" to be "irritating and offensive," Catherine seems ultimately to concur with Edward's notion that a woman best leave the business of money to men (401, 402). Thus, when as early as the third chapter of the novel, Catherine Vernon has turned sixty-five and decided to find someone to replace her in the bank, she does not think of recruiting a young woman, but instead "selected two hopeful young men to carry on her work," Edward and Harry. Later, when in an act reminiscent of John Vernon's, Edward has stolen money from the bank, sending it into collapse, Catherine disapproves of Hester's desire to follow in her footsteps and conduct the business of the bank:

"It is a great pity," she said, "a girl like you, that instead of teaching or doing needlework, you should not go to Vernon's, as you have a right to do, and work there."

"I wish I could," Hester said, with eager eyes.

"They tell me you wanted to do something like what I had done. Ah! you did not know it was all to be done over again. This life is full of repetitions. People think the same thing does not happen to you twice over, but it does in my experience. You would soon learn. A few years' work, and you would be an excellent man of business; but it can't be."

"Why cannot it be? You did it. I should not be afraid—"

"I was old. I was past my youth. All that sort of thing was over for me." (492–93)

Catherine clearly sees herself as an exception to the rule; moreover, she has been the exceptional woman of business not because of any personal goal but because circumstances required her to rise to the occasion. Instead of the challenge, responsibility, and power she herself has experienced, Catherine holds out for Hester the possibility of marriage to Harry or to Roland Ashton, as "it is better in the end" (493). Catherine's insistence that Hester marry leads the reader along with Hester to the understanding that the commercial empowerment of Catherine Vernon is to remain an anomaly, not the beginning of a new tradition. The angel in the house wins out over the woman in the marketplace.

Jane Lewis writes in *Women in England* (1984) that "the cult of domesticity stressed the sanctity of the home as a refuge from the rapid economic, political and social change outside the home and from the competitive values of the marketplace" (113). While it may well be true that the home was intended to serve as such a refuge, it cannot be denied that even the most angelic of women in the home had some ties to the marketplace if only indirectly as keeper of the budget. As Luce Irigaray has pointed out, in the Western world, woman has been herself to the marketplace as commodity (172). Exemplary of this financial phenomenon is Defoe's Moll Flanders, who commodifies her physical self to survive, to get security, and to gain social standing. That woman could enter the marketplace not as commodity but as an authority and a commercial player, that woman could transact some business other than that of marriage was a revolutionary idea in a society where according to Irigaray men historically "make commerce *of* them [women], but . . . do not enter into any exchanges *with* them" (172). This idea of a woman's participation in the world of money and finance on an equal footing with men was one that a writer like Margaret Oliphant began to imagine. As breadwinner for her and her brother's children, Oliphant perhaps more than some of her contemporaries appreciated the business skills it took to live in a world where money and mammon determine the quality of one's reality and the terms of one's existence. Charlotte Brontë may have helped support her father's household with her teaching and writing, Elizabeth Gaskell may have bought her husband a house, and George Eliot ensured an income for Lewes and his sons, yet for a writer like Oliphant, money and the ability to conduct business were not merely additional feathers in the headdress of the angelic woman. They were becoming a necessity. Though Oliphant and her sister writers may not have been ready either to educate women or to accept women in the positions of tellers and bankers, they supported the idea that women should, in the words of *Hester*'s narrator, "understand business and be ready for any emergency" (6). Then too, they began to explore the idea of women entering the worlds of business and finance and handling money in ways traditionally exercised exclusively by men.

NOTES

1. The phrase "getting and spending" is taken from William Wordsworth's poem "The World Is Too Much with Us" in *English Romantic Writers*, ed. David Perkins (New York: Harcourt, Brace, and World, 1967), 289. Thomas Carlyle, *Past and Present*, ed. Richard D. Altick (1843; rpt. New York: New York University Press, 1977), 149.

See Norman Russell's very informative *The Novelist and the Mammon: Literary Responses to the World of Commerce in the Nineteenth Century* (Oxford: Clarendon Press, 1986), which "duly acknowledge[s] the importance of prevailing economic theories" and "examines the responses of Victorian novelists to the thriving commercial life of the city, the world, of stockjobbers and brokers, financiers and insurance promoters" (vii). While Russell mentions two or three women writers who focused on banking and commerce in their novels (e.g., Catherine Gore in *The Banker's Wife* [1843], Harriet Martineau in *Berkeley the Banker* [1833], Dinah Mulock Craik in *John Halifax, Gentleman* [1856]) it is very clear in both Russell's book and in the fiction of the women writers he mentions that "the bankers, brokers, insurers, bill-discounters" (1), the purveyors of money and capitalism, were men.

2. See Martha Vicinus' edition, *Suffer and Be Still: Women in the Victorian Age* (Bloomington: Indiana University Press, 1972). Vicinus herself borrows the phrase from Sara Ellis's *The Daughters of England* (London, 1845).

3. In *The Lives of Victorian Gentlewomen*, Peterson provides an interesting insight into the relations between gentlewomen and the idea of earning money. Peterson observes that "there were solid practical grounds" for the attitude that earning money was "beneath a lady's dignity":

A gentlewoman earning her own living fell outside the circle of social activities that would keep her in touch with her own kind. A ball that lasted until 3 A.M., for example, was not conducive to alert employment the following day. More important, the very fact of having to earn a living demonstrated to the world, and to prospective suitors in particular, that a woman had no effective, economically viable family. A good match was one in which each partner brought to the marriage social and economic resources and safeguards . . . that would sustain the new family being created. The social message of earning a living was the fact of an economically crippled family. In addition, a lady's working would rob of employment those who needed it—those whom it was her social responsibility to aid. (120–21)

Not only her ability to maintain social contacts, but also her role as the consumer bearing witness to her husband's financial powers and her status as the domestic angel who gives instead of depriving others, in this case of needed employment—these might be compromised if the lady earned money.

4. Writers like Carlyle and Dickens did, however, worry that relationships were getting to be based upon the artificial and unfulfilling cash nexus.

5. Lower- and upper-middle- and upper-class women in some cases exercised significant economic power. Though Elizabeth Roberts focuses on the years 1890–1940, she describes a working-class tradition in which women had significant control over family finances and were in fact "financial controllers." Thus, "all earning children gave their wages to their mother for her to dispose of as she thought best. Similarly, 'good' husbands were expected to hand over their wages without any deductions having been made. There were variations in the operation of this custom. Some wives were so strict that their husbands received no pocket money at all. One worked as a waiter at the local pub, and was expected to rely on his tips for pocket money; another was allowed to keep his overtime pay, but not a penny of his wages," *A Woman's Place: An Oral History of Working-Class Women 1890–1940* (Oxford: Basil Blackwell, 1984), 110–11.

M. Jeanne Peterson in *Family, Love, and Work in the Lives of Victorian Gentlewomen* (Bloomington: Indiana University Press, 1989) asserts that "money, its ownership, and its management were a fact" in the case of "one circle of upper-middle-class women" she studies, the Pagets. Dwelling on such legal arrangements as the wills and marriage settlements that set these women apart, Peterson contends that "in the upper-middle-class family a gentlewoman was usually empowered by the private legal creations of marriage settlements, wills, and trusts. As a consequence, the Victorian gentlewoman had a sphere of power, a realm of autonomous existence, based on the financial resources inherited from parents, settled on her at marriage, and made available to her as a widow. The world of money . . . was not forbidden to gentlewomen" (131).

6. Because Miss Ainsley is an old maid without the protection of brother, father, or husband she is accustomed to fending for herself economically. As one who by unfortunate necessity transacts many of her own financial affairs, the old maid is in part exempt from the socioeconomic requirement that women not engage

in significant monetary transactions. Here though, Miss Ainsley's role is suitably angelic because charitable.

7. M. Jeanne Peterson does a fine job of demonstrating how a gentlewoman could be "empowered by the private legal creations of marriage settlements, wills, and trusts in *Lives of Victorian Gentlewomen*. As Peterson points out,

> wills and marriage settlements gave women power over marriage portions and legacies. Such monies gave women a separate financial sphere. She was not subject to a husband's control in these matters, but neither did she, by these arrangements, have any direct influence over him or the family's finances. It is important to look to the "family purse" for a measure of women's role in money matters. Women's roles in family financial management included both the mundane household matters that were part of middle-class women's lives and major responsibilities related to family finance. (124)

8. In *The Feminization of American Culture* (New York: Avon Books, 1977), Ann Douglas gives an interesting analysis of woman's role as consumer in the United States, where

> the ideal woman whom the counselors and educators wished to shape was to exert moral pressure on a society in whose operations she had little part, and to spend money—or have it spent on her—in an economy she could not comprehend. She was in embryo both a saint and a consumer. Naturally the lady and her advisors underplayed her status as consumer and overplayed her status as saint. They were largely ignorant of the developing economic situation of which they were a part; they were more aware of the sincerity of their conscious religious motivations than of the reality of the economic forces which partially determined them. . . . In actual fact . . . the two roles, saint and consumer, were interlocked and mutually dependent; the lady's function in a capitalist society was to appropriate and preserve both the values and the commodities which her competitive husband, father, and son had little time to honor or enjoy; she was to provide an antidote and a purpose for their labor. (69–70)

As Douglas herself comments, in the roles of angel and consumer the American woman in the nineteenth century may well have out-Victorianed the Victorians (3).

REFERENCES

Austen, Jane. *Persuasion*. New York: Signet, 1965.

Brontë, Charlotte. *Shirley*. New York: Penguin, 1974.

Carlyle, Jane Welsh. "Budget of a Femme Incomprise." *Life of Jane Welsh Carlyle* by Mrs. Alexander Ireland. New York: Charles L. Webster, 1891.

Carlyle, Thomas. *Past and Present*. 1848. Ed. Richard D. Altick. New York: New York University Press, 1977.

Defoe, Daniel. *Moll Flanders*. Ed. James Sutherland. Boston: Houghton Mifflin, 1959.

Eliot, George. *The Mill on the Floss*. New York: Penguin, 1974 (originally published 1860).

Engels, Friedrich. "The Origins of the Family, Private Property, and the State." *Feminism: The Essential Historical Writings*. Ed. Miriam Schneir. New York: Random House (Vintage), 1972.

Gaskell, Elizabeth. *Cranford and Cousin Phillis*. Ed. Peter Keating. Middlesex, England: Penguin, 1976.

Gilman, Charlotte Perkins. *Women and Economics. The Feminist Papers: From Adams to de Beauvoir*. Ed. Alice S. Rossi. New York: Columbia University Press, 1973.

Heilbrun, Carolyn G. *Writing a Woman's Life*. New York: Norton, 1988.

Hunt, Linda C. *A Woman's Portion: Ideology, Culture, and the British Female Novel Tradition*. New York: Garland, 1988.

Irigaray, Luce. *This Sex Which Is Not One*. Trans. Catherine Porter with Carolyn Burke. Ithaca, N.Y.: Cornell University Press, 1977.

Lewis, Jane. *Women in England 1870–1950: Sexual Divisions and Social Changes*. Bloomington: Indiana University Press, 1984.

Linton, Eliza Lynn. *Ourselves*. London: Chatto and Windus, 1884.

Martineau, Harriet. "On Marriage." *Harriet Martineau on Women*. Ed. Gayle Graham Yates. New Brunswick, N.J.: Rutgers University Press, 1985.

Moers, Ellen. *Literary Women*. Garden City, N.Y.: Doubleday (Anchor), 1977.

Mulock, Dinah. *About Money and Other Things: A Gift Book*. New York: Harper, 1887.

Oliphant, Margaret. *Hester: A Story of Contemporary Life*. New York: Penguin (Virago), 1984 (originally published 1883).

Peterson, M. Jeanne. *Family, Love, and Work in the Lives of Victorian Gentlewomen*. Bloomington: Indiana University Press, 1989.

Reed, John R. *Victorian Conventions*. Athens, Ohio: Ohio University Press, 1975.

Thompson, Dorothy Lampen. *Adam Smith's Daughters*. New York: Exposition Press, 1973.

Vicinus, Martha. *Suffer and Be Still: Women in the Victorian Age*. Bloomington: Indiana University Press, 1972.

Wordsworth, William. "The World Is Too Much with Us." *English Romantic Writers*. Ed. David Perkins. New York: Harcourt, Brace, and World, 1967.

Displaced Persons: The Cost of Speculation in Charles Dickens' *Martin Chuzzlewit*

Raymond L. Baubles, Jr.

When Adam Smith in *The Wealth of Nations* addresses the concept of *value*, he locates its source in labor:

What is bought with money or with goods is purchased with labour. . . . It was not by gold or by silver, but by labour that all the wealth of the world was originally purchased; and its value, to those who possess it, and who want to exchange it for some new productions, is precisely equal to the quantity of labour which it can enable them to purchase or command. (133)

But a curious phenomenon has taken place since Adam Smith's time. A displacement has occurred which has shifted *value* from the labor, goods, or services acquired by or exchanged for money to the money itself. In other words, my worth is no longer measured by my capacity for labor or by the quality of my goods but by the number of dollars which I generate or possess.

This transmogrification is not a recent one; it began in the late eighteenth and nineteenth centuries. For reasons and through a process too complex to analyze here, financial transactions acquired primary importance and financial entrepreneurs—bankers, stockbrokers, speculators—became more important participants in the economies of nations; money became a commodity in itself, acquiring a life of its own as the concept of profit was disconnected from the products which generated it.

This disembodiment is more than a matter of economics. It has serious social and moral consequences. As money itself becomes the primary commodity, the scramble for dollars or pounds can corrupt social relationships, destroy social responsibility, and lead to a disintegration of moral values and the loss of a sense of self.

The nineteenth-century British novelists were well aware of the terrific power of money and of the insidious effects it could have on the individual caught up by its allure. Time and again, the plot of the Victorian novel hinges upon the acquisition of money or the lack thereof, the misplaced will or its hidden codicil, the real or rumored existence of a natural son, the late second marriage with its threat of renewed fertility—as the various characters watch their anticipated fortunes rise and fall with the rapidity of stock market transactions and speculate on futures as if they were dealing in a commodities market. In many nineteenth-century novels, social relationships are cultivated only insofar as they bring the promise of monetary profit, and moral dilemmas rarely reach the level of consciousness.

Charles Dickens, who well understood the workings of the financial markets, addresses these concerns and illustrates the human cost of financial speculation, of money transactions gone awry, in many of his novels, perhaps most fully in *Martin Chuzzlewit*. Characterized as a novel which "could be defined as Dickens' first elaborate attack on the money worship of commercialized man" (Miller 132), in which "the ugly, disfiguring effect of money as a social force is the central and organizing concern" (Engel 103), *Martin Chuzzlewit* is predominantly about *self*[1] and "the inherent lunacy of commerce" (G. Smith 47). But it should be noted that it is commerce of a particular sort—the commerce in money rather than in goods, in paper currency detached from any substance whatsoever. And just as the money is disembodied, so too are those who speculate in or deal with it. Ironically, although *self* is a central motif of the novel, the various characters have no self. Altering their identities at whim, chamelionlike in their behaviors, most of Dickens' speculators lack a stable center of identity. What Dickens seems to indicate in this early work is that those who choose to speculate do so at the considerable cost of their humanity. Indeed, they sacrifice their humanity on the altar of mammon, a concern with disembodied profit resulting in a displacement of person.

Emblematic of this disintegration of the human spirit is Montague Tigg, through whom "Dickens is suggesting that there is a fundamental identity between shabby, down-at-the-heel roguery and expansive financial manipulation" (G. Smith 48). Tigg is an unctuous character who adapts his demeanor to the immediate moment. In his third and most significant appearance,[2] now "no longer Montague Tigg but Tigg Montague" (429; ch. 27), he is the chairman of the board of the Anglo-Bengalee Disinterested Loan and Life Assurance Company. In this company, Dickens' most extended and comprehensive analysis of the operations of a bubble enterprise, the reader sees the emptiness and corruption at its core. Little more than a board composed of a chairman and a secretary, "everything else being a light-hearted little fiction" (434; ch. 27),[3] its capital assets amounting to "[a] figure of two, and as many oughts after it as the printer can get into the same line" (429; ch. 27), underwritten by fictional property in Bengal (hence, its name), preying upon small investors who have the most to lose, the Anglo-Bengalee operates in the manner of many of the joint-stock companies of the day,[4] financial bubbles floated by unscrupulous promoters for the sole purpose of gaining other people's money.

In an attempt to seduce Jonas Chuzzlewit to become a partner in the company, Tigg details the duplicity which underlies its operations. When a prospective client approaches the Anglo-Bengalee for a loan to be secured by himself and two others, he is urged to insure his own life for double the amount and to urge his cosigners to purchase policies also. Because the loan is usually desperately needed, Tigg's proposal is more often than not accepted. In addition to charging "the highest lawful interest" (the only instance in which the company operates within the law) to be paid in advance, the amount provided to the borrower is further reduced by the premium on the life assurance policy. As Tigg describes the process,

We're not exactly soft upon B; for besides charging B the regular interest, we get B's premium, and B's friends' premiums, and we charge B for the bond, and, whether we accept him or not, we charge B for "inquiries" (we keep a man, at a pound a week, to make 'em), and we charge B a trifle for the secretary; and, in short, my good fellow, we stick it into B, up hill and down dale, and make a devilish comfortable little property out of him. (445; ch. 27)

To Tigg, clients are chattel, not people. B, as an individual, is displaced; he becomes the equivalent of the thoroughbred horse pulling Tigg's cabriolet. Other policies are equated with office furniture; in the past, when some of the original ones fell in, Tigg says only that "we had a couple of unlucky deaths that brought us down to a grand piano" (446; ch. 27). He suggests that Jonas, in joining the company, abjure both truth and responsibility; not content to keep his moral bankruptcy private, his counsel, in the event of a recurrence of such a situation, is given "in so low a whisper, that only one disconnected word was audible, and that imperfectly. But it sounded like 'Bolt' " (446; ch. 27). The smarminess which he employs is indicative of his unscrupulousness. If Tigg is willing to help Jonas, it is solely because Tigg will benefit. He baldly states, "We companies are all birds of prey: mere birds of prey. The only question is, whether, in serving our own turn, we can serve yours too: whether in double-lining our own nest, we can put a single lining into yours" (441; ch. 27). A moral bankrupt more than willing to bankrupt others financially for his own ease and comfort, Tigg operates with no other end in mind than the increase of capital. He has no sense of social or moral responsibility. People are property to be exchanged for material possessions; the death of a client is disturbing only because it leads to his own financial loss. There are no grand (or even grandiose) plans for the betterment of society, no investment in capital improvements (for, in this venture, there is little fixed capital), no reinvestment in secondary enterprises for the improvement of the quality of life other than one's own, least of all no intent to honor the policies themselves; there is simply the continuous accumulation of raw capital seemingly for its own sake. About this there is something inherently distasteful since Tigg is promoting a company speculating in human lives. And in the sacrifice of others' humanity in that enterprise, Tigg has sacrificed his own as well.

But he is not alone in such venal behavior nor in the payment of such a price. For the varied plots in the novel all revolve around the contemplated acquisition of someone else's property; all the characters are engaged in speculative ventures of one sort or another, and all lack, as a result, a core identity and moral center. Mere bundles of affections, largely a group of charlatans and *poseurs*, they seek the main chance that will enrich them with the least amount of effort at someone else's expense.

Foremost among them is Seth Pecksniff, a disingenuous schoolmaster-architect and land surveyor who seems never to have worked at his vocations a day in his life.

Mr. Pecksniff's professional engagements, indeed, were almost, if not entirely, confined to the reception of pupils; for the collection of rents, with which pursuit he occasionally varied and relieved his graver toils, can hardly be said to be a strictly architectural employment. *His genius lay in ensnaring parents and guardians, and pocketing premiums.* (13; ch. 2, my emphasis)

The architectural enterprise is simply a Pecksniffian variation of Tigg's Anglo-Bengalee with one innovation. Pecksniff steals much more than money from his apprentices; he steals their ideas as well. He sets them to the task of drafting original plans, telling them that "it really is in the finishing touches alone, that great experience and long study in these matters tell" (88; ch. 6):

There were cases on record in which the masterly introduction of an additional back window, or a kitchen-door, or half a dozen steps, or even a water-spout, had made the design of a pupil Mr. Pecksniff's own work, and had brought substantial rewards into the gentleman's pocket. But such is the magic of genius, which changes all it handles into gold! (88; ch. 6)

As bankrupt in morals as he is in ideas (in another context he states, "There is nothing personal in morality" [14; ch. 2] without any comprehension of the ironic applicability of his remark), pharisaical and parasitical, Pecksniff is an even more distasteful, more depraved character than Tigg. Tigg makes no pretense about his treatment of others as objects, openly acknowledging his dishonesty and duplicity to his coconspirators; Pecksniff, however, is far more devious, coyly (but ineffectively) dissembling even when he does not have to do so. With feigned innocence and ingenuousness, Pecksniff tries to mask what is really a mean-spirited brutality toward others. Beneath his smug, self-satisfied air lies a contempt for all humanity; the moralistic platitudes to which he gives voice throughout the novel are belied by his actions.

This disparity between word and deed illustrates an utter disdain for others, a disdain which extends to the very language he uses and which emphasizes his moral vacuity. Like Alice's Humpty Dumpty, "Mr. Pecksniff was in the frequent habit of using any word that occurred to him as having a good sound, and rounding a sentence well, without much care for its meaning" (15; ch. 2). As Sucksmith points out in a most impressive study of Dickensian rhetoric, "[Dickens] deliberately resorts to forced rhetorical figures to betray the insincerity which lies behind the various poses of Pecksniff" (57).

But it is more than mere insincerity and hypocrisy which Pecksniff's use of words reflects; the substitution of manner for matter reveals his lack of an *authentic* personality.[5] This condition is significantly different from and far more demeaning than alienation. As Trilling points out in another context,[6] "[I]t is not the estrangement of the self from the self. . . . Rather, it is the transformation of the self into what is not human" (123). The inauthentic person is, in essence, self-less. For Pecksniff, identity is pose, a continual tailoring of his character and behavior to fit his notions of what others expect or desire of him in order to achieve monetary gain. In shaping himself entirely by external considerations and concerns, in being consistent only in his inconsistency, he becomes inauthentic.

This annihilation of self is motivated by financial reward, either real or anticipated. Pecksniff's emotional life is sterile, superseded by economic considerations. Even his expression of sorrow to Mr. Todgers over the loss of his wife is undercut by the inappropriately appended observation "She had a small property" (149; ch. 9). In this regard, Pecksniff is little different in kind from Tigg; and their enterprises are remarkably similar.

However, Dickens levels his most scathing indictment of speculators and speculation at their American cousins. Renouncing all subtlety in his analysis of the American enterprise, Dickens accuses its operatives of the most meretricious and contemptible behavior. Major Pawkins is the embodiment of all the worst in the American character. His object, no different from that of all Americans, is the acquisition of dollars:

All their cares, hopes, joys, affections, virtues, and associations seemed to be melted down into dollars. Whatever the chance contributions that fell into the slow cauldron of their talk, they made the gruel thick and slab with dollars. Men were weighed by their dollars, measures gauged by their dollars; life was auctioneered, appraised, put up, and knocked down for its dollars. *The next respectable thing to dollars was any venture having their attainment for its end.* (273; ch. 16, my emphasis)

In this sweeping denunciation of a system that places more value on the accumulation of wealth for its own sake than on any substantial product or labor which that wealth should represent, Dickens maintains that the American character is inherently dehumanized, base, and corrupt. Contrary to their rather sanctimonious attitude, the Americans demonstrate the same moral vacuity as the English, a vacuity which extends to their use of language also; for, like Pecksniff, they use it loosely and casually and frequently with the deliberate intention to mislead and defraud. In *Martin Chuzzlewit*, the emphasis on money on both sides of the Atlantic is capable of engulfing all who would make capital acquisition their ultimate goal, destroying the very fabric of their humanity.

No one escapes ridicule. "Dickens's great fault is his predilection for very mean and despicable characters, out of proportion in number; and, besides, he makes goodness contemptible" (Robinson 645). For the most part, those characters who should function as moral touchstones are themselves monstrous and grotesque. Even Old Martin Chuzzlewit is consumed by his wealth. Obsessed by the desire to protect his fortune, he becomes a thoroughgoing misanthrope and divorces himself from every human impulse; his behavior borders on the reprehensible.

Among the rest of the characters, there is no one who merits the reader's respect or admiration. Indeed, every character in this novel is, like the boarders at Todgers', reduced to a "turn" (144; ch. 9); in no other work does Dickens dehumanize his cast of characters to the extent that he does here. Many of his contemporaries would find themselves in agreement with Henry Crabb Robinson's assessment: "Aug. 24th [1844]. . . . I finished *Chuzzlewit* at night; a book that I do not wish to look into a second time, so generally disgusting are the characters and incidents of the tale" (646). Despite generally favorable reviews (Collins 183), *Martin Chuzzlewit* held little appeal for the reading public, so harsh was its portrait of society and so relentless its bitter tone.

The commercial enterprise, more precisely the commerce in dollars or pounds, does not establish the selfishness and self-centered nature of the characters in this novel so much as it demonstrates their lack of centered selves and their repudiation of all things human. Driven by profit, guided by the principle "Do other men, for they would do you" (181; ch. 11), they reduce themselves and others to mere chattel, valuable only insofar as and to the extent that they can generate profit. Pecksniff berates Mrs. Todgers: "To worship the golden calf of Baal, for eighteen shillings a week! . . . To barter away that precious jewel, self-esteem, and cringe to any mortal creature—for eighteen shillings a week!" (168–69; ch. 10)— but it is not for her betrayal of her humanity that he does so; what offends him is that she does it so cheaply when there was a greater profit to be made.

This will not be the last time that Dickens turns to an examination of these issues and comes to the same conclusions. Ten years later, in *Little Dorrit*, and twenty years later, in *Our Mutual Friend*, he presents far bleaker pictures of the social and moral havoc wrought by financial speculation.

But the message remains the same. In Victorian England, just as, architecturally, main-street facades of respectable houses and shops often conceal an appalling poverty behind them (Marcus 266), so the possession of money frequently masks a moral penury within. In striving for profit for its own sake, disconnected from any commodity produced by labor and, indeed, from labor itself, the financial speculators betray an inner emptiness, a lack of moral values which prevents them from seeing or realizing their own humanity. Because they view their associations in monetary terms, they reduce others to objects, depriving them of their humanity and precluding the development of trust. As a result, the Tiggs and Pecksniffs of the world themselves become objects, commodities to be used and discarded as soon as they have served their purpose.

NOTES

1. Both Steven Marcus in *Dickens from Pickwick to Dombey* (New York: Simon and Schuster, 1965) and J. Hillis Miller in *Charles Dickens: The World of His Novels* (Bloomington: Indiana University Press, 1969) acknowledge this, but their interpretations of Dickens' treatment are significantly different from one another as they are also from my own.

2. In chapter 27, Tigg, who beforehand seemed a minor character hovering on the fringes of the novel, assumes a larger role in its business, now an essential catalyst in the plot.

3. Charles Dickens, *Martin Chuzzlewit* (Oxford: Oxford University Press, 1989). Because of the availability of many reliable editions of the text of Dickens' novels, I have included chapter citations as well as page numbers for ease of reference.

4. That Dickens' portrait is not an exaggerated one is attested to by the fact that "the scandalous activities of a type of promoter personified in *Martin Chuzzlewit* (1843) by one Mr. Tigg Montague . . . were the immediate impetus and occasion of the appointment, in 1841, of a parliamentary committee 'to inquire

into the state of the laws respecting joint-stock companies, with a view to the greater security of the public' " (Hunt 90).

5. I refer here to Lionel Trilling's distinction between authenticity and sincerity. Authenticity, he states, suggests "a more strenuous moral experience than 'sincerity' does, a more exigent conception of the self and of what being true to it consists of, a wider reference to the universe and man's place in it, and a less acceptant and genial view of the social circumstances of life" (11).

6. Trilling is contrasting Hegelian and Marxist concepts of alienation, but his remarks are apt within the present discussion. It is also interesting to note that he observes that, according to Marx, "[m]oney, in short, is the principle of the inauthentic in human existence" (124).

REFERENCES

Collins, Philip, ed. *Dickens: The Critical Heritage*. New York: Barnes & Noble, 1971.

Dickens, Charles. *Martin Chuzzlewit*. Oxford: Oxford University Press, 1989 (originally published 1843).

Engel, Monroe. *The Maturity of Dickens*. Oxford: Oxford University Press, 1959.

Hunt, Bishop Carleton. *The Development of the Business Corporation in England 1800–67*. Cambridge, Mass.: Harvard University Press, 1936.

Marcus, Steven. "Reading the Illegible." *The Victorian City: Images and Reality*. 2 vols. Ed. H. J. Dyos and Michael Wolff. London: Routledge & Kegan Paul, 1973. 257–76.

Miller, J. Hillis. *Charles Dickens: The World of His Novels*. Bloomington: Indiana University Press, 1969.

Robinson, Henry Crabb. *Henry Crabb Robinson on Books and Their Writers*. Vol. 2. Ed. Edith J. Morley. London: J. M. Dent and Sons, 1938.

Smith, Adam. *The Wealth of Nations Books I–III*. Intro. by Andrew Skinner. New York: Penguin Classics, 1986 (originally published 1776).

Smith, Grahame. *Dickens, Money, and Society*. Berkeley and Los Angeles: University of California Press, 1968.

Sucksmith, Harvey Peter. *The Narrative Art of Charles Dickens: The Rhetoric of Sympathy and Irony in His Novels*. Oxford: The Clarendon Press, 1970.

Trilling, Lionel. *Sincerity and Authenticity*. Cambridge: Harvard University Press, 1972.

Blood and Money in Bram Stoker's *Dracula*: The Struggle Against Monopoly

ROBERT A. SMART

Capital is dead labour which, vampire-like, lives only by sucking living labour, and lives the more, the more labour it sucks.

Karl Marx, *Capital*

Bram Stoker's 1897 masterpiece *Dracula* in fact contains two quite different stories. The most familiar one is the gothic tale of Count Dracula, the vampire, who preys on the London public for just over three months, from 8 August in an undisclosed year to 5 November of the same year. In this time, he seduces the fair Lucy Westenra (whose name is clearly symbolic), and transforms her into his evil minion, a voluptuous creature whose advances can scarcely be resisted by the stalwart band of vampire killers. Dracula nearly succeeds in getting Mina Harker as well, the heroine of the novel, and her fate hangs in the balance until the final moments of the novel. But the end of the story is too well-known by now to create much suspense and anxiety in the modern reader: the evil bloodsucker is chased back to his ancient home in Eastern Europe, where the now-virile Jonathan Harker (who marries Mina while lying in bed in Budapest, ill of a "brain fever") stabs the Transylvanian Count in the heart just as day crosses into night, the time when Dracula is least powerful. This Mina is saved, England is saved, and the Harkers bear a young son as testimony to Jonathan's restored vigor and manhood.

But there is a second story, more ambivalent and complex than the gothic tale, which is in fact a morality tale about money. This second story, embedded more deeply in the structure of the novel, is about money and free enterprise, wherein the dangers of monopoly—symbolized by the greedy Count Dracula—are successfully thwarted by the combined enterprise of a young band of entrepreneurs. Chief among them is Jonathan Harker, who has risen in a very short time from clerk in a London solicitor's office to full partner and owner of the firm. His meteoric rise to riches, success, and virility is matched against the greedy acquisitiveness of the Count, whose desire for blood leaves him young and immortal, and transforms his victims into servile, empty minions. In the words of Franco Moretti, "Stoker's Dracula . . . is a rational entrepreneur who invests his gold to expand his dominion: to conquer the City of London" (84).

Blood is the symbolic connector between the two stories. "Blood is the life" in the gothic tale, and indeed Dracula lives and is rejuvenated by the blood he takes from his victims, who then become "undead," *nosferatu*, imprisoned in a sort of suspended state between real life and real death until they can be ritually exorcized of the demon's curse. It's worth noting here that none of the vampires, not even Dracula himself, desires this existence, and they all die with peaceful looks on their faces once the brutal exorcism is finished. In the second story, blood is money, the "life substance" of a free economy. A free flow of money is vital to an evolved capitalist economy, while the concentration of money and capital in the hands of a few monopolists staunches both free capital flow and movement up or down the socioeconomic ladder. Jonathan Harker's rapid rise to the head of his law firm would be impossible in a monopolized system. From the very beginning of the novel, money and blood are linked, and become the vital substances at stake in the struggle for power between Dracula and the four determined vampire killers. Money, in the form of cash and securities, provides Dracula access to London, after he has exchanged his family treasure through the Royal Bank of London; money inherited by Jonathan Harker from Mr. Peter Hawkins, his generous employer, revitalizes the sick young man—"I was impotent" (225)—and makes it possible for him to strike the final blow against Dracula; and it is money—taken from all the men in the vampire killer gang—which eventually defeats the evil Count, prompting Mina Harker by the end of the novel to extol the "wonderful power of money." This story, I suggest, is the more complex of the two, and the one which creates, inevitably, some rather interesting contrasts to the moral simplicities of the gothic tale. We must begin with Jonathan Harker, apprentice solicitor.

As I mentioned earlier, Jonathan Harker comes to Count Dracula to complete some real estate transactions with him, and to fulfill, it turns out, his apprenticeship as a young solicitor. In fact, Harker's determination to prove his worth as a financial solicitor blinds him for a while to the weird goings-on in Dracula's castle. Harker learns two things during his initial meetings with the Count: the Rumanian nobleman has certainly done his homework in learning all one can learn from books about England, and secondly, Dracula is himself quite a good solicitor, with a good knowledge of how money can be used to obtain power, and how to cover all but the most discrete transactions along the way. At the end of the conversation, Harker remarks in his journal that "he [the Count] certainly left me under the impression that he would have made a wonderful solicitor, for there was nothing that he did not think of or foresee" (44). A mere twenty pages later, the madness in Dracula's methodology becomes clear to Harker, as well as the role he has played in it: "This was the being I was helping to transfer to London, where perhaps for centuries to come, he might, among its teeming millions, satiate his lust for blood, and create a new and ever widening circle of semi-demons to batten on the helpless" (67). Harker's close association with the vampire is symbolized by the fact that Dracula for a time becomes Jonathan Harker, dressing in his suits and hat, if only to allay local suspicion about the fate of the young Brit. There can be no mistake, however, by the end of this section in Jonathan Harker's journal: Dracula is a monopolist, plainly and evilly, and he has gained access to an unwary London through the very financial practices which were designed to preserve and abet free, competitive enterprise.

The symbolic function of blood as both food for the gothic vampire and as a symbol for money in a free economic system is established by Dracula. In fact, it is only when Harker realizes that Dracula drinks human blood that the connection between blood and money becomes clear to him, prompting the horrified lament I've just noted. We understand the threat which is posed by monopoly in the gothic terms of the vampire story, a metaphoric connection which Harker fails to make until nearly seventy pages and one week into the story. From this point in the story on, the blood/money metaphor drives both levels of the novel.

Because of this, the act of sucking blood in the novel takes on a different meaning as symbolic of the monopolist's work. The clearest picture of this process is given by Lucy Westenra (obviously Westenra, symbol of the pure and vital West) as she describes Dracula's first attack on British soil:

Then I have a vague memory of something long and dark with red eyes, just as we saw in the sunset, and something very sweet and very bitter all around me at once; and then I seemed sinking into deep green water, and there was a singing in my ears, as I have heard there is to drowning men; and then everything seemed passing away from me; my soul seemed to go out from my body and float about the air. (121)

Key in this experience is the separation of the soul from Lucy's body, which is symbolically the loss of individuation and freedom, leaving only a human shell, devoid of human will. That is in fact what happens to Dracula's victims and, Stoker warns, is the fate as well of free societies which are unwittingly victimized by foreign monopolies. Lucy eventually loses her fight with the vampire and becomes his minion. Interestingly, she then becomes a highly sexed, voluptuous creature who also threatens the unity of the small band of entrepreneurs, especially her fiancé Arthur Holmwood, Lord Godalming. She is "saved," however, by the men and ritually destroyed as a will-less creature of the night to regain her place as a human being but not before raising some interesting questions about Victorian sexuality and money. In fact, Dracula's swift and nearly undetected acquisition of four estates in all the compass points of London is paralleled by his attacks on Lucy Westenra and, later, upon Mina Harker. When he is finally feeling the pressure from his hunters and confronts them in his second house, he taunts them by saying, "Your girls that you all love are mine already; and through them you and others shall yet be mine—my creatures, to do my bidding and to be my jackals when I want to feed. Bah!" (365). Quite clearly, property is represented in the novel by the women, one of whom (Lucy) is proposed to by all the men save Jonathan Harker, who is already affianced to Mina. In fact, Lucy at one point jests in a letter to Mina that she wishes she could marry them all and that the law should be changed to allow it. This is an unusual remark for a proper Victorian maid and may account for the ease with which she falls into Dracula's power. She has the acquisitive instinct of the monopolist, something we do not see anywhere in Mina's character.

Earlier, in what is probably the most exciting scene of the novel, Dracula had come into the Harkers' bedroom, where Jonathan lies powerless (again!) on the bed, while the Count pulls Mina to his breast, forcing her to drink his blood, thereby introducing a powerful foreign substance (his blood) into her body. In other words, she becomes more like him and loses herself in the process. This is significant later in the story. Dracula's words to the small band of men as they've just burst in on the scene reveal once again his intention to possess completely what he covets, symbolized here by the blood of the women loved by the men who are chasing him. He says to Mina, "And you, their best beloved one, are now to me flesh of my flesh; blood of my blood; kin of my kin; my bountiful wine-press for a while; and shall be later on my companion and my helper. . . . when my brain says 'Come!' to you, you shall cross land or sea to do my bidding" (343). The importance of this scene in the novel, aside from its shocking perversity, lies in the progression of Dracula's description of Mina Harker, now the only woman left to the men. She is first separate, "You," then the most beloved of the men; then ("now") becomes a part of Dracula—identical with him—and is finally dehumanized to a crude tool, a "wine-press." This is what he wishes for a "companion and helper": not a partner or colleague, but a half-human and will-less minion who will do his bidding without question.

In the story of these two women, Stoker crystallizes the fear of monopoly which actually concerned some observers of late Victorian society. As Franco Moretti observed, "Dracula is a true monopolist: solitary and despotic, he will not brook competition. Like monopoly capital his ambition is to subjugate the last vestiges of the liberal era and destroy all forms of economic independence" (92). The horror of the vampire's attack is compounded by the analogous connection to Britain's economic well-being.

With the attack on Mina Harker, the novel focuses less evenly between the two stories, and the economic allegory in *Dracula* becomes more prominent. Dracula attacks no one else for pleasure as he had with Lucy and Mina, and he is preoccupied with leaving the country he had once planned to dominate. Once Jonathan Harker and Mina are married, Dracula's attack on Mrs. Harker constitutes a rape, and he violates a social and moral institution in addition to the person of Mina Harker. This was not true of Lucy Westenra, who was only recently affianced; she was lost to the Rumanian Count. The situation is different with the Harkers, for once Mina is violated, Jonathan Harker pursues Dracula with a fervor matched only by the vampire's greed and inhumanity. "He was never so resolute, never so strong, never so full of volcanic energy as at present" (273). First of all, Harker undoes the harm he did at the start by using Dracula's financial manipulations to track him and ultimately to trap him. Through with his apprenticeship, Harker uses his experience and knowledge as a solicitor to track the coffins of dirt which Dracula imported to England as a safeguard for his survival, and so also discovers the vast real estate holdings of the vampire: "The systematic manner in which this was done made me think that he could not mean to confine himself to two sides of London. He was now fixed on the far east of the northern shore, on the east of the southern shore, and on the south" (311). By means of retracing Dracula's carefully concealed financial steps, Harker and the others manage to trap him briefly in his Piccadilly estate. Before he arrives, papers and deeds which represent his power and the means to expand it are burned by the hunters, even as they admire the large stock of money and treasure in the corner.

The next scene is crucial. We could say that Dracula is killed twice in the novel: once at the end, obviously, when Jonathan Harker's knife slashes into his heart, and once also before that, here in this scene before he leaves England. The band of hunters has been alerted by Mina that Dracula is headed toward them, as they rifle through the Count's possessions, waiting for him to walk into a prepared trap. Eventually, he does arrive, eluding the trap fairly easily, and then confronts all of them, quite angry by now for their having destroyed so many of his coffins. The

first to move against Dracula is Jonathan Harker, who has been insulted
as a man and husband (and as an entrepreneur) by the "rape" of Mina
which takes place earlier. Harker leaps forward trying to stab Dracula with
his long-bladed kukri knife, hoping to destroy the old bloodsucker. "The
blow was a powerful one; only the diabolical quickness of the Count's
leap back saved him. A second less and the trenchant blade had shorn
through is heart. As it was, the point just cut the cloth of his coat, making
a wide gap whence a bundle of banknotes and a stream of gold fell out"
(364). At first, the speaker—Dr. John Seward, a psychologist—calls Harker's attack a failure, albeit a narrow one. But we have to understand the
symbolic dimensions of this scene to appreciate its significance in the
text. Dracula the monopolist receives a fatal blow in this scene, since it
is the draining away of his money and resources—his "blood"—which
will defeat his plans to conquer England. Moreover, the combined money
("blood") of the vampire hunters poses a threat too great for the old
vampire to withstand. It is this very development which Mina Harker
refers to by her comment extolling the "wonderful power of money,"
forgetting momentarily that this same power when used by someone like
Dracula can have very opposite results. Before Harker can raise another
blow against Dracula, the vampire "swept under Harker's arm ere his
blow could fall, and, grasping a handful of the money from the floor,
dashed across the room, and threw himself at the window" (365). Coins
leaking from the slashed pocket can be heard tinkling to the pavement,
leaking from Harker's "wound," as Dracula leaves his former safe haven
forever. Clearly, Dracula has received his "death-blow" in this scene, at
least Dracula in his persona as monopolist. It remains for the gothic vampire to meet his inevitable fate at the gates of Castle Dracula. As though
to drive the point home, Van Helsing, the Dutch leader of the vampire
killers, "put the money remaining into his pocket; took the title deeds
in the bundle as Harker had left them and swept the remaining things
into the open fireplace, where he set fire to them with a match" (365).
The tide has turned in the struggle.

In a remarkable journal entry written in Eastern Europe, Jonathan Harker describes all the modern contrivances which the band of vampire
killers has arrayed against the retreating Count, who now has to rely on
the medieval technology (horses, carts, rafts) of his native Transylvania
to convey him home. The relatively "high-tech" nature of the equipment
and the seemingly unending supply of cash to purchase it and to provide
well-placed bribes gives Harker cause for optimism, despite Mina's precarious situation, and he exclaims, "Judge Moneybag will settle this case,
I think!" (397). There can be no doubt after this that the novel will end
as an economic struggle, with the vast resources of the "corporation" of
vampire hunters massed against the considerable but ultimately lesser
capital of the Rumanian Count. The simplistic moral dichotomy of pol-

lution versus purity which Stoker used to describe the battle over Lucy has largely been abandoned for the economic combat of the marketplace.

The focal point of this struggle is Mina Harker since she is the last woman ("possession") left to the band of vampire killers. More important, she has been "baptized" by the Count and made to drink his blood, thereby making her like him as Lucy never was. The significance of this lies in the realization that she is half monster, half human, with both sides locked in a desperate struggle. At first, this is a huge disappointment to Harker and his companions since Mina's knowledge of the group's plans can be known by Dracula: he simply reads her mind and the part of her which is monster cannot resist his will. Soon, however, the team turns this situation to their advantage as they understand that they too can "read" Dracula's mind. At sunrise or at sunset, the crossing hours of the day, Dracula is at his most vulnerable and thereby, under hypnosis, Mina can be made to reveal all that he thinks and senses. This proves to be of enormous worth to the group since they can nearly always find and track down the vampire in his desperate escape to the castle. For Mina, this situation is considerably vexing, for she must seriously consider the possibility that she will become a vampire like her companion Lucy. To that end, she extracts a solemn promise from all the men, even her reluctant spouse, that she is to be killed and exorcized as a matter of pity for her, should the time ever come. The closer the group gets to the castle, the less power Van Helsing has over her and the more she resembles the vampire. Once again, however, the difference is made by money and by the willingness of those who have it to give it freely: "And, too, it made me think of the wonderful power of money! What can it not do when it is properly applied; and what might it do when basely used! I felt so thankful that Lord Godalming is so rich, and that both he and Mr. Morris [a Texas financier], who also has plenty of money, are willing to spend it so freely" (423). Here is the moral nub of the novel: money by itself is not evil, but its purposes can be made evil depending on the intentions of those who have it. The Count's purposes are base and so he must be defeated, just as the group's purposes are noble and so they must be victorious.

By contrast, it was not money which the men pooled to save poor Lucy Westenra, but blood. In the final days of her mortal life, she was given several infusions of blood from all of the men, including the septuagenarian Van Helsing, who calls the exchange of blood "a marriage," ironically fulfilling Lucy's earlier desire to marry all the men who had proposed to her. But blood divorced from its real metonymic base—money—is not adequate and the efforts of the men are all in vain. Lucy is lost to the monopolist. But they are not about to make the same mistake with Mina. The vast sum of money expended by the group allows them to intercept the Count just before his castle, and, in a very dramatic moment, allows Jonathan Harker to kill the evil vampire just as the final moments of sunset ebb away. Mina, of course, is completely free of the vampire's curse after his death, and the whole nightmarish experience is revisited seven years later, when the group—minus Quincy Morris, the American, who is killed by Dracula's bodyguards—returns to the decaying castle. The point of this visit, we learn in a note at the end of the novel, is to assure the prosperity and perseverance of the intrepid entrepreneurs, through the birth of Jonathan and Mina's son, whose birth date, appropriately, is the day of Quincy Morris's death. Thus the unfortunate American entrepreneur lives on in the Harker's son, who is also named Quincy, a scarcely veiled allusion to Britain's paternity in the development of American enterprise.

Finally, Stoker's "second novel" is not without ambivalences and contradictions. To name two of them, we simply have to look closely at Jonathan Harker's role in the novel. No one in the novel seems willing to recognize that the system championed by the vampire killers against the monopolist Count is the very same system which he used so successfully to create his sinister monopoly. Unavoidably, Stoker is forced to show us that capitalism as practiced in Europe and America in the nineteenth century can engender either a free competitive market system or a feudal monopoly system. The only difference, he seems to suggest, lies in the intentions of the principals. A second point which is richly suggestive occurs when Mina describes for us in a letter the enhanced status of her husband, following the death of his benefactor/employer Mr. Hawkins: "Jonathan Harker, a solicitor, a partner, rich, master of his business" (206). Quite clearly, we can suggest that Harker's vigorous opposition to Dracula comes only once he is in a financial position to compete with the Count. Before this, he is always powerless and prostrate before the vampire, unable to match his economic and psychological power. All that changes with Harker's inheritance and, shortly after, with the attack on Mina, which becomes a competition for property between the two men. Again, Stoker would have us believe it is mostly the intention and purpose of the contestant which determines the difference between entrepreneur and vampire.

REFERENCES

Moretti, Franco. "Dialectic of Fear." *Signs Taken for Wonders: Essays in the Sociology of Literary Forms*. London: Verso, 1988.
Stoker, Bram. *Dracula*. London: Penguin Books, 1979 (originally published 1897).

Index

About the Contributors

ANDREI ANIKIN is a professor at the Institute of World Economics and International Relations of the Academy of Sciences in Moscow, Russia. His research interests include economics, literature, and history.

RAYMOND L. BAUBLES, JR. is a professor of English at Western Connecticut State University. He has recently completed his doctoral dissertation, entitled "Finance and Folly: The Speculative Investor in Nineteenth-Century British History and Literature." He is now working on a study of John Law and the "Mississippi Bubble."

DAVID T. COURTWRIGHT is a professor and chairman of the Department of History, Philosophy, and Religious Studies at the University of North Florida. He has published *Dark Paradise: Opiate Addiction in America, 1923–1965*. He is currently working on a book about single men and social disorder in American history.

VANESSA D. DICKERSON is a professor of English at Rhodes College and was previously a member of the faculty of the University of Virginia. Her interest is in both Victorian literature and contemporary African-American women writers. She has published several articles on these subjects, which have appeared in books and journals. She is presently completing a critical study of the ghost fiction of Victorian women.

JOHN LOUIS DIGAETANI is a professor of English at Hofstra University, where he writes about opera, literature, and business communication. His books include *Richard Wagner and the Modern British Novel, Pen-*

etrating Wagner's Ring, Puccini the Thinker, An Invitation to the Opera, A Search for a Postmodern Theater, and *The Handbook of Executive Communication*. His essays have appeared in *The Wall Street Journal, Opera News, Opera Monthly, The Drama Review, Modern Fiction Studies*, and other journals.

RICHARD G. DOTY is the Curator of the National Numismatic Collection, National Museum of American History, Smithsonian Institution. He has written five books and numerous articles, mostly on numismatics, particularly numismatic technology.

ANDREW ECONOMOPOULOS is a professor of Economics at Ursinus College in Collegeville, Pennsylvania. He has written several essays dealing with the history of the antebellum banking industry, which have been published in *The Journal of Money, Credit, and Banking, Explorations in Economic History*, and *The Atlantic Economic Journal*.

SANDRA K. FISCHER is a professor of English at the University of Albany, State University of New York. She is author of *Econolingua: A Glossary of Coins and Economic Language in Renaissance Drama* and essays on drama and poetry in various journals. Her current project is a book-length study called *Shakespeare and the Poetics of Value*.

JOHN A. FREY is Chairman of Romance Languages and Literatures at George Washington University. He has published articles on Baudelaire, Marie de France, Louis Desprez, Verlaine, Balzac, and Chateaubriand. He has also published books on Mallarmé, Zola, and Hugo.

HELEN L. HARRISON is a professor of French at Dickinson College in Carlisle, Pennsylvania. Her research and publications have focused on seventeenth-century French theater, particularly the textual interplay of money and language as media of exchange and as indicators of social status. She is currently finishing a book on seventeenth-century French comedy.

MICHAEL J. HAUPERT is a professor of Economics and associate director of the Center for Economic Education at the University of Wisconsin at La Crosse. His research interests include the historical evolution of financial institutions, particularly the American banking industry.

JOANN P. KRIEG is a professor of English at Hofstra University. Her books include *Long Island Architecture, Walt Whitman: Here and Now*, and *Epidemics in the Modern World*.

CATHERINE L. LAWSON is a professor of Economics at Central Connecticut State University where she is a member of both the economics and honors faculties. Dr. Lawson teaches and researches in the areas of macroeconomic policy and the history of economic thought. She has published and is a frequent conference presenter on the topics of economic theory and policy.

ROBERT A. LEONARD is a professor of Linguistics at Hofstra University. His principle research interests are theoretic semantics, especially as applied to intercultural linguistics and other intercultural meaning systems. Currently teaching courses in linguistics, Swahili, crosscultural and international area studies, Dr. Leonard is the author of encyclopedia, book, and journal articles.

THOMAS M. LUCKETT is a professor of History at Portland State University in Portland, Oregon. He is currently preparing a book on the economic origins of the French Revolution, as well as a critical edition of François-Maximilien Misson's *A Cry from the Desert*.

LEE MORRISSEY is a doctoral candidate in English literature at Columbia University. His research interests include eighteenth- and nineteenth-century British literature.

CLIFTON W. POTTER, JR. is a professor and Chairman of the Department of History at Lynchburg College in Virginia where he has been a member of the faculty since 1965. His principal research efforts have been devoted to the study of British numismatics with an emphasis on the use of medallic art as propaganda in the reign of Elizabeth I.

JEFFREY POWERS-BECK is a professor of English at East Tennessee State University. He recently completed his dissertation, entitled "The Tangled Thread: Sacred Song, Secular Concerns, and the Shape of Herbert's Career," at Indiana University.

PATRICIA REYNAUD is a professor of Literature, Culture, and Society in the department of French and Italian at Miami University. Born in France, she graduated from the Sorbonne and the Institut d'Etudies Politiques in Paris. Two of her articles on literature and economics have been published in *Diacritics* and *Nineteenth-Century French Studies*. Her forthcoming book, *Fiction et faillité: Economie et métaphores dans* MADAME BOVARY investigates the interaction between money and literary representation in Gustave Flaubert's novel.

ROBERT A. SMART is a professor of English at Bradford College, and holder of the Dorothy Bell Endowed Chair in Writing. He is the author of *The Nonfiction Novel* and founding editor of *The Writing Teacher*, published by the National Poetry Foundation.

ELLEN STEPHENS has a Master's Degree in Industrial/Organizational Psychology from Montclair State College. After many years in the business world, she is interested in issues that pertain to the workplace. She is pursuing further research in motivation and interviewing techniques.

ALEX SZOGYI is a professor in the Department of Romance Languages of Hunter College of the City University of New York. He specializes in modern French theater and writes on this topic.

JOHN ULRICH is a professor of English at Mansfield University. His interests include Victorian literature, symbolic exchange theory, and animation historiography.

Hofstra University's
Cultural and Intercultural Studies
Coordinating Editor, Alexej Ugrinsky

Lyndon Baines Johnson and the Uses of Power
(Editors: Bernard J. Firestone and Robert C. Vogt)

Eighteenth-Century Women and the Arts
(Editors: Frederick M. Keener and Susan E. Lorsch)

Suburbia Re-examined
(Editor: Barbara M. Kelly)

James Joyce and His Contemporaries
(Editors: Diana A. Ben-Merre and Maureen Murphy)

The World of George Sand
(Editors: Natalie Datlof, Jeanne Fuchs, and David A. Powell)

Richard M. Nixon: Politician, President, Administrator
(Editors: Leon Friedman and William F. Levantrosser)

Watergate and Afterward: The Legacy of Richard M. Nixon
(Editors: Leon Friedman and William F. Levantrosser)

Immigration and Ethnicity: American Society—"Melting Pot" or "Salad Bowl"?
(Editors: Michael D'Innocenzo and Josef P. Sirefman)

Johann Sebastian: A Tercentenary Celebration
(Editor: Seymour L. Benstock)

Cold War Patriot and Statesman: Richard M. Nixon
(Editors: Leon Friedman and William F. Levantrosser)

Jimmy Carter: Foreign Policy and Post-Presidential Years
(Editors: Herbert D. Rosenbaum and Alexej Ugrinsky)

The Presidency and Domestic Policies of Jimmy Carter
(Editors: Herbert D. Rosenbaum and Alexej Ugrinsky)